America's Best Recipes

☆☆☆

A 1989 HOMETOWN COLLECTION

America's Best Recipes

Oxmoor
House®

ISBN: 0-8487-0765-6
ISSN: 0898-9982

Manufactured in the United States of America
First Printing 1989

Executive Editor: Ann H. Harvey
Production Manager: Jerry Higdon
Associate Production Manager: Rick Litton
Art Director: Bob Nance
Production Assistant: Theresa Beste

America's Best Recipes: A 1989 Hometown Collection

Editor: Janice L. Krahn
Copy Editor: Mary Ann Laurens
Editorial Assistants: Kay Hicks, Kelly E. Hooper
Director, Test Kitchen: Julie Fisher
Test Kitchen Home Economists: Nancy C. Earhart,
    Vanessa Taylor Johnson, Chrissy Pieroni, Kathleen
    Royal, Gayle Hays Sadler, Paula N. Saunders, Jill Wills
Senior Photographer: Jim Bathie
Photo Stylist: Kay E. Clarke
Senior Designer: Cynthia R. Cooper
Designer: Jane Bonds

Project Consultants: Meryle Evans, Audrey P. Stehle

Scenic Illustrations by Dana Moore
Food Illustrations by Wade Gilbreath

Cover: *Savor the cuisine of the Southwest with Chicken
    Tacos (page 32), Flan (page 27), and edible cactus
    pads (see Cactus Mexicano, page 44).*

Frontispiece: *A picturesque harbor scene in Stonington,
    Connecticut*

Oxmoor House, Inc., is also the publisher of *Cooking
Light* books. For subscription information for *Cooking
Light* magazine, write to *Cooking Light*®, P.O. Box C-549,
Birmingham, Alabama 35283.

Contents

Introduction

From America's celebrated hometown cookbooks come over four hundred all-new recipes featured in *America's Best Recipes - A 1989 Hometown Collection*. To discover the distinctive dishes that make American cuisine unique, we have covered the miles for you, collecting treasured recipes from your family, friends, and acquaintances throughout the country. Our experienced food writers searched hundreds of current community cookbooks across America before choosing the recipes that best reflect current food trends, regional cuisines, and just plain "good cooking." In addition, we asked the cookbook committee chairpersons to nominate recipes they considered to be their "cream of the crop." Over six hundred of the submitted recipes were rigorously tested, judged, and retested by our staff of home economists to ensure that they indeed are the outstanding, reliable recipes we would all be eager to prepare in our own homes for family and friends. The result is *America's Best Recipes*—a collection of over four hundred of these recipes, representing every region of the country. Some recipes are simple, some are challenging, and all are terrific! Special attention was focused upon the increasing popularity of Southwestern Cuisine in "Celebrate the Southwest"—a special chapter highlighting the cookbooks and flavorful recipes from the border states.

This national community cookbook salutes the dedicated volunteers who have successfully raised funds to help meet the needs of their communities. We encourage you to review the Acknowledgments at the back of this book, order other cookbooks that are of interest to you, and contribute to the success of the nonprofit organizations responsible for creating the fascinating community cookbooks that are featured in *America's Best Recipes - A 1989 Hometown Collection*.

The Editors

Celebrate
the Southwest

The Mission San Antonio de Valero, more commonly known as the Alamo, was founded in 1718 by the Franciscans and was later converted to the fortress where Davy Crockett and James Bowie lost their lives fighting Santa Anna's army during the Texas Revolution.

☆☆☆

Southwestern Cuisine

Contrary to popular belief, Southwestern Cuisine is not all "hot," but it is certainly sizzling in terms of its popularity across the country. A blending of cultures has led to a rich and diversified cuisine—one which Southwesterners feel strongly about preserving. Although there is regional variation in Southwestern fare, the cuisine is bound together by common ingredients, cooking techniques, and flavor blends. Across America, we are becoming familiar with the vibrant flavors and colors of the dishes coming from the border states. The distinctive, hearty, and robust flavors that are inherent in Mexican cookery have become our own.

The Southwest is a melting pot of cultures, and, consequently, the roots of its cuisine are numerous and variegated as well. Southwestern Cuisine is heavily influenced by a Mexican Cuisine that has evolved over centuries based upon Mexico's geography, climate, indigenous foods, and native cultures. The Spaniards, Mexicans, Anglos, and Indians each contributed unique food traditions, making for a complementary blend of rich flavors. During the sixteenth century, the Spaniards perhaps had the strongest influence on the cuisine of the native Indians by introducing them to such foods as rice, wheat, peanuts, chocolate, garlic, onions, avocados, citrus fruits, and chile peppers. Beef, pork, and, consequently, lard used for frying are part of the Spanish heritage. Heretofore, Indians used a dry-griddle cooking method and relied on vegetables and spices that were readily available, including squash, dried beans, potatoes, corn, vanilla, and cinnamon.

Today, regions of Mexico have distinct cooking traditions resulting from differences in climates, topography, and locally available ingredients. Northern Mexico, with its dry climate, is best known for its beef, wheat, and cheese-based dishes. In central Mexico, there is a corn-based cuisine featuring tortilla-based dishes such as tamales and enchiladas, as well as freshwater fish, pork, poultry, and goat. The cuisine of the Southeastern peninsula, the Yucatan, is noted for its tropical fruits and sea-food. Certain traditional dishes, such as tortillas, tacos, enchi-ladas, guacamole, custards, chicken soups, and refried beans, can be found throughout the various regions of Mexico with rela-tively minor variations in their ingredients.

North of the Mexican border, Americans have created their own regional versions of Mexican cookery by adapting traditional Mexican dishes and cooking techniques to suit their own ingre-dients and taste preferences. The foods differ from state to state in the West and Southwest, but the rich flavors and fiesta-like atmosphere of Southwestern Cuisine remains the same. In Texas, Tex-Mex Cuisine has its roots in northern Mexico-style cookery, and is identified by the use of fresh and dried chiles, tortillas, barbecued meats, cheeses, tacos, and tamales. In New Mexico, the cuisine has a heavy Spanish influence and is known as Santa Fe style, featuring puffy breads, an abundance of chiles, and an ingredient unique to New Mexico cookery—blue corn. Arizona's southwestern cookery has strong Indian roots and utilizes ingredients such as cactus pads (nopales), beef jerky, mild green chiles, wheat tortillas, dried beans, and rice. Californians have produced a lightened Mexican cuisine, known as Cal-Mex, which successfully combines Mexican Cuisine with touches of Italian and Oriental cookery, starring fresh seafood, fruits and vegetables, mild chile sauces, and cilantro.

Southwestern Cuisine has a sunny, comfortable casualness about it that is warm and inviting. Eating in the Southwest is a celebration! We invite you to celebrate Southwestern Cuisine with this flavorful collection of authentic Southwestern fare beginning on page 14.

The Essential Chile

More chiles are produced and consumed than any other seasoning in the world. Chiles are used in a variety of ways ranging from spice to vegetable. Chiles, native to Mexico, are grown in over one hundred varieties, and each has its own unique characteristics. Due to the increased popularity of Southwestern Cuisine, chiles have become readily available in the United States.

Chile Language

Learning about the chile can seem complicated in terms of classification and terminology, but don't be intimidated by the convoluted terms for the different chile varieties. Although there are many definitions of the terms "chile" and "pepper," most people agree that "chile" refers to the hot variety and "pepper" refers to the sweet variety. Confusion arises because the exact same chile can be found under several different names, depending upon its stage of development and the geographic region in which it was cultivated. Chile names are essentially based upon their color, shape, place of origin, and level of hotness.

Chile Heat

The hotness level of a chile can vary within a given variety and can be affected by the climate of the growing region and the time of year the chile is grown. A mild chile and a fiery hot chile, amazingly, can grow on the same plant. The hotness level of a chile is determined by a substance called capsaicin which is found mainly in the veins of the chile—the thin inner membrane to which the seeds are attached. The stem end of the chile is the hottest portion. There is a rule of thumb that one can follow when trying to identify a mild or hot chile—usually the lighter green the skin of a chile and the blunter the tip, the milder the chile. Small dark green chiles with pointed tips are often the hottest chiles available. Fresh and dried red chiles with various hotness levels and flavor characteristics are often used in combination with one another to add flavor balance to a dish.

Capsaicin can cause painful burning or a rash when it comes in contact with skin, so take precautions when handling all chiles whether they are fresh, dried, canned, or ground. Protect your skin by wearing rubber gloves and washing your hands with warm, soapy water after handling chiles. Work with chiles under cold running water and not hot water, which will release irritating vapors. Take care you do not rub your eyes or touch your face after you have handled a chile. If you do get capsaicin in your eyes or on your skin, flush the affected area with cold water.

Identifying Chiles

Fresh Chiles

When buying fresh chiles, choose those that are firm and plump with a shiny, unblemished skin. Fresh chiles will keep for two weeks when refrigerated in a loosely sealed plastic bag lined with paper towels.

Roasting and peeling chiles enhance their flavor as well as remove their tough, transparent skin. To roast chiles, pierce near the stem with a knife. Place the chiles on a baking sheet, and broil until uniformly blistered, turning often. Transfer the chiles to a plastic bag and seal. After standing 10 to 15 minutes, the chiles will be ready to peel.

The **Anaheim** chile, also called a California green chile, is a light green to medium yellow-green chile with some orange tint. The chile is slightly twisted in shape with a round tip and firm, thick flesh. The chile ranges from 4 to 6 inches long and 1½ inches wide. Anaheims have a mild flavor with a slight bite. The Anaheim chile is the most common chile in American markets. Canned green chiles can be substituted for Anaheim chiles.

The **jalapeño** or "Texas Pickle" is a small dark to bright green or red chile that measures 2 to 3 inches long and ¾ inch wide. It is plump but not round, with a blunt tip and slightly tapered end. The hotness level of the jalapeño varies from hot to very hot. Pickled jalapeños are an acceptable substitute.

The **poblano** chile is a large dark green chile that resembles an elongated sweet green pepper with a characteristic pointed end. It measures 3½ to 5 inches long and has a flavor that varies from mild to hot. The milder poblanos are considered to be very versatile chiles. If poblano chiles are unavailable, sweet green peppers can be successfully substituted.

The **serrano** is a dark green chile that is sometimes allowed to ripen to red. The chile is smaller and thinner than a jalapeño, measuring 1 to 1½ inches long and ⅜ to ½ inch wide. The serrano has a thin outer skin and a pointed tip and is an extremely hot chile. Pickled jalapeños can be substituted.

Dried Red Chiles

Dried red chiles are vine-ripened green chiles which turn from green to yellow then orange to red as they ripen. The chiles are picked and then dried in the sun or an oven. Dried chiles are sold separately or in a long, knotted strand called a ristra. If stored in a cool, dry place, dried chiles will keep for several months.

To prepare dried chiles for cooking, wipe off any surface dust from the chiles. To soften the chiles and intensify their flavor, roast the chiles about 1 minute in a greaseless skillet, being careful not to scorch them. Set the roasted chiles in a colander, and rinse under cold water while slitting them lengthwise to stem, seed, and devein.

The **ancho** chile is the most common dried chile. It is the dried form of the ripened poblano chile. Fairly large and triangular in shape, it has a wrinkled and medium to dark reddish-brown skin. The ancho is a full-flavored chile with a hotness level ranging from mild to medium hot. Ground chile powder can be substituted for anchos, using ½ teaspoon for each fresh ancho chile.

Chipotles are dried, ripened jalapeños that are smoked over mesquite. They are hot chiles with a dull reddish-brown color with a wrinkled skin.

Pasillas, also called the Chile Negros in southern California markets, are slender and about 6 inches long with wrinkled, blackish-brown skins. Pasillas are usually very hot, and are often used in combination with anchos.

The **cayenne** is a small, narrow dark red chile that is fiery hot and used almost exclusively in its dried form.

Guacamole with Homemade Salsa

4 medium avocados, peeled
and coarsely chopped
1 medium tomato, seeded
and coarsely chopped

1 green onion, finely chopped
½ cup Homemade Salsa
Fresh cilantro sprigs
(optional)

Combine avocado, tomato, chopped green onions, and ½ cup Homemade Salsa in a large serving bowl, tossing gently to mix well. Garnish with fresh cilantro sprigs, if desired. Serve with tortilla chips. Yield: 4 cups.

Homemade Salsa

2 jalapeño peppers, seeded
and chopped
6 guero (hot yellow) peppers,
seeded and chopped
2 large tomatoes, seeded and
chopped
8 cloves garlic, minced
1 (14.5-ounce) can stewed
tomatoes, undrained and
chopped

¼ cup plus 2 tablespoons
vegetable oil
½ teaspoon salt
1 tablespoon chopped fresh
cilantro
1 teaspoon dried whole
oregano
½ teaspoon pepper

Combine all ingredients in a large mixing bowl, tossing gently to mix well. Serve any remaining Homemade Salsa as a condiment over fried eggs, cold meats, poultry, or hamburgers, or as a dip with tortilla chips. Yield: 4 cups.

Delicious Decisions
The Junior League of San Diego, California

Chile con Queso

1 large onion, finely chopped
1 tablespoon bacon drippings
2 (10-ounce) cans tomatoes
with green chiles,
undrained
1 (4-ounce) can chopped
green chiles, undrained

1 teaspoon salt
⅛ teaspoon pepper
4 cups (16 ounces) shredded
process American cheese

Sauté onion in bacon drippings in a large skillet until tender. Drain tomatoes with chiles, reserving juice; coarsely chop tomatoes. Add tomatoes with chiles, chopped green chiles, salt, and pepper to onion; cover and cook over medium-low heat 15 minutes. Add cheese; cook over low heat, stirring constantly, until cheese melts. Thin cheese mixture to desired consistency by adding reserved tomato liquid, one tablespoon at a time. Serve warm with tortilla chips. Yield: 4 cups.   Sandy Baggett

Diamonds in the Desert
The Woman's League of Ozona, Texas

Mexican Stuffed Cheese

1 (2-pound) round Cheddar cheese (6 inches in diameter)
1 (16-ounce) can refried beans
1 (4-ounce) can chopped green chiles, drained
1 medium tomato, seeded and chopped
2 cloves garlic, minced
¼ teaspoon dried whole oregano
¼ teaspoon ground coriander
¼ teaspoon hot sauce
5 (8-inch) corn tortillas
2 tablespoons vegetable oil

Hollow out center of cheese round, leaving a shell about ½-inch thick. Set shell aside. Shred cheese; set aside.

Combine refried beans and next 6 ingredients in a medium saucepan. Cook over medium heat, stirring often, until thoroughly heated. Set aside.

Fry tortillas, one at a time, in hot oil 3 to 5 seconds on each side or just until tortillas are softened. Drain on paper towels.

Line a 10-inch quiche dish or pieplate with softened tortillas. Place cheese shell on top of tortillas; fill cheese shell with refried bean mixture. Top with reserved shredded cheese. Bake stuffed cheese shell at 350° for 30 minutes or until cheese melts and bean mixture is thoroughly heated. Serve immediately with tortilla chips. Yield: 16 appetizer servings.

Purple Sage and Other Pleasures
The Junior League of Tucson, Arizona

Super Nachos

½ pound ground beef
½ pound bulk chorizo
1 large onion, chopped
½ teaspoon salt
½ teaspoon pepper
2 (16-ounce) cans refried
  beans
2 (4-ounce) cans chopped
  green chiles, drained

3 cups (12 ounces) shredded
  Cheddar cheese
¾ cup commercial taco sauce
9 green onions, chopped
1 cup chopped ripe olives
2 (6-ounce) cans frozen
  avocado dip, thawed
1 (8-ounce) carton
  commercial sour cream

Cook ground beef, sausage, and onion in a large skillet until meat is browned, stirring to crumble meat. Drain well; add salt and pepper. Set aside.

Spread beans in a 13- x 9- x 2-inch baking dish; layer meat mixture, green chiles, cheese, and taco sauce on top of beans. Bake, uncovered, at 350° for 15 minutes or until cheese melts and mixture is thoroughly heated. Remove from oven. Sprinkle green onions and olives evenly over top of mixture. Top evenly with avocado dip and sour cream. Serve warm with tortilla chips. Yield: 16 appetizer servings.

Con Mucho Gusto
The Desert Club of Mesa, Arizona

Quesadillas (Cheese-Filled Tortillas)

16 (8-inch) flour tortillas
2 cups (8 ounces) shredded
  mild Cheddar or Monterey
  Jack cheese

1 onion, thinly sliced
1 jalapeño pepper, seeded
  and minced

Lay 1 tortilla on a hot, lightly greased griddle; top with ¼ cup cheese, 1 onion slice, and ½ teaspoon minced jalapeño pepper. Place another tortilla on top. Cook over medium heat 1 minute; turn tortilla over, and cook 1 minute or until cheese melts. Remove from heat, and cut into 8 wedges. Repeat procedure with remaining ingredients. Yield: about 5 dozen.

Celebrate San Antonio
The Junior Forum of San Antonio, Texas

Stuffed Jalapeño Peppers

1 (8-ounce) package cream
  cheese, softened
¼ cup mayonnaise
2 hard-cooked eggs, finely
  chopped
1 tablespoon finely chopped
  onion

¼ teaspoon garlic salt
2 (7-ounce) cans whole
  pickled jalapeño peppers,
  drained

Combine first 5 ingredients in a medium bowl, stirring well. Cut peppers in half lengthwise; remove seeds and veins. (Wear rubber gloves when working with peppers.) Stuff pepper halves with cream cheese mixture. Cover and chill. Yield: about 2½ dozen.

Celebrate San Antonio
The Junior Forum of San Antonio, Texas

Ceviche

1 pound white fish, red
  snapper, or sole, boned,
  skinned, and cut into
  ½-inch cubes
⅔ cup fresh lemon juice
½ cup vegetable juice
  cocktail
2 tablespoons green chile
  salsa
1 large tomato, finely chopped
1 large carrot, scraped and
  thinly sliced

6 green onions, finely
  chopped
½ cup chopped celery
⅓ cup sliced pimiento-stuffed
  olives
⅓ cup finely chopped green
  pepper
1 clove garlic, minced
½ cup chopped fresh parsley
½ cup chopped fresh cilantro
1 tablespoon capers
¼ teaspoon salt

Place fish in a glass bowl (do not use metal); add lemon juice. Cover and marinate in refrigerator 24 hours, tossing occasionally. Drain. Rinse fish with cold water, and drain again. Combine vegetable juice cocktail and remaining ingredients; stir in fish. Cover and chill at least 2 hours. Serve with tortilla chips. Yield: 6 to 8 appetizer servings.

Delicious Decisions
The Junior League of San Diego, California

Traditional Sangría

¾ cup sugar
Rind of 1 orange, cut into
   thin strips
¾ cup freshly squeezed
   orange juice (about 3
   oranges)
Rind of 1 lemon, cut into
   thin strips

½ cup freshly squeezed
   lemon juice (about 3
   lemons)
1 cup brandy
1 quart Burgundy or other
   dry red wine
1 (33.8-ounce) bottle club
   soda, chilled

Combine all ingredients except club soda in a large pitcher, stirring to dissolve sugar. Add club soda just before serving. Serve over ice. Yield: 2½ quarts.

Winning at the Table
The Junior League of Las Vegas, Nevada

Margaritas

Salt
5 cups crushed ice
¾ cup tequila
1 (6-ounce) can frozen
   limeade concentrate, thawed
   and undiluted

¼ cup Triple Sec
¾ cup lemon-lime carbonated
   beverage, chilled
Lime slices

Dip rims of margarita glasses in water, then in salt; shake to remove excess salt. Combine ice and remaining ingredients except lime slices in container of an electric blender; cover and process until smooth. Pour beverage into salt-rimmed glasses; garnish with lime slices. Yield: 5 cups.   Roger Borgelt

Lone Star Legacy II
The Junior Forum of Austin, Texas

Homemade Flour Tortillas

4 cups all-purpose flour
⅛ teaspoon baking powder
2 teaspoons salt

⅔ cup shortening
1 cup plus 3 tablespoons hot
   water

Combine flour, baking powder, and salt; stir well. Cut in shortening with a pastry blender until mixture resembles coarse meal. Gradually add water, stirring until mixture forms a dough.

Divide dough into 24 equal portions. Roll each with a rolling pin to a very thin circle, about 6 inches in diameter, turning dough and rolling both sides.

Place an ungreased skillet over medium heat; cook tortillas 2 minutes on each side or until lightly browned, being careful not to let tortillas wrinkle. (Pat tortillas lightly with a spatula while browning the second side.) Serve warm. Yield: 2 dozen.   Marian Reed

Lone Star Legacy II
The Junior Forum of Austin, Texas

Mexican Cornbread

1 cup yellow cornmeal
1 cup all-purpose flour
1 tablespoon plus 1 teaspoon
   baking powder
½ teaspoon salt
½ cup instant nonfat dry
   milk powder
2 tablespoons sugar
2 eggs

1 cup water
⅓ cup vegetable oil
1 cup (4 ounces) shredded
   Cheddar cheese
1 (4-ounce) can chopped
   green chiles, drained
1 tablespoon butter or
   margarine

Combine first 6 ingredients; make a well in center of mixture. Beat eggs until foamy; add water and oil, mixing well. Add egg mixture to cornmeal mixture, stirring just until dry ingredients are moistened. Stir in cheese and chiles.

Melt butter in an 8-inch square baking pan. Pour batter into pan, and bake at 375° for 30 to 35 minutes or until cornbread is golden brown. Yield: 8 servings.   S. D. Jackman

Lone Star Legacy II
The Junior Forum of Austin, Texas

Churros (Spanish Fritters)

1 cup sugar
2 teaspoons ground cinnamon
1 cup water
2 tablespoons butter or
   margarine
2 tablespoons shortening

1 tablespoon sugar
½ teaspoon salt
½ cup white cornmeal
½ cup all-purpose flour
2 eggs, lightly beaten
Peanut oil

Combine 1 cup sugar and cinnamon; set aside.

Combine water, butter, shortening, 1 tablespoon sugar, and salt in a large saucepan; bring to a boil. Add cornmeal and flour all at once, stirring vigorously over low heat about 1 minute or until mixture leaves sides of pan and forms a smooth ball. Remove from heat, and cool slightly.

Add eggs to flour mixture, beating with a wooden spoon until batter is smooth.

Pour oil to a depth of 3 inches into a large Dutch oven or heavy deep skillet; heat oil to 375°. Fill a pastry bag fitted with star tip No. 4 with batter. Pipe batter in 8-inch-long strips into hot oil. Fry until golden brown, turning once. Drain on paper towels.

Sprinkle cinnamon sugar over warm Churros. Serve immediately. Yield: about 2 dozen.

Celebrate San Antonio
The Junior Forum of San Antonio, Texas

Sopaipillas

4 cups all-purpose flour
1 tablespoon baking powder
1 teaspoon salt

3 tablespoons shortening
1⅓ cups hot water
Vegetable oil

Combine flour, baking powder, and salt in a large mixing bowl; cut in shortening with a pastry blender until mixture resembles coarse meal. Gradually stir in hot water, mixing well. (Dough will be sticky.) Turn dough out onto a lightly floured surface, and knead 5 to 10 times. Cover and let rest 30 minutes.

Roll dough to ⅛-inch thickness, and cut into 3-inch squares. Pour oil to a depth of 3 inches into a Dutch oven; heat oil to 370°. Gently place dough squares in oil, a few at a time. Spoon hot oil over dough until Sopaipillas are lightly browned. Drain well on paper towels. Serve Sopaipillas with honey and butter or margarine. Yield: about 3 dozen.   Brandi and Cynthia Bradford

Lone Star Legacy II
The Junior Forum of Austin, Texas

Bolillos (Mexican Rolls)

1 cup warm water (105° to 115°)

1 tablespoon plus 1½ teaspoons sugar

1 package dry yeast

1 tablespoon salt

2 tablespoons butter or margarine

1 cup water

6 cups all-purpose flour

1 teaspoon cornstarch

½ cup cold water

Combine 1 cup warm water, sugar, and yeast in a large mixing bowl; let stand 5 minutes.

Combine salt, butter, and 1 cup water in a small saucepan; heat until butter melts. Cool to 105° to 115°.

Stir butter mixture into yeast mixture. Add 2½ cups flour; beat at medium speed of an electric mixer until blended. Add remaining 3½ cups flour to make a soft dough.

Turn dough out onto a lightly floured surface; knead 10 minutes. Cover and let rise in a warm place (85°), free from drafts, 1½ hours or until doubled in bulk.

Punch dough down, and divide into 16 equal portions. Shape each portion into a 4- x 1½-inch loaf-shaped roll. Place on greased baking sheets. Cover and let rise in a warm place, free from drafts, 35 minutes or until doubled in bulk.

Score tops of rolls with scissors, making slashes ¾-inch deep and 2 inches long.

Dissolve cornstarch in ½ cup cold water in a small saucepan; bring to a boil. Let cool slightly. Brush each roll with cornstarch mixture. Bake at 375° for 35 to 40 minutes or until rolls are golden brown. Yield: 16 rolls.

Celebrate San Antonio
The Junior Forum of San Antonio, Texas

Pan Dulce

1 package dry yeast
¾ cup warm water
  (105° to 115°)
¾ cup sugar
3 tablespoons butter or
  margarine,
  melted
2 eggs, beaten
½ teaspoon salt

3½ cups all-purpose flour
1 cup sugar
1 cup all-purpose flour
1 teaspoon ground
  cinnamon
⅛ teaspoon salt
½ cup butter or margarine
1 egg yolk

Dissolve yeast in warm water in a large mixing bowl; let yeast mixture stand 5 minutes. Add ¾ cup sugar, melted butter, 2 beaten eggs, and ½ teaspoon salt to yeast mixture, and beat at medium speed of an electric mixer until ingredients are well blended. Gradually add 3½ cups flour, beating until mixture is smooth. (Dough will be sticky.)

Place dough in a well-greased bowl, turning to grease top. Cover and let rise in a warm place (85°), free from drafts, 1½ hours or until doubled in bulk.

Punch dough down; turn out onto a lightly floured surface, and knead until dough is smooth and elastic (2 to 3 minutes). Shape dough into 18 balls, and place 2 inches apart on greased baking sheets. Flatten each ball slightly.

Combine 1 cup sugar, 1 cup flour, ground cinnamon, and ⅛ teaspoon salt in a medium mixing bowl; cut in ½ cup butter with a pastry blender until mixture resembles coarse meal. Stir in egg yolk. Shape mixture into 18 balls; roll each ball to a 3-inch circle on a lightly floured surface. Using a metal spatula, place one circle on top of each roll. (Circles should completely cover the top of each roll.)

Score through topping and halfway through roll with a sharp knife, forming a swirl or a crisscross design. Cover and let rise in a warm place, free from drafts, 30 minutes or until doubled in bulk. Bake at 400° for 10 minutes or until lightly browned. Serve warm. Yield: 1½ dozen.

Purple Sage and Other Pleasures
The Junior League of Tucson, Arizona

Pasteles de Cacao (Cocoa Cakes)

½ cup butter or margarine, softened
1 cup sugar
3 eggs
¾ cup cocoa

1½ cups all-purpose flour
1 tablespoon baking powder
⅛ teaspoon salt
⅔ cup milk
1 teaspoon vanilla extract

Cream butter; gradually add sugar, beating at medium speed of an electric mixer until light and fluffy. Add eggs, one at a time, beating after each addition.

Combine cocoa, flour, baking powder, and salt; add to creamed mixture alternately with milk, beginning and ending with flour mixture. Stir in vanilla.

Spoon batter into paper-lined muffin pans, filling two-thirds full. Bake at 375° for 15 to 20 minutes. Remove from pans, and let cool on wire racks. Yield: 16 cakes.

Purple Sage and Other Pleasures
The Junior League of Tucson, Arizona

Mexican Cookies

1 (3-inch) stick cinnamon, broken into fine pieces
5 cups all-purpose flour
2 cups sugar
1 tablespoon baking powder
½ teaspoon baking soda

Pinch of salt
2 eggs, beaten
1 teaspoon vanilla extract
2 cups shortening
Cinnamon sugar

Roast cinnamon in a skillet over medium heat 2 to 3 minutes, stirring occasionally. Combine cinnamon pieces, flour, and next 4 ingredients in a large mixing bowl; stir well. Add eggs and vanilla; mix well. Knead in shortening until mixture forms a dough.

Shape dough into ¾-inch balls; place on ungreased cookie sheets. Slash top of each cookie with a shallow X. Bake at 350° for 15 minutes. Cool slightly on cookie sheets; dip tops of cookies in cinnamon sugar. Let cool completely on wire racks. Yield: 10 dozen.

Celebrate San Antonio
The Junior Forum of San Antonio, Texas

Mexican Wedding Cookies

1 cup butter
¾ cup sifted powdered sugar
1 teaspoon vanilla extract
2 cups all-purpose flour

1 cup finely chopped pecans
1½ cups sifted powdered
  sugar

Cream butter; gradually add ¾ cup powdered sugar, beating until light and fluffy. Stir in vanilla. Add flour to creamed mixture, beating well. Stir in pecans. Shape dough into 1-inch balls. Place 1 inch apart on ungreased cookie sheets. Bake at 325° for 25 minutes or until browned. Roll in 1½ cups powdered sugar; cool completely on wire racks. Roll again in powdered sugar. Yield: 4 dozen.

Purple Sage and Other Pleasures
The Junior League of Tucson, Arizona

Pumpkin Empanadas

1 (16-ounce) can pumpkin
¾ cup sugar
1 teaspoon ground allspice
4 cups all-purpose flour
½ cup sugar
1 tablespoon plus 1 teaspoon
  baking powder

1 teaspoon salt
1⅓ cups shortening
1 cup milk
Milk
¼ cup sugar
½ teaspoon ground cinnamon
1 egg white, lightly beaten

Combine first 3 ingredients; stir well, and set aside.

Combine flour, ½ cup sugar, baking powder, and salt; cut in shortening with a pastry blender until mixture resembles coarse meal. Sprinkle 1 cup milk evenly over surface, stirring with a fork until dry ingredients are moistened. Shape into a ball; roll to ⅛-inch thickness on a lightly floured surface. Cut into 4-inch circles.

Place 1 tablespoon pumpkin mixture in center of each circle. Moisten edges with milk; fold in half, and press edges together to seal. Combine ¼ cup sugar and cinnamon. Brush empanadas with egg white, and sprinkle with sugar mixture. Place on ungreased baking sheets, and bake at 450° for 6 to 8 minutes or until golden brown. Yield: about 3 dozen.   Beverly Bone

Lone Star Legacy II
The Junior Forum of Austin, Texas

Buñuelos (Fried Tortilla Pastries)

5 cups all-purpose flour
2 tablespoons sugar
2 teaspoons baking powder
1 teaspoon salt

¼ cup shortening
2 cups hot water or milk
Vegetable oil
Cinnamon sugar

Combine flour, sugar, baking powder, and salt in a large mixing bowl. Cut in shortening with a pastry blender until mixture resembles coarse meal. Make a well in center of mixture. Add hot water, stirring until mixture forms a dough. Cover and let stand 1 hour.

Divide dough in half. Cover one half of dough, and set aside. Divide other half of dough into 15 balls. Roll each on a lightly floured surface to a thin circle about 7 inches in diameter. Fry one at a time in deep hot oil (375°) until crisp and golden. Drain on paper towels. Sprinkle with cinnamon sugar. Repeat procedure with remaining half of dough. Yield: 2½ dozen.

Celebrate San Antonio
The Junior Forum of San Antonio, Texas

Dulce con Nueces (Brown Sugar Pralines)

2 cups sugar
1 cup firmly packed dark
   brown sugar
1 teaspoon baking soda
⅛ teaspoon salt
1 cup buttermilk

⅔ cup light corn syrup
2 tablespoons butter, melted
2 teaspoons vanilla extract
1½ cups pecan halves
1 teaspoon hot water

Combine sugars, soda, salt, buttermilk, and corn syrup in a small Dutch oven, mixing well. Cook over medium-low heat, stirring occasionally, until mixture reaches soft ball stage (234°). Remove from heat; add butter and vanilla, stirring until mixture begins to thicken. Add pecans, and stir until mixture is thick and creamy. Stir in water. Working rapidly, drop mixture by rounded tablespoonfuls onto wax paper; let stand until firm. Remove from wax paper, and store in an airtight container. Yield: 2½ dozen.

Crème de Colorado
The Junior League of Denver, Colorado

Mexican Fried Ice Cream

½ gallon French vanilla ice
   cream
4 to 5 cups corn flakes,
   coarsely crushed
1 tablespoon plus 1 teaspoon
   ground cinnamon

Vegetable oil
Honey
Sweetened whipped cream
Cinnamon-Sugar Tortillas

Place 8 scoops of ice cream on a baking sheet; freeze ice cream balls at least 1 hour or until firm.

Combine crushed corn flakes and cinnamon in a shallow dish. Roll each ice cream ball in corn flake mixture, coating well. Place coated ice cream balls on baking sheet. Cover and freeze several hours or until very firm.

Fry ice cream balls in deep hot oil (375°) for 10 to 20 seconds or until golden brown. Drain on paper towels, and serve immediately with honey, sweetened whipped cream, and Cinnamon-Sugar Tortillas. Yield: 8 servings.

Cinnamon-Sugar Tortillas

¼ cup sugar
½ teaspoon ground cinnamon

4 (8-inch) flour tortillas
Vegetable oil

Combine sugar and cinnamon, stirring well; set aside. Cut each tortilla into 4 wedges. Heat ½ inch of oil in a large skillet to 350°. Fry tortilla wedges, a few at a time, 1 minute or until golden brown. Drain well on paper towels, and sprinkle with sugar mixture. Yield: 16 tortillas.

Crème de Colorado
The Junior League of Denver, Colorado

Capirotada (Mexican Bread Pudding)

½ (1-pound) loaf French
   bread, toasted
1 cup firmly packed brown
   sugar
1 cup water
1 (3-inch) stick cinnamon

1 cup sliced cooking apple
1 cup raisins
1 cup chopped walnuts
8 ounces Monterey Jack
   cheese, cubed

Break toasted bread into bite-size pieces, and set aside.

Combine brown sugar, water, and cinnamon stick in a small saucepan; cook over medium heat, stirring occasionally, until sugar dissolves. Cover, reduce heat, and simmer 5 minutes. Remove and discard cinnamon stick; set aside.

Layer half of bread, sliced apple, raisins, chopped walnuts, Monterey Jack cheese, and brown sugar syrup in a 13- x 9- x 2-inch baking dish. Repeat layers, ending with syrup. (Make sure bread is soaked with syrup.) Bake at 350° for 15 minutes. Serve warm with ice cream. Yield: 8 servings.   Antonia Herrera

Around the World, Around Our Town
Friends of the San Pedro Library
San Pedro, California

Flan

¾ cup sugar
¼ cup water
3 eggs, lightly beaten
2 cups milk
½ cup sugar

1 teaspoon vanilla extract
Orange sections (optional)
Sliced fresh strawberries
   (optional)

Combine ¾ cup sugar and water in a heavy saucepan; place over medium heat, and cook, stirring constantly with a wooden spoon, until sugar crystallizes into lumps (about 15 minutes). Continue to cook, stirring constantly, until sugar melts and turns a light golden brown (about 15 minutes). Pour hot caramel mixture into six 6-ounce custard cups or an 8-inch round cakepan. Set aside.

Combine eggs, milk, ½ cup sugar, and vanilla in a large mixing bowl; beat with a wire whisk. Pour egg mixture over caramelized sugar in custard cups or pan. Place cups or pan in a large shallow baking dish. Pour hot water to a depth of 1 inch into dish.

Bake at 300° for 1 hour or until a knife inserted near center comes out clean. Remove cups or pan from water, and cool. To serve, loosen edge of custard with a spatula; invert onto serving plate. If desired, garnish with orange sections and sliced strawberries. Yield: 6 servings.

Crème de Colorado
The Junior League of Denver, Colorado

Huevos Rancheros

3 tablespoons unsalted butter
or margarine, divided
4 eggs
2 (8-inch) flour tortillas
1½ cups (6 ounces) shredded
Cheddar cheese

¼ cup commercial salsa
3 tablespoons commercial
sour cream
Additional commercial salsa

Melt 1 tablespoon butter in a 10-inch crêpe pan, and heat until hot enough to sizzle a drop of water. Cook eggs over low heat to desired degree of doneness; keep warm.

Melt 1 tablespoon butter in crêpe pan over medium heat. Place 1 tortilla in pan, and cook 30 to 45 seconds or until softened; turn tortilla over. Place 2 eggs, ¾ cup cheese, and 2 tablespoons salsa on tortilla; fold in half. Cover and cook 1 minute or until cheese melts. Turn tortilla over; cover and cook 1 minute.

Repeat procedure with remaining ingredients. Top each serving of Huevos Rancheros with a dollop of sour cream and salsa. Yield: 2 servings.

Crème de Colorado
The Junior League of Denver, Colorado

Breakfast Burritos

¼ pound bulk chorizo
2 tablespoons finely chopped
onion
2 tablespoons finely chopped
green pepper
2 eggs
2 tablespoons milk
¼ teaspoon freshly ground
pepper

1 tablespoon butter or
margarine
4 (8-inch) flour tortillas
1 medium tomato, peeled,
seeded, and chopped
½ cup (2 ounces) shredded
Cheddar cheese
Burrito Sauce

Cook sausage, onion, and green pepper in a large skillet until meat is browned and vegetables are tender, stirring to crumble meat; drain and set aside.

Beat eggs, milk, and pepper in a small mixing bowl. Melt butter in an 8-inch skillet over medium heat; add egg mixture. As mixture starts to cook, gently lift edges with a spatula, and tilt pan so that uncooked portion flows underneath. When egg mixture is set, remove from heat.

Spoon sausage mixture off center of each tortilla. Top sausage mixture with eggs, chopped tomato, and shredded cheese.

Fold the edge of tortilla nearest filling up and over filling just until mixture is covered. Fold opposite side of tortilla to center; roll up and secure with a wooden pick. Repeat folding procedure with remaining tortillas. Place on a baking sheet. Bake at 350° for 15 minutes or until burritos are thoroughly heated. Serve with warm Burrito Sauce. Yield: 4 servings.

Burrito Sauce

1 cup chopped onion
2 tablespoons vegetable oil
3½ cups finely chopped
   tomato
1 (4-ounce) can chopped
   green chiles, undrained
½ teaspoon sugar
½ teaspoon salt

¼ teaspoon garlic salt
⅛ teaspoon freshly ground
   pepper
2 tablespoons minced fresh
   parsley
2 tablespoons minced fresh
   cilantro

Sauté chopped onion in oil in a skillet 5 minutes or until tender. Add chopped tomato, chopped green chiles, sugar, salt, garlic salt, and pepper to onion in skillet; simmer 15 minutes or until mixture is slightly thickened, stirring occasionally. Stir in minced fresh parsley and cilantro. Yield: 3 cups.

Crème de Colorado
The Junior League of Denver, Colorado

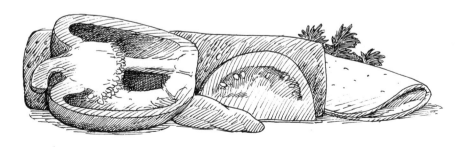

Fajitas

1 (1½-pound) flank steak
¾ cup fresh lime juice
½ cup freshly squeezed
 orange juice
¼ cup tequila
¼ cup vegetable oil
4 cloves garlic, minced
3 green onions, minced
1 teaspoon salt

1 teaspoon Worcestershire
 sauce
¾ teaspoon paprika
½ teaspoon pepper
12 (8-inch) flour tortillas
Pico de Gallo
2 cups (8 ounces) shredded
 Monterey Jack or Cheddar
 cheese

Trim and discard excess fat from steak; place steak in a large shallow dish. Combine lime juice, orange juice, tequila, oil, minced garlic, green onions, salt, Worcestershire sauce, paprika, and pepper, stirring well. Pour marinade over meat. Cover and marinate steak in refrigerator 24 hours, turning occasionally.

Remove steak from marinade, reserving marinade. Grill steak over hot coals 4 to 5 minutes on each side or to desired degree of doneness, basting frequently with marinade. Slice steak diagonally across grain into thin slices.

Wrap tortillas in aluminum foil, and bake at 325° for 15 minutes or until thoroughly heated. Divide meat evenly among tortillas. Top each serving of meat with Pico de Gallo and shredded Monterey Jack cheese; wrap tortilla around filling. Serve Fajitas with remaining Pico de Gallo. Yield: 6 servings.

Pico de Gallo

4 large tomatoes, seeded and
 chopped
1 cup chopped green onions
2 or 3 jalapeño peppers,
 seeded and minced
¼ cup lemon juice

3 tablespoons chopped fresh
 cilantro
Salt to taste
1 teaspoon freshly ground
 pepper
2 avocados

Combine chopped tomato, green onions, minced jalapeño pepper, lemon juice, cilantro, salt, and pepper in a medium bowl, stirring gently. Cover and chill at least 6 hours. Just before serving, peel and chop avocados, and add to tomato mixture. Yield: 6 cups.

California Heritage Continues
The Junior League of Pasadena, California

Chimichangas

1 (4-pound) boneless top
   round roast, cut into
   ½-inch cubes
1 medium onion, chopped
1 clove garlic, crushed
2 tablespoons vegetable oil
2 (4-ounce) cans chopped
   green chiles, undrained
1 (16-ounce) can whole
   tomatoes, undrained and
   chopped

2 teaspoons salt
⅛ teaspoon dried whole
   oregano
12 (8-inch) flour tortillas
Vegetable oil
Shredded lettuce
1 cup (4 ounces) shredded
   Cheddar cheese
1 (8-ounce) carton
   commercial sour cream
1 cup commercial salsa

Place beef in a large ungreased skillet; cover and cook over medium-low heat for 1½ to 2 hours or until moisture has evaporated (do not stir).

Sauté chopped onion and garlic in 2 tablespoons vegetable oil in a medium skillet until tender. Add chopped green chiles to onion mixture in skillet, and cook 2 to 3 minutes.

Drain tomatoes, reserving liquid. Add chopped tomatoes, onion mixture, salt, and oregano to beef, stirring well. Cook over medium heat until mixture is thoroughly heated, adding reserved tomato liquid if mixture becomes too dry. Set beef mixture aside.

Wrap tortillas in aluminum foil, and bake at 325° for 15 minutes or until thoroughly heated.

Spoon about ½ cup of beef mixture off center of a tortilla. Fold the edge nearest filling up and over filling, just until mixture is covered. Fold opposite sides of tortilla to center, and roll up. Secure with a wooden pick. Repeat filling and rolling procedure with remaining beef mixture and tortillas.

Fry filled tortillas in deep hot oil 2 to 3 minutes or until golden brown, turning once. Drain well on paper towels; remove wooden picks. Arrange Chimichangas over shredded lettuce-lined serving platter. Top with cheese, sour cream, and salsa. Serve immediately. Yield: 12 servings.

Purple Sage and Other Pleasures
The Junior League of Tucson, Arizona

Arroz con Pollo (Chicken with Rice)

1 (3½-pound) broiler-fryer, cut up
¾ cup olive oil
1 small onion, chopped
1 clove garlic, minced
1 cup uncooked long-grain rice
2½ cups canned diluted chicken broth
½ cup tomato sauce
½ teaspoon salt
½ teaspoon curry powder
¼ teaspoon pepper
⅛ teaspoon ground saffron
¾ cup frozen English peas, thawed
¼ cup sliced fresh mushrooms

Brown chicken in hot oil in a Dutch oven over medium-high heat. Drain chicken on paper towels. Reserve 1 tablespoon drippings in Dutch oven. Sauté onion and garlic in drippings until tender. Stir in rice, chicken broth, tomato sauce, salt, curry powder, pepper, and saffron. Place chicken over rice mixture. Bring to a boil; cover, reduce heat, and simmer 25 minutes. Add peas and mushrooms. Cover and cook 5 to 10 minutes or until rice and chicken are tender. Yield: 4 to 6 servings.   Thomaline Aguallo Buchan

Around the World, Around Our Town
Friends of the San Pedro Library
San Pedro, California

Chicken Tacos

4 chicken breast halves
1 teaspoon salt
1 medium onion, chopped
1 tablespoon butter or margarine
1 cup chopped tomato
2 teaspoons ground cumin
½ teaspoon salt
½ teaspoon garlic salt
½ teaspoon pepper
¼ cup picante sauce
10 commercial taco shells
1 cup shredded lettuce
1 cup (4 ounces) shredded Cheddar cheese
Fresh cilantro sprigs (optional)

Place chicken in a large saucepan; add water to cover and 1 teaspoon salt. Bring to a boil; cover, reduce heat, and simmer 20 minutes or until tender. Drain, reserving ¼ cup broth. Remove skin, bone chicken, and cube meat; set aside. Sauté onion in butter in a skillet until tender. Stir in chicken, tomato, and next 4 ingredients.

Cover, reduce heat, and simmer 5 minutes. Stir in reserved broth and picante sauce. Simmer, uncovered, 15 minutes. Spoon about ¼ cup chicken mixture into each taco shell; top each with shredded lettuce and cheese. Garnish with fresh cilantro sprigs, if desired. Yield: 5 servings.   Annette Dow

Lone Star Legacy II
The Junior Forum of Austin, Texas

Chicken Tostadas

1 clove garlic, minced	1¾ cups vegetable oil
2 tablespoons vegetable oil	6 (6-inch) flour tortillas
3 cups shredded cooked chicken breast	½ small head iceberg lettuce, thinly sliced
1 (4-ounce) can diced green chiles, drained	1 cup (4 ounces) shredded Cheddar cheese
½ cup commercial sour cream	2 tomatoes, chopped
	Avocado Dressing

Sauté garlic in 2 tablespoons oil in a saucepan until tender. Stir in chicken, chiles, and sour cream. Cook over medium heat until thoroughly heated; remove from heat, and keep warm.

Heat 1¾ cups oil in a 10-inch skillet over medium heat. Fry tortillas, one at a time, 30 seconds on each side or until lightly browned. Drain on paper towels. Arrange lettuce on each tortilla; top with chicken mixture. Sprinkle with cheese and tomato, and top with Avocado Dressing. Yield: 6 servings.

Avocado Dressing

3 tablespoons vegetable oil	½ teaspoon salt
2 tablespoons cider vinegar	1 avocado, peeled and chopped
2 teaspoons minced pickled jalapeño pepper	1 tomato, chopped
½ teaspoon sugar	

Combine all ingredients in a small bowl; stir gently to combine. Cover and chill. Yield: 2 cups.

Crème de Colorado
The Junior League of Denver, Colorado

Chicken Enchiladas with Tomatillo Sauce

2 (3-ounce) packages cream cheese, softened
⅓ cup half-and-half
2 cups shredded cooked chicken
¾ cup finely chopped onion
½ teaspoon salt
Tomatillo Sauce, divided
12 (8-inch) corn tortillas

Vegetable oil
¾ cup (3 ounces) shredded Cheddar cheese
¾ cup (3 ounces) shredded Monterey Jack cheese
Shredded lettuce
Chopped tomato
Ripe olives
Commercial sour cream

Combine cream cheese and half-and-half in a large bowl; beat at medium speed of an electric mixer until smooth. Add chicken, onion, and salt, stirring well.

Pour 2 cups Tomatillo Sauce into a 13- x 9- x 2-inch baking dish; set aside.

Fry tortillas, one at a time, in 2 tablespoons oil in a skillet 5 seconds on each side or just until tortillas are softened; add additional oil, if necessary. Drain on paper towels.

Spread each tortilla with 1 tablespoon Tomatillo Sauce. Place ¼ cup chicken mixture in center of each tortilla, and roll up tortillas. Place filled tortillas, seam side down, in prepared baking dish. Pour 2½ cups Tomatillo Sauce over tortillas. Cover with aluminum foil, and bake at 350° for 20 minutes. Remove foil, and sprinkle enchiladas with cheeses. Bake, uncovered, an additional 5 minutes or until cheese melts. Serve with shredded lettuce, chopped tomato, ripe olives, sour cream, and remaining Tomatillo Sauce. Yield: 6 to 8 servings.

Tomatillo Sauce

24 fresh tomatillos, husked
4 to 6 serrano chiles, seeded and minced
3 cups canned diluted chicken broth

2 tablespoons cornstarch
¼ cup water
1 teaspoon salt
2 tablespoons chopped fresh cilantro

Combine tomatillos, chiles, and chicken broth in a large Dutch oven. Bring to a boil; reduce heat, and simmer 7 to 10 minutes.

Combine cornstarch and water; stir until smooth. Gradually add cornstarch mixture to tomatillo mixture, stirring until mixture thickens. Stir in salt and cilantro. Bring mixture to a boil, and boil 5 minutes. Remove from heat; let cool slightly.

Transfer tomatillo mixture in batches to container of an electric blender or food processor; cover and process until mixture is smooth. Yield: 6 cups.

Crème de Colorado
The Junior League of Denver, Colorado

Shrimp and Jicama Salad with Chile Vinegar

5 cups water	4 large tomatoes, sliced
1 pound unpeeled small fresh shrimp	4 large fresh tomatillos, husked and sliced
Chile Vinegar	Fresh cilantro sprigs (optional)
2 cups peeled, shredded jicama	

Bring water to a boil; add shrimp, and cook 3 to 5 minutes. Drain well; rinse in cold water. Chill. Peel and devein shrimp.

Pour ⅓ cup Chile Vinegar over shrimp, and toss gently. Pour ⅓ cup Chile Vinegar over jicama, and toss gently. Arrange tomato slices and tomatillo slices on individual salad plates; top evenly with jicama mixture. Place shrimp mixture over jicama mixture. Pour remaining Chile Vinegar over salads. Garnish with fresh cilantro sprigs, if desired. Yield: 4 servings.

Chile Vinegar

⅔ cup white wine vinegar	3 tablespoons minced fresh cilantro
¼ cup sugar	2 tablespoons seeded, minced jalapeño pepper
⅛ teaspoon salt	

Combine vinegar, sugar, salt, cilantro, and jalapeño pepper in a medium mixing bowl; stir with a wire whisk until well blended. Yield: 1¼ cups.

Crème de Colorado
The Junior League of Denver, Colorado

Black Bean, Corn, and Bell Pepper Salad

1 cup dried black beans
1 (10-ounce) package frozen corn, thawed
1 medium-size green pepper, chopped
1 medium-size sweet red pepper, chopped
1 jalapeño pepper, seeded and chopped
3 green onions, thinly sliced
2 tablespoons minced fresh parsley
2 tablespoons olive oil
3 tablespoons fresh lime juice
Salt and pepper to taste
Lettuce leaves (optional)

Sort and wash beans; place in a large saucepan. Cover with water 2 inches above beans; let soak at least 8 hours. Drain beans, and cover with fresh water; cook 1 hour or until tender. Drain well, and let beans cool. Combine beans, corn, green pepper, red pepper, jalapeño pepper, green onions, and parsley in a large bowl. Add olive oil, lime juice, salt, and pepper; stir gently to combine. Serve on lettuce leaves, if desired. Yield: 6 servings.

Crème de Colorado
The Junior League of Denver, Colorado

Fresh Hot Sauce

4 jalapeño peppers, seeded
4 poblano chiles, seeded
6 medium tomatoes, peeled, coarsely chopped, and divided
3 large cloves garlic, chopped
1 teaspoon salt
¼ teaspoon coarsely ground pepper
¼ teaspoon honey
½ cup chopped green onions
¼ cup chopped fresh cilantro

Combine peppers, chiles, half the tomatoes, garlic, salt, pepper, and honey in container of an electric blender; cover and process until finely chopped. Place in a large bowl. Stir in remaining tomatoes, green onions, and cilantro. Cover and chill 1 hour. Serve as a dip with tortilla chips or as an accompaniment to scrambled eggs or beef. Yield: 7 cups.   Sandy Baggett

Diamonds in the Desert
The Woman's League of Ozona, Texas

Red Chile Sauce

24 dried red chiles
2 cloves garlic

3 cups water
2 teaspoons salt

Wash chiles; remove stems, seeds, and veins. Place chiles on a baking sheet. Bake at 250° for 10 to 15 minutes, turning often with tongs. Let cool. Rinse chiles with cold water; drain.

Place chiles and garlic in container of an electric blender or food processor; cover and process 10 seconds or until finely chopped. Add water and salt; cover and process 3 to 5 minutes or until mixture is pureed. Store in refrigerator. Serve with beef, chicken, or eggs. Yield: 3¼ cups.

Cooking with the Santa Fe Opera
The Santa Fe Opera Guild
Santa Fe, New Mexico

Gazpacho

½ cup tomato juice
4 cups peeled, seeded, and chopped tomato (about 3 pounds)
1¼ cups peeled, seeded, and chopped cucumber (about 1 pound)
½ cup minced green pepper
½ cup minced onion
2 cups tomato juice, chilled
⅓ cup olive oil

3 tablespoons vinegar
1 clove garlic, minced
2 to 3 tablespoons lemon juice
1 teaspoon salt
½ teaspoon paprika
½ teaspoon pepper
¼ teaspoon hot sauce
Croutons (optional)
Commercial sour cream (optional)

Pour ½ cup tomato juice into ice cube trays to form 6 cubes; freeze. Combine chopped tomato, cucumber, green pepper, onion, and 2 cups tomato juice in a large bowl; stir gently to combine. Add oil and next 7 ingredients; stir gently. Cover and chill at least 4 hours. To serve, ladle soup into chilled bowls, and place a tomato juice cube in each serving. If desired, garnish each serving with croutons and a dollop of sour cream. Yield: 8 cups.

Purple Sage and Other Pleasures
The Junior League of Tucson, Arizona

Tortilla Soup

1 small onion, chopped
1 (4-ounce) can chopped
green chiles, drained
2 cloves garlic, minced
2 tablespoons vegetable oil
1 cup peeled, chopped tomato
1 (10½-ounce) can beef
bouillon
1 (10¾-ounce) can chicken
broth, undiluted
1½ cups water
1 (12-ounce) can tomato juice

1 teaspoon salt
1 teaspoon ground cumin
1 teaspoon chili powder
¼ teaspoon pepper
2 teaspoons Worcestershire
sauce
3 (6-inch) corn tortillas, cut
into ½-inch strips
¼ cup (1 ounce) shredded
Cheddar cheese
1 avocado, peeled and
chopped

Sauté onion, chiles, and garlic in oil in a large Dutch oven until tender. Add tomato and next 9 ingredients. Bring to a boil; cover, reduce heat, and simmer 1 hour. Stir in tortilla strips and cheese; simmer 10 minutes or until tortillas are softened and cheese melts. Garnish with chopped avocado. Yield: 7 cups.

Con Mucho Gusto
The Desert Club of Mesa, Arizona

Caldo de Pollo (Mexican Chicken Soup)

1 (3½- to 4-pound)
broiler-fryer, cut up
4 medium zucchini, cut into
1-inch pieces
1 cup corn, cut from cob
1 large onion, cut into 1-inch
pieces

4 medium tomatoes, cut into
wedges
2 teaspoons cumin seeds
½ teaspoon ground red
pepper
Salt and pepper to taste

Combine all ingredients in a large Dutch oven. Bring to a boil; cover, reduce heat, and simmer 1½ hours. Remove chicken from soup. Remove skin, bone chicken, and dice meat. Add chicken to soup, and cook an additional 15 minutes. Yield: 9 cups.

Celebrate San Antonio
The Junior Forum of San Antonio, Texas

Sopa de Maiz (Mexican Corn Soup)

7 medium ears fresh corn
1 cup canned diluted chicken broth
¼ cup butter or margarine
2 cups milk
1 teaspoon ground cumin
1 clove garlic, minced
1 (4-ounce) can chopped green chiles, undrained
⅛ teaspoon hot sauce
1 teaspoon ground white pepper
8 (6-inch) corn tortillas
2 cups vegetable oil
½ teaspoon salt
1 cup (4 ounces) shredded Monterey Jack cheese with jalapeño peppers
1 cup diced tomato
2 cups diced cooked chicken
1 (8-ounce) jar salsa
1 (4-ounce) can sliced ripe olives, drained
1 (8-ounce) carton commercial sour cream
8 green onions, sliced
1 medium avocado, peeled and diced

Cut corn from cobs, scraping cobs to remove all milk. Combine corn and broth in container of an electric blender; cover and process until smooth. Melt butter in a Dutch oven; add pureed corn mixture, and simmer 5 minutes, stirring constantly. Stir in milk, cumin, and garlic; bring to a boil. Add chiles, hot sauce, and white pepper; reduce heat, and simmer, uncovered, 30 minutes.

Stack tortillas, and cut into 1-inch pieces. Fry tortillas in a skillet in 2 cups hot oil (375°) until golden. Drain on paper towels; sprinkle with salt. Add cheese to soup, stirring until melted. To serve, place 2 tablespoons tomato and ¼ cup chicken in 8 soup bowls. Ladle soup into bowls. Top with tortillas, salsa, olives, sour cream, green onions, and avocado. Yield: 8 cups.

Crème de Colorado
The Junior League of Denver, Colorado

Black Bean Soup

1½ cups dried black beans
6 to 8 cups canned diluted
  chicken broth
1 cup chopped onion
1 cup chopped celery
1 cup shredded carrots
2 tablespoons butter or
  margarine, melted
1 cup shredded red potatoes

1 bay leaf
2 cloves garlic, minced
1 teaspoon dried whole
  oregano
½ teaspoon freshly ground
  pepper
3 tablespoons fresh lemon
  juice
Lemon slices (optional)

Sort and wash beans; place in a large Dutch oven. Cover with water 2 inches above beans; let soak 20 hours. Drain beans, and return to Dutch oven. Add chicken broth; bring to a boil. Cover, reduce heat, and simmer 3 to 4 hours.

Sauté chopped onion, celery, and shredded carrot in butter in a large skillet 3 to 5 minutes or until vegetables are tender. Add vegetable mixture, potato, bay leaf, minced garlic, oregano, and pepper to beans; stir well. Bring to a boil; cover, reduce heat, and simmer 45 minutes or until beans are tender. Remove and discard bay leaf, and stir in lemon juice just before serving. Garnish each serving with a lemon slice, if desired. Yield: 8 cups.

Crème de Colorado
The Junior League of Denver, Colorado

Hot Red Chili

20 dried red chiles, washed
  and seeded
4 pounds coarsely ground
  beef
1 medium onion, chopped
4 or 5 cloves garlic, minced
1 teaspoon vegetable oil
1½ teaspoons salt

1 teaspoon ground oregano
1 teaspoon ground cumin
¼ teaspoon pepper
1 (8-ounce) can tomato sauce
¾ cup water
2 to 3 tablespoons masa
  harina
2 tablespoons water

Place chiles with water to cover in a medium saucepan; cover and simmer until tender. Drain, reserving ¼ cup liquid. Place chiles and reserved liquid in container of an electric blender or food processor; cover and process until smooth. Set aside.

Cook ground beef, chopped onion, and minced garlic in vegetable oil in a large Dutch oven until meat is browned, stirring to crumble meat. Add pureed peppers, salt, oregano, cumin, and pepper. Stir in tomato sauce and ¾ cup water. Cover and bring to a boil; reduce heat, and simmer 3 to 4 hours, adding water, if necessary. Combine masa harina and 2 tablespoons water, stirring well. Add to beef mixture, stirring gently. Cook until mixture is slightly thickened. Yield: 8 cups.   Janice Kallman

Lone Star Legacy II
The Junior Forum of Austin, Texas

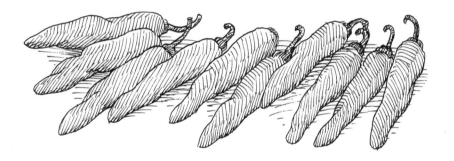

Santo Domingo Red Chili with Pork

1 (4-pound) boneless pork
   roast, trimmed and cut into
   ½-inch cubes
¼ cup lard or bacon
   drippings, melted

8 to 12 dried red chiles,
   washed and seeded
4 cups water
1 clove garlic
1 teaspoon salt

Cook pork in lard in a large Dutch oven until meat is browned and juices from meat have evaporated.

Combine chiles, water, and garlic in container of an electric blender or food processor; cover and process until mixture is smooth. Add chile mixture to pork; stir in salt. Bring to a boil; reduce heat, and simmer, uncovered, 1 hour or until pork is tender, stirring occasionally. Yield: 7 cups.

Cooking with the Santa Fe Opera
The Santa Fe Opera Guild
Santa Fe, New Mexico

Arroz Mexicano (Mexican Rice)

1 cup uncooked long-grain
  rice
2 tablespoons vegetable oil
1 clove garlic
½ teaspoon salt
1 small onion, chopped
1 carrot, scraped and diced
2 tomatoes, peeled and
  chopped

1 cup water
1 cup canned diluted chicken
  broth
⅓ cup frozen English peas,
  thawed
½ teaspoon salt

Sauté rice in vegetable oil in a large heavy saucepan until rice is lightly browned. Mash garlic with ½ teaspoon salt to form a paste; add to rice. Stir in chopped onion and diced carrot. Cook over medium heat, stirring occasionally, until vegetables are tender. Add chopped tomato, and cook 2 minutes. Add water; cover and simmer until water is absorbed. Stir in chicken broth, peas, and ½ teaspoon salt; cover and simmer 30 to 40 minutes or until mixture is thoroughly heated. Yield: 5 cups.

Purple Sage and Other Pleasures
The Junior League of Tucson, Arizona

Maquechou

8 ears fresh corn
2 tablespoons vegetable oil
½ cup finely chopped onion
¼ cup finely chopped green
  pepper

1 large tomato, peeled and
  diced
1½ teaspoons sugar
¾ teaspoon salt
¼ teaspoon pepper

Cut corn from cobs, scraping cobs well to remove all milk. Heat vegetable oil in a large saucepan; add corn, chopped onion, green pepper, diced tomato, sugar, salt, and pepper, stirring well. Cover and simmer 15 to 20 minutes or until mixture is thoroughly heated, stirring occasionally. Yield: 6 servings.   Julie Sentell

Lone Star Legacy II
The Junior Forum of Austin, Texas

Black Beans

1 pound dried black beans	1 teaspoon salt
4 cups water	½ teaspoon pepper
1 (¼-pound) slab of bacon or	Commercial sour cream
5 slices bacon	(optional)
2 green onions, chopped	
1 tablespoon chopped fresh	
cilantro or parsley	

Sort and wash beans; place in a large Dutch oven. Cover with water 2 inches above beans; let soak 8 hours. Drain.

Combine beans, 4 cups water, bacon, green onions, cilantro, salt, and pepper; bring mixture to a boil. Cover, reduce heat, and simmer 3 hours or until beans are tender. Uncover and simmer 30 to 45 minutes or until liquid is reduced. (Bean mixture should be slightly soupy.) Remove and discard bacon before serving. Ladle into bowls, and, if desired, garnish each serving with a dollop of sour cream. Yield: 10 servings.   Julie Sentell

Lone Star Legacy II
The Junior Forum of Austin, Texas

Refried Beans

1 pound dried pinto beans	½ cup vegetable oil
7 cups water	1 teaspoon salt
1 clove garlic, minced	½ cup (2 ounces) shredded
1 slice bacon, chopped	Cheddar cheese

Sort and wash beans thoroughly; place in a large Dutch oven. Add water, garlic, and bacon. Bring to a boil. Cover, reduce heat, and simmer 2½ hours or until beans are tender. Drain.

Heat oil in a large saucepan; add beans and salt. Mash beans. Stir in cheese; cook over medium heat, stirring often, until cheese melts. Yield: 8 servings.   Antonia Herrera

Around the World, Around Our Town
Friends of the San Pedro Library
San Pedro, California

Cactus Mexicano

2 pounds nopales (cactus
  pads)
1 large tomato, diced
1 small onion, chopped

1 clove garlic, minced
½ cup chopped fresh cilantro
1½ teaspoons salt
½ teaspoon pepper

Carefully remove thorns and eyes from nopales with a sharp knife; trim outer edges, and cut nopales into ½-inch pieces. Place in a saucepan with water to cover; bring to a boil. Reduce heat, and simmer 30 to 40 minutes or until tender. Drain and let cool.

Combine nopales, tomato, and remaining ingredients, tossing gently to combine. Yield: 6 servings.   Carmen Vasquez

Lone Star Legacy II
The Junior Forum of Austin, Texas

Mexican Zucchini

4 cups thinly sliced zucchini
¾ cup chopped celery
½ large onion, chopped
½ cup sliced sweet red or
  green pepper
2 tablespoons olive oil
½ cup picante sauce

1½ teaspoons dried whole
  basil, crushed
1 teaspoon salt
½ teaspoon freshly ground
  pepper
1 cup (4 ounces) shredded
  Monterey Jack cheese

Sauté zucchini, celery, onion, and sweet red pepper in oil in a large skillet 3 minutes, stirring constantly. Add picante sauce, basil, salt, and pepper; stir well. Cover and cook over medium heat 3 to 5 minutes or until vegetables are tender. Add cheese, stirring until cheese melts. Serve immediately. Yield: 6 servings.

Crème de Colorado
The Junior League of Denver, Colorado

Appetizers & Beverages

Now a ghost town nestled against the snow-capped mountains of Colorado, the abandoned Victorian buildings and pool hall on Main Street in Eureka seem to echo with the sights, sounds, and libations of more exciting days gone by.

☆☆☆

Shoepeg Corn Dip

1 (12-ounce) can shoepeg
  corn, drained
1 cup (4 ounces) shredded
  sharp Cheddar cheese
¼ cup grated Parmesan
  cheese

1 cup commercial sour cream
½ cup mayonnaise
1 to 2 tablespoons grated
  onion
Fresh parsley sprigs
  (optional)

Combine first 6 ingredients; stir well. Chill several hours. Garnish with fresh parsley sprigs, if desired. Serve with taco chips or crackers. Yield: 3½ cups.

Palette to Palate
The Junior League of St. Joseph and Albrecht Art Museum
St. Joseph, Missouri

Horseradish Dip

1 (16-ounce) carton
  commercial sour cream
1 tablespoon minced green
  onions
1 clove garlic, crushed
1 tablespoon paprika
1½ teaspoons dried
  horseradish

1 teaspoon salt
1 teaspoon dried whole
  tarragon, crushed
½ teaspoon pepper
¼ teaspoon garlic salt

Combine all ingredients; stir well. Chill at least 3 hours. Serve with an assortment of fresh vegetables. Yield: about 2 cups.

California Treasure
The Junior League of Fresno, California

Roasted Red Peppers

15 medium-size sweet red
  peppers (about 5 pounds),
  cut into strips
1 (2¼-ounce) can sliced ripe
  olives, undrained
⅓ cup fine, dry
  breadcrumbs
1 teaspoon salt
1 teaspoon pepper
1 teaspoon dried whole
  oregano
2 cloves garlic, minced
¼ cup olive oil

Combine all ingredients in a large bowl; stir well. Spread mixture evenly in 2 shallow roasting pans. Bake at 325° for 1 hour.

Transfer mixture in batches to container of an electric blender or food processor; cover and process until smooth. Place red pepper mixture in a large serving bowl; serve at room temperature with assorted crackers. Yield: about 5 cups.   Marcia Thaler

As You Like It
St. Bernard's School
New York, New York

Spinach Madeleine

2 (10-ounce) packages frozen
  chopped spinach
¼ cup butter or margarine
2 tablespoons all-purpose
  flour
2 tablespoons chopped
  onion
½ cup evaporated milk
1 (6-ounce) roll jalapeño
  cheese, sliced
1 tablespoon prepared
  horseradish
1 teaspoon Worcestershire
  sauce
¾ teaspoon celery salt
½ teaspoon salt
½ teaspoon pepper
½ cup soft breadcrumbs

Cook spinach according to package directions. Drain well, reserving ½ cup liquid. Set aside.

Melt butter in a medium saucepan over low heat; add flour, stirring until smooth. Cook 1 minute, stirring constantly. Add chopped onion, and cook 1 minute. Gradually stir in milk and ½ cup reserved spinach liquid. Cook over medium heat, stirring constantly, until mixture is thickened and bubbly. Stir in jalapeño cheese, horseradish, Worcestershire sauce, celery salt, salt, and pepper. Cook, stirring constantly, until cheese melts. Stir in spinach.

Pour spinach mixture into a 1½-quart casserole. Top with breadcrumbs. Bake at 350° for 20 minutes or until thoroughly heated. Serve with an assortment of fresh vegetables. Yield: about 3 cups.

Bound to Please
The Junior League of Boise, Idaho

Salmon Mousse

1 envelope unflavored gelatin
¼ cup cold water
½ cup whipping cream
1 (8-ounce) package cream cheese
1 cup commercial sour cream
1 teaspoon lemon juice
1 teaspoon Worcestershire sauce
⅛ teaspoon garlic salt
⅛ teaspoon hot sauce
½ cup grated onion

3 tablespoons chopped fresh chives
2 tablespoons chopped fresh parsley
1 to 2 tablespoons prepared horseradish
1 pound smoked salmon, chopped
Shredded lettuce
Sliced pimiento-stuffed olives
Shredded carrot

Soften gelatin in water 1 minute. Place whipping cream in a small saucepan over medium heat; cook until thoroughly heated. Add gelatin mixture, stirring until gelatin dissolves. Set aside.

Place cream cheese in a heavy saucepan. Cook over medium-low heat until softened, stirring constantly. Stir in sour cream, lemon juice, Worcestershire sauce, garlic salt, and hot sauce. Stir in gelatin mixture, onion, chives, parsley, and horseradish. Gently stir in salmon. Spoon mixture into a greased 5-cup fish-shaped mold. Cover and chill until firm.

Unmold mousse onto a serving platter lined with shredded lettuce. Garnish mousse with sliced olives and shredded carrot. Serve with crackers. Yield: 5 cups.   Elaine Wolfe

Beyond the Village Gate
The Parmadale Children's Village
Parma, Ohio

Layered Seafood Spread

2½ cups water
¾ pound unpeeled medium-size fresh shrimp
1 (8-ounce) package cream cheese, softened
¼ cup lemon juice
1 tablespoon mayonnaise
½ teaspoon seasoned salt
½ teaspoon lemon-pepper seasoning

¼ teaspoon Worcestershire sauce
1 (12-ounce) jar cocktail sauce
2 cups (8 ounces) shredded Monterey Jack cheese
3 green onions, chopped
½ cup chopped green pepper
½ cup sliced ripe olives

Bring water to a boil; add shrimp, and cook 3 to 5 minutes. Drain well; rinse with cold water. Chill. Peel and devein shrimp. Chop half the shrimp. Chill chopped shrimp and remaining whole shrimp.

Beat cream cheese at medium speed of an electric mixer until light and fluffy. Add lemon juice, mayonnaise, seasoned salt, lemon-pepper seasoning, and Worcestershire sauce, and beat until smooth. Spread mixture into a 10-inch circle on a large serving platter. Cover and chill at least 30 minutes.

Spread cocktail sauce evenly over cream cheese mixture. Layer chopped shrimp, shredded Monterey Jack cheese, and remaining ingredients except whole shrimp over cocktail sauce. Top with whole shrimp. Cover and chill thoroughly. Serve with assorted crackers. Yield: 25 appetizer servings.

Uptown Down South
The Junior League of Greenville, South Carolina

Oysters Rockefeller Spread

2 (10-ounce) packages frozen chopped spinach, thawed and drained
1 (12-ounce) container Standard oysters, undrained
¼ cup butter or margarine
1 clove garlic, minced

¼ cup all-purpose flour
⅓ cup chopped green onions
⅓ cup chopped fresh parsley
1 teaspoon salt
1 teaspoon anchovy paste
¼ teaspoon ground red pepper

Press spinach between paper towels to remove excess moisture. Set spinach aside.

Place oysters and oyster liquor in a saucepan. Bring to a boil. Remove from heat; let stand 5 minutes or until edges of oysters curl. Drain oysters, reserving liquor. Add water to liquor to make 1 cup, if necessary. Chop oysters. Set oyster liquor and oysters aside.

Melt butter in medium saucepan over low heat; add garlic, and sauté 1 minute. Add flour, stirring until smooth. Cook 1 minute, stirring constantly. Gradually add reserved oyster liquor; cook over medium heat, stirring constantly, until mixture is thickened and bubbly. Stir in spinach, chopped oysters, green onions, parsley, salt, anchovy paste, and red pepper. Serve in a chafing dish with party rye bread. Yield: 3⅓ cups.

The Kentucky Derby Museum Cookbook
The Kentucky Derby Museum
Louisville, Kentucky

Tarheel Crocks

2 cups (8 ounces) shredded
  sharp Cheddar cheese
2 hard-cooked eggs, mashed
¾ cup mayonnaise
8 pimiento-stuffed olives,
  chopped
1 teaspoon chopped fresh
  parsley

1 teaspoon Worcestershire
  sauce
¾ teaspoon grated onion
½ teaspoon salt
¼ teaspoon paprika

Combine all ingredients in a large mixing bowl; stir well. Pack cheese mixture into a cheese crock. Store in refrigerator. Serve with crackers. Yield: 2¼ cups.

Even More Special
The Junior League of Durham and Orange Counties,
North Carolina

Chutney Cheese Balls

3 (8-ounce) packages cream
  cheese, softened
1 cup commercial sour cream
1 cup chopped raisins
1 cup chopped salted peanuts
8 slices bacon, cooked and
  crumbled

½ cup chopped green onions
1 tablespoon plus 1 teaspoon
  curry powder
⅓ cup flaked coconut
⅓ cup minced fresh parsley
2 tablespoons chutney

Combine cream cheese and sour cream in a large bowl; beat at medium speed of an electric mixer until smooth. Add raisins and next 4 ingredients, stirring well. Shape mixture into 2 balls. Combine coconut and parsley; roll cheese balls in coconut mixture. Cover and chill at least 4 hours. Top each cheese ball with chutney before serving. Serve with crackers. Yield: 5½ cups.

Winning at the Table
The Junior League of Las Vegas, Nevada

Garlic Cheese Ball

2 (8-ounce) packages cream
  cheese, softened
4 cups (16 ounces) shredded
  sharp Cheddar cheese
1 or 2 large cloves garlic,
  crushed
¼ teaspoon ground red
  pepper
⅓ cup chopped
  pimiento-stuffed olives

1 (4-ounce) jar diced
  pimiento, undrained
1 teaspoon Worcestershire
  sauce
½ cup chopped walnuts or
  pecans
Paprika

Combine first 7 ingredients, stir well. Stir in walnuts. Shape mixture into 2 cheese balls, and sprinkle with paprika. Chill 8 hours. Serve with crackers. Yield: 4¾ cups.   Brenda Phillips

Down Home in High Style
The Houston Academy
Dothan, Alabama

Artichoke-Parmesan Strudel

1 medium onion, finely
  chopped
2 cloves garlic, minced
¼ cup butter or margarine
3 (6-ounce) jars marinated
  artichoke hearts, drained
  and chopped
1 (8-ounce) package cream
  cheese, softened
1 cup cottage cheese
1¼ cups freshly grated
  Parmesan cheese
3 eggs, beaten

½ cup cracker crumbs
1 teaspoon garlic salt
1 teaspoon dried whole
  marjoram
1 teaspoon minced fresh
  parsley
¾ teaspoon dried whole
  tarragon
15 (18½- x 12-inch) sheets
  frozen phyllo pastry,
  thawed and divided
1 cup butter or margarine,
  melted

Sauté onion and garlic in ¼ cup butter in a skillet until tender. Add artichoke hearts and next 9 ingredients; cook over medium heat 5 minutes or until cheeses melt, stirring often. Set aside.

Place 1 phyllo sheet on a flat surface (keep remaining phyllo covered with a damp towel); brush with melted butter. Layer 4 phyllo sheets on first sheet, brushing each sheet with melted butter.

Spread one-third artichoke mixture crosswise, 1 inch from narrow end of phyllo. Starting at narrow end, carefully roll up jellyroll fashion. Tuck ends under. Carefully place on a lightly greased baking sheet; repeat procedure with remaining phyllo and artichoke mixture. Brush rolls with remaining melted butter. Bake at 350° for 30 minutes or until lightly browned. Cut into 1-inch slices, and serve warm. Yield: 30 appetizer servings.

Very Innovative Parties
The Loma Linda University School of Dentistry Auxiliary
Loma Linda, California

Chippewa Quiche

⅓ cup uncooked wild rice
Pastry for 9-inch pie
1½ cups diced ham (about ½ pound)
2 cups (8 ounces) shredded Swiss cheese

2 tablespoons butter or margarine
½ cup diced green pepper
3 green onions, minced
4 eggs
1 cup whipping cream

Cook wild rice according to package directions. Line bottom of a 13- x 9- x 2-inch baking pan with pastry. Prick pastry with a fork. Bake at 450° for 5 to 6 minutes. Let cool completely.

Layer cooked wild rice, diced ham, and shredded Swiss cheese over pastry; set aside.

Melt butter in a small skillet over medium heat. Add green pepper and green onions, and sauté until tender. Sprinkle sautéed vegetables over cheese. Beat eggs and whipping cream until well blended. Pour egg mixture over mixture in pan. Bake at 375° for 35 to 45 minutes or until set. Let cool slightly; cut into 1½-inch squares. Serve immediately. Yield: 30 appetizer servings.

Wild Rice, Star of the North
The 1006 Summit Avenue Society
St. Paul, Minnesota

Mushroom Tarts

24 slices white bread
¼ cup butter or margarine, melted
¼ cup minced green onions
¼ cup butter or margarine, melted
½ pound fresh mushrooms, finely chopped
2 tablespoons all-purpose flour
1 cup whipping cream

1 tablespoon plus 1½ teaspoons minced fresh chives
1 tablespoon minced fresh parsley
½ teaspoon salt
½ teaspoon lemon juice
⅛ teaspoon ground red pepper
Grated Parmesan cheese

Cut a 3-inch circle from each slice of bread, using a 3-inch biscuit cutter. Brush miniature (1¾-inch) muffin pans with melted butter.

Gently fit bread rounds into miniature muffin pans, forming cups. Brush bread with remaining melted butter. Bake at 400° for 10 minutes or until lightly browned. Let cool in pan.

Sauté green onions in ¼ cup butter in a large heavy skillet 1 minute. Stir in mushrooms; cook, uncovered, 10 minutes. Remove from heat, and stir in flour. Gradually stir in whipping cream. Bring mixture to a boil over medium heat; cook 1 minute or until mixture is thickened and bubbly. Remove from heat; stir in chives and next 4 ingredients.

Spoon mushroom mixture evenly into toast cups. Sprinkle Parmesan cheese over mushroom mixture. Bake at 350° for 10 minutes. Serve immediately. Yield: 2 dozen.   Bonnie Harris

Let's Table It
The Vermont Center for Independent Living
Montpelier, Vermont

Chicken-Almond Puffs

1 cup chicken broth
½ cup butter or
   margarine
1 cup all-purpose flour
¼ teaspoon salt
4 eggs

½ cup diced cooked
   chicken
2 tablespoons chopped
   blanched almonds,
   toasted
⅛ teaspoon paprika

Combine chicken broth and butter in a medium saucepan; bring to a boil. Combine flour and salt; add all at once to broth mixture, stirring vigorously over low heat until mixture leaves sides of pan and forms a smooth ball. Remove from heat, and let cool slightly.

Add eggs, one at a time, beating with a wooden spoon after each addition; beat until batter is smooth. Stir in chicken, almonds, and paprika. Drop by heaping teaspoonfuls 2 inches apart onto ungreased baking sheets. Bake at 450° for 10 minutes; reduce heat to 350°, and bake 5 to 10 minutes or until golden brown. Serve immediately. Yield: 4 dozen.

Out of Our League, Too
The Junior League of Greensboro, North Carolina

Empanaditas

2 cups butter, softened
2 (8-ounce) packages cream
  cheese, softened
1 teaspoon salt
4 cups all-purpose flour
1 pound ground beef
¾ cup finely chopped onion
3 cloves garlic, crushed

¼ cup plus 1 tablespoon
  finely chopped salad olives
2 (4-ounce) cans chopped
  green chiles, undrained
¼ cup raisins, chopped
¼ teaspoon salt
2 egg yolks, beaten
¼ cup milk

Combine butter, cream cheese, and 1 teaspoon salt in a large bowl; beat at medium speed of an electric mixer until smooth. Add flour, 1 cup at a time, kneading until well blended. Shape pastry into an 8- x 6-inch rectangle; chill several hours or overnight.

Combine ground beef, onion, and garlic in a large skillet; cook over medium heat until meat is browned and onion is tender, stirring to crumble meat. Stir in olives, chiles, raisins, and ¼ teaspoon salt; cook until liquid has evaporated. Let cool.

Remove pastry from refrigerator, and let stand at room temperature 30 minutes. Divide pastry in half; roll half of pastry to ¼-inch thickness on a lightly floured surface. Cut into 24 (3-inch) circles. Place about 2 teaspoons meat mixture on half of each pastry circle. Fold circles in half, making sure edges are even. Press edges of filled pastries together firmly, using a fork dipped in flour. Repeat with remaining pastry and meat mixture. Place pastries on lightly greased baking sheets.

Combine egg yolks and milk; stir well. Brush over tops of pastries. Bake at 375° for 12 to 15 minutes or until pastries are golden brown. Yield: 4 dozen.

Cooking with the Santa Fe Opera
The Santa Fe Opera Guild
Santa Fe, New Mexico

Kielbasa Appetizers

1 (12-ounce) jar apricot
  preserves
2 tablespoons lemon juice
2 teaspoons Dijon mustard

½ teaspoon ground ginger
1 pound kielbasa, cut into
  ¼-inch pieces

Combine all ingredients except kielbasa in a medium saucepan, and stir well. Cook over low heat 2 to 3 minutes, stirring constantly. Add kielbasa, and cook until sausage is thoroughly heated. Serve warm. Yield: 5 dozen.   Julia W. Kozikowski

Na Zdrowie II
The Women's Auxiliary-Polish American Club of Agawam
Feeding Hills, Massachusetts

Chicken Waikiki

**4 chicken breast halves,
 skinned and boned**
¼ cup lemon juice
¼ cup dry sherry
**3 tablespoons Worcestershire
 sauce**

**½ cup finely chopped
 macadamia nuts**
½ cup fine, dry breadcrumbs
½ cup all-purpose flour
2 eggs, beaten
Chutney Sauce

Cut chicken into 1-inch pieces. Combine lemon juice, sherry, and Worcestershire sauce in a medium bowl. Add chicken pieces, tossing to coat well. Cover tightly, and marinate chicken in refrigerator at least 30 minutes.

Combine macadamia nuts and breadcrumbs in a small bowl. Remove chicken pieces from marinade, discarding marinade. Dredge chicken in flour; dip in beaten egg, and dredge in macadamia nut mixture. Place chicken on a lightly greased 15- x 10- x 1-inch jellyroll pan. Bake at 350° for 25 to 30 minutes or until done. Serve warm with Chutney Sauce. Yield: 4½ dozen.

Chutney Sauce

¾ cup mayonnaise
**¼ cup prepared
 mustard**

**3 tablespoons chutney,
 finely chopped**

Combine all ingredients in a small bowl, stirring well. Cover and chill. Yield: 1 cup.   Adele Davis

We, The Women of Hawaii Cookbook
We, The Women of Hawaii
Waialua, Oahu

Blue Cheese-Stuffed Shrimp

6 cups water
2 dozen unpeeled jumbo
  fresh shrimp
1 (3-ounce) package cream
  cheese, softened
1 ounce blue cheese, crumbled

½ teaspoon prepared mustard
1 teaspoon finely chopped
  green onions
¾ cup finely chopped fresh
  parsley

Bring water to a boil; add shrimp, and cook 3 to 5 minutes. Drain well; rinse with cold water. Chill. Peel and devein shrimp. Butterfly shrimp, leaving tails intact.

Combine cream cheese and next 3 ingredients in a bowl. Stuff each shrimp with 1 teaspoon cheese mixture. Roll cut side of shrimp in parsley. Cover and chill at least 1 hour. Yield: 2 dozen.

Celebrated Seasons
The Junior League of Minneapolis, Minnesota

Savory Cheese Wafers

1 (8-ounce) round fully
  ripened Brie
½ cup butter or margarine,
  cut into pieces
1¼ cups all-purpose flour
2 teaspoons dry mustard

½ teaspoon salt
⅛ teaspoon ground white
  pepper
1 egg, beaten
1 teaspoon water
1 cup finely chopped walnuts

Remove and discard rind from cheese. Cut cheese into small pieces. Position knife blade in food processor bowl. Add cheese, butter, and next 4 ingredients. Cover and process 30 seconds or until mixture forms a ball and pulls away from sides of bowl.

Shape dough into two 8-inch logs. Combine egg and water in a shallow container. Dip logs in egg mixture, turning to coat. Transfer to wax paper, and let dry slightly. Roll logs in chopped walnuts; cover and chill thoroughly. Cut logs into ½-inch slices. Place slices on ungreased baking sheets; bake at 425° for 12 to 15 minutes or until lightly browned. Let cool on wire racks. Yield: 2½ dozen.

Boston Tea Parties
The Museum of Fine Arts
Boston, Massachusetts

Sweet-and-Spicy Almonds

3 tablespoons peanut oil
2 cups whole blanched
  almonds
½ cup plus 1 tablespoon
  sugar, divided

1½ teaspoons salt
1½ teaspoons ground cumin
1 teaspoon ground red
  pepper

Heat oil in a large heavy skillet over medium heat. Add almonds; sprinkle with ½ cup sugar. Cook 10 to 15 minutes or until almonds are golden brown and sugar is melted, stirring frequently. Remove from heat; transfer to a large bowl. Add remaining 1 tablespoon sugar, salt, cumin, and red pepper. Toss almonds gently to coat well. Spread coated almonds in a single layer on wax paper; let cool. Store in an airtight container. Yield: 2 cups.

The Gathering
The Blue Bird Circle
Houston, Texas

Cocktail Pecans

3 tablespoons butter or
  margarine, melted
3 tablespoons Worcestershire
  sauce
1 teaspoon salt
½ teaspoon ground
  cinnamon

¼ teaspoon garlic powder
¼ teaspoon ground red
  pepper
Dash of hot sauce
1 pound pecan halves

Combine melted butter, Worcestershire sauce, salt, cinnamon, garlic powder, red pepper, and hot sauce in a large bowl, stirring well. Add pecan halves to mixture, stirring gently to coat well. Spread coated pecans in a single layer in a 15- x 10- x 1-inch jellyroll pan. Bake at 300° for 25 to 30 minutes, stirring frequently. Drain pecans on paper towels; let cool. Store in an airtight container. Yield: 5 cups.

Jean Goodrich

Santa Barbara: 200 Years of Good Taste
The Santa Barbara Historical Society-Docent Council
Santa Barbara, California

Uncle Tench's Whiskey Punch

3 quarts boiling water
18 regular-size tea bags
4 cups sugar
6 (25.4-ounce) bottles whiskey

2 (25.4-ounce) bottles rum
1 quart lemon juice
3⅓ cups orange juice

Pour boiling water over tea bags; cover and steep 5 minutes. Remove tea bags, squeezing gently. Add sugar to tea, stirring until sugar dissolves.

Pour sweetened tea into a large glass container. Add whiskey and remaining ingredients, stirring well. Cover tightly, and let stand at room temperature one week. Serve punch over crushed ice. Yield: about 3 gallons.   Anne Goodpasture

Keeping the Feast
The Episcopal Church Women of St. Thomas Church
Abingdon, Virginia

Pink Lady Punch

1 quart cranberry juice
cocktail
1 quart pineapple juice

1½ cups sugar
2 quarts ginger ale, chilled

Combine cranberry juice cocktail, pineapple juice, and sugar in a large container; stir until sugar dissolves. Chill. Stir in ginger ale just before serving. Yield: 1 gallon.   Leola Helvin

Parker's Blue Ribbon Recipes
The Parker Ward Relief Society
St. Anthony, Idaho

Hot Apple Cider Punch

1 gallon apple cider	1 medium orange, sliced
1 quart ginger ale	2 (3-inch) sticks cinnamon
¾ cup red cinnamon candies	1½ teaspoons whole cloves

Pour apple cider and ginger ale into a 30-cup percolator. Place candies and remaining ingredients in percolator basket. Perk through complete cycle of percolator. Serve hot. Yield: 1¼ gallons.

Unbearably Good!
The Junior Service League of Americus, Georgia

Miami "Vise"

1 quart vanilla ice cream, softened	3 tablespoons crème de banana
3 tablespoons white crème de menthe	3 tablespoons white crème de cacao

Combine all ingredients in container of an electric blender; cover and process until smooth. Serve immediately. Yield: 4 cups.

Make It Miami
The Guild of the Museum of Science, Inc.
Miami, Florida

Spiced Iced Coffee

6 cups hot coffee	10 whole allspice
¼ cup sugar	2 black peppercorns
2 (6-inch) sticks cinnamon	Half-and-half
10 whole cloves	Sugar

Combine first 6 ingredients; stir well. Let stand at room temperature 1 hour. Strain and serve over cracked ice. Serve with half-and-half and sugar. Yield: 6 cups.   Helen Schrader

The Cooks' Book
The Nightingale-Bamford School
New York, New York

Café Brûlot

¼ cup plus 2 tablespoons
   sugar
8 (3-inch) strips lemon rind
4 (3-inch) strips orange rind
4 (3-inch) sticks cinnamon,
   broken in half, or ½
   teaspoon ground cinnamon
10 whole cloves

4 whole allspice or ½
   teaspoon ground allspice
1½ cups brandy, divided
½ cup curaçao or other
   orange-flavored liqueur
   (optional)
4 cups hot coffee

Combine first 6 ingredients in a chafing dish; crush slightly, using the back of a spoon. Combine 1 cup brandy and, if desired, curaçao in a small saucepan. Heat just until thoroughly heated (do not boil); pour into chafing dish.

Place remaining ½ cup brandy in a small saucepan with a long handle. Heat just long enough to produce fumes (do not boil). Remove from heat; ignite and pour over ingredients in chafing dish. Add coffee. Ladle into demitasse cups, and serve immediately. Yield: 6 cups.

Artist's Palate Cookbook
New Orleans Museum of Art-Women's Volunteer Committee
New Orleans, Louisiana

Spiced Tea

3 cups water
⅔ cup sugar
4 whole cloves
2 (2-inch) sticks cinnamon

2 tablespoons loose tea
⅔ cup orange juice, chilled
⅓ cup lemon juice, chilled
2⅓ cups ice water

Combine 3 cups water, sugar, cloves, and cinnamon sticks in a medium saucepan. Bring to a boil, and boil 5 minutes. Strain and pour over tea; let steep 3 minutes. Strain. Stir in juices and ice water. Serve immediately. Yield: 6 cups.   Mrs. C. V. Whitney

The Great Entertainer Cookbook
The Buffalo Bill Historical Center
Cody, Wyoming

Breads

A water mill, such as this restored one built in 1797 next to Clear Creek in Tennessee, was commonly used to harness the power of water to grind grain into flour and meal products that could be used for baking.

☆☆☆

Cranberry-Raisin Bread

4 cups all-purpose flour
1¾ cups sugar
1 tablespoon baking
powder
1 teaspoon baking soda
1½ teaspoons salt
½ cup unsalted butter or
margarine
2 eggs

1 tablespoon grated orange
rind
1½ cups orange juice
2 cups fresh or frozen
cranberries, thawed and
coarsely chopped
1 cup raisins
Cranberry Butter

Combine flour, sugar, baking powder, soda, and salt in a large mixing bowl; cut in ½ cup unsalted butter with a pastry blender until mixture resembles coarse meal.

Combine eggs, orange rind, and orange juice in a large mixing bowl; add flour mixture, stirring well. Gently fold in chopped cranberries and raisins.

Pour batter into two greased 9- x 5- x 3-inch loafpans. Bake at 350° for 1 hour and 10 minutes or until a wooden pick inserted in center comes out clean. Cool in pans 10 minutes; remove bread from pans, and let cool on wire racks. Serve bread with Cranberry Butter. Yield: 2 loaves.

Cranberry Butter

1 cup fresh or frozen
cranberries, thawed
1 cup sifted powdered
sugar

½ cup unsalted butter,
softened
1 tablespoon lemon juice

Place cranberries and powdered sugar in container of an electric blender or food processor. Cover and process until cranberries are finely minced, scraping sides of processor bowl occasionally. Add butter and lemon juice; process until smooth.

Transfer Cranberry Butter to a serving bowl. Cover and chill until firm. Yield: 1¼ cups.

California Heritage Continues
The Junior League of Pasadena, California

Pear Bread

½ cup unsalted butter or margarine, softened
1 cup sugar
2 eggs
1 teaspoon vanilla extract
2 cups all-purpose flour
1 teaspoon baking powder
½ teaspoon baking soda
½ teaspoon salt
⅛ teaspoon ground nutmeg
¼ cup buttermilk
1 cup peeled, cored, and coarsely chopped pear
½ cup chopped pecans (optional)

Cream butter; gradually add sugar, beating well at medium speed of an electric mixer. Add eggs, one at a time, beating after each addition. Stir in vanilla.

Combine flour, baking powder, soda, salt, and nutmeg in a medium bowl; add to creamed mixture alternately with buttermilk, beginning and ending with flour mixture. Gently fold in chopped pear and, if desired, pecans.

Spoon batter into a well-greased 9- x 5- x 3-inch loafpan. Bake at 350° for 50 to 60 minutes or until a wooden pick inserted in center comes out clean. Cool in pan 10 minutes; remove from pan, and let cool on a wire rack. Yield: 1 loaf.

Boston Tea Parties
The Museum of Fine Arts
Boston, Massachusetts

Oregon Prune Bread

2 cups boiling water
2 cups prunes, pitted and chopped
2 teaspoons baking soda
2 tablespoons butter or margarine, softened
1¼ cups sugar
1 egg
4 cups all-purpose flour
2 teaspoons baking powder
1 teaspoon salt
1 teaspoon vanilla extract
1 cup walnuts, chopped

Combine water, prunes, and baking soda in a large mixing bowl; stir well. Set aside, and let cool.

Cream butter; gradually add sugar, beating at medium speed of an electric mixer until light and fluffy. Add egg, beating well. Drain prune mixture, reserving liquid. Set prunes and liquid aside. Combine flour, baking powder, and salt; add to creamed mixture alternately with reserved liquid from prunes, beginning and ending with flour mixture. Stir in prunes, vanilla, and walnuts.

Pour batter into two greased 8½- x 4½- x 3-inch loafpans. Bake at 350° for 1 hour or until a wooden pick inserted in center comes out clean. Cool in pans 10 minutes; remove from pans, and let cool on wire racks. Yield: 2 loaves.

Rave Revues
Lakewood Center Associates, Lakewood Center for the Arts
Lake Oswego, Oregon

Chocolate-Almond Zucchini Bread

3 eggs
1 cup sugar
1 cup firmly packed brown sugar
1 cup vegetable oil
1 teaspoon vanilla extract
2 (1-ounce) squares unsweetened chocolate, melted

2 cups shredded zucchini
2 cups all-purpose flour
1 teaspoon baking soda
½ teaspoon baking powder
1 teaspoon salt
1 teaspoon ground cinnamon
1 cup slivered almonds

Beat eggs in a large mixing bowl at medium speed of an electric mixer until thick and lemon colored. Add sugar, brown sugar, vegetable oil, and vanilla, beating well. Stir in melted chocolate and shredded zucchini.

Combine flour, soda, baking powder, salt, and cinnamon in a medium mixing bowl; add flour mixture to zucchini mixture, stirring just until dry ingredients are moistened. Fold in almonds.

Spoon batter into two well-greased 9- x 5- x 3-inch loafpans. Bake at 350° for 50 to 60 minutes or until a wooden pick inserted in center of each loaf comes out clean. Let bread cool in pans 10 minutes; remove loaves from pans, and let bread cool completely on wire racks. Yield: 2 loaves.

A Pinch of Salt Lake
The Junior League of Salt Lake City, Utah

Poppy Seed Bread

2 cups sugar
4 eggs
3 cups all-purpose flour
1 tablespoon plus 1 teaspoon
  baking powder
½ teaspoon salt
1 (12-ounce) can evaporated
  milk
1 cup vegetable oil
½ cup poppy seeds

Beat sugar and eggs in a large bowl at medium speed of an electric mixer until well blended. Combine flour, baking powder, and salt; set aside. Combine milk and oil. Add flour mixture to sugar mixture alternately with milk mixture, beginning and ending with flour mixture. Stir in poppy seeds.

Pour batter into two greased 8½- x 4½- x 3-inch loafpans. Bake at 350° for 50 minutes or until a wooden pick inserted in center comes out clean. Cool in pans 10 minutes; remove from pans, and let cool on wire racks. Yield: 2 loaves.   Lucie Kelly

A Visual Feast
The Founders Society, Detroit Institute of Arts
Detroit, Michigan

Apple and Cream Cheese Coffee Cake

½ cup butter or margarine,
  softened
1 (8-ounce) package cream
  cheese, softened
1 cup sugar
2 eggs
1 teaspoon almond extract
1¾ cups all-purpose flour
1 teaspoon baking powder
½ teaspoon baking soda
¼ teaspoon salt
¼ cup milk
½ cup sugar
2 tablespoons all-purpose
  flour
1 teaspoon ground cinnamon
4 cups peeled, sliced cooking
  apples
2 tablespoons lemon juice

Cream butter and cream cheese in a large mixing bowl; gradually add 1 cup sugar, beating at medium speed of an electric mixer until light and fluffy. Add eggs, one at a time, beating after each addition. Stir in almond extract.

Combine 1¾ cups flour, baking powder, soda, and salt in a medium bowl; add flour mixture to creamed mixture alternately with milk, beginning and ending with flour mixture. Mix well after each addition.

Pour batter into a greased and floured 13- x 9- x 2-inch baking pan. Combine ½ cup sugar, 2 tablespoons flour, and cinnamon in a small mixing bowl. Dip apple slices in lemon juice. Combine apple slices and cinnamon mixture, tossing gently to coat well. Arrange apple slices on top of batter. Bake at 350° for 50 to 60 minutes or until a wooden pick inserted in center comes out clean. Serve warm. Yield: 12 servings.

Faye Wilhelmi

Good Cooking Cookbook
United Lutheran Church
Langdon, North Dakota

Overnight Coffee Cake

¾ cup butter or margarine, softened
1 cup sugar
2 eggs
1 cup commercial sour cream
2 cups all-purpose flour
1 teaspoon baking powder
1 teaspoon baking soda
1 teaspoon ground nutmeg
½ teaspoon salt
¾ cup firmly packed brown sugar
½ cup pecans, chopped
1 teaspoon ground cinnamon

Cream butter in a large mixing bowl; gradually add 1 cup sugar, beating at medium speed of an electric mixer until light and fluffy. Add eggs, one at a time, beating after each addition. Add sour cream, mixing well.

Combine flour and next 4 ingredients; add to creamed mixture, mixing well. Pour batter into a greased and floured 13- x 9- x 2-inch baking pan.

Combine brown sugar, chopped pecans, and cinnamon in a small mixing bowl, stirring well. Sprinkle brown sugar mixture evenly over batter. Cover and chill 8 hours. Uncover and bake at 350° for 35 to 45 minutes or until a wooden pick inserted in center comes out clean. Yield: 12 servings.

The Market Place
The Junior Woman's Club of Augusta, Georgia

Peanut Butter and Jelly Muffins

2 cups all-purpose flour
½ cup sugar
2½ teaspoons baking
  powder
½ teaspoon salt

¾ cup peanut butter
2 eggs, lightly beaten
¾ cup milk
¼ cup strawberry preserves

Combine flour, sugar, baking powder, and salt in a large bowl; cut in peanut butter with a pastry blender until mixture resembles coarse meal. Make a well in center of mixture. Combine eggs and milk; add to dry ingredients, stirring just until moistened.

Spoon half of batter into greased muffin pans, filling one-third full; top each muffin with ¾ teaspoon strawberry preserves. Spoon remaining batter into muffin pans, filling two-thirds full. Bake at 400° for 15 to 17 minutes or until lightly browned. Remove from pans immediately. Yield: 16 muffins.   Nonie Slavitz

A Slice of Nantucket
St. Mary's Guild, St. Mary-Our Lady of the Isle Church
Nantucket, Massachusetts

Sour Cream-Corn Muffins

1 cup yellow cornmeal
1 cup all-purpose flour
¼ cup sugar
2 teaspoons baking powder
½ teaspoon baking soda

1½ teaspoons salt
2 eggs, lightly beaten
1 cup commercial sour cream
¼ cup butter or margarine,
  melted

Combine cornmeal, flour, sugar, baking powder, soda, and salt in a large bowl; make a well in center of mixture. Combine eggs, sour cream, and butter; add to dry ingredients, stirring just until dry ingredients are moistened. Spoon batter into greased miniature (1¾-inch) muffin pans, filling three-fourths full. Bake at 425° for 10 to 12 minutes. Remove muffins from pans immediately, and serve warm. Yield: 2 dozen.

Crème de LA Coast
Small World Guild-Childrens Hospital of Orange County,
California

Scones

¼ cup currants
¼ cup boiling water
2 cups all-purpose flour
2 tablespoons sugar
2½ teaspoons baking powder
½ teaspoon salt

⅓ cup shortening
1 egg, lightly beaten
½ cup plus 2 tablespoons
  milk, divided
1 tablespoon sugar

Combine currants and water; let stand 10 minutes. Drain well, and set aside.

Combine flour, 2 tablespoons sugar, baking powder, and salt in a large mixing bowl; cut in shortening with a pastry blender until mixture resembles coarse meal. Add currants to dry ingredients, stirring well.

Combine beaten egg and ½ cup milk in a small bowl; add milk mixture to dry ingredients, stirring just until dry ingredients are moistened. Turn dough out onto a lightly floured surface, and knead lightly 4 or 5 times.

Divide dough in half. Roll each half to a circle ¼-inch thick. Cut each circle into 6 pie-shaped wedges. Place wedges on a lightly greased baking sheet; brush with remaining 2 tablespoons milk. Sprinkle remaining 1 tablespoon sugar evenly over wedges. Bake at 450° for 10 to 12 minutes or until lightly browned. Serve warm. Yield: 1 dozen.

Sherry A. Liles

Calling All Cooks Two
The Telephone Pioneers of America
Birmingham, Alabama

Olive-Nut Appetizer Bread

2 packages dry yeast
1 cup warm water (105° to 115°)
1 cup milk
3 tablespoons sugar
2 tablespoons butter or margarine
2 teaspoons salt
4½ cups all-purpose flour
2 cups (8 ounces) shredded sharp Cheddar cheese
¾ cup sliced pimiento-stuffed olives
¾ cup chopped walnuts

Dissolve yeast in warm water in a large mixing bowl; let stand 5 minutes. Combine milk, sugar, butter, and salt in a saucepan; heat until butter melts, stirring occasionally. Cool to 120° to 130°. Gradually add milk mixture and flour to yeast mixture, stirring until smooth. Stir in cheese, olives, and walnuts.

Place batter in a well-greased bowl. Cover and let rise in a warm place (85°), free from drafts, 1 hour or until doubled in bulk.

Stir batter well. Spoon batter into a well-greased 10-inch Bundt pan. Bake at 350° for 50 minutes. Remove bread from pan, and let cool on a wire rack. Yield: one 10-inch loaf.

Artist's Palate Cookbook
New Orleans Museum of Art-Women's Volunteer Committee
New Orleans, Louisiana

Proscuitto and Onion Bread

1 package dry yeast
¼ cup warm water (105° to 115°)
1 cup milk
½ cup butter or margarine
2 eggs, beaten
½ cup (2 ounces) chopped proscuitto
2 tablespoons minced onion
½ teaspoon salt
4 cups all-purpose flour
1 tablespoon milk
2 tablespoons sesame seeds

Dissolve yeast in warm water in a large mixing bowl, and let stand 5 minutes.

Combine milk and butter in a saucepan; heat until butter melts, stirring occasionally. Cool to 105° to 115°. Add milk mixture, eggs, proscuitto, onion, and salt to yeast mixture, stirring until blended. Add flour, stirring well (dough will be sticky).

Place dough in a well-greased 1½-quart soufflé dish. Brush top with 1 tablespoon milk; sprinkle with sesame seeds. Cover and let rise in a warm place (85°), free from drafts, 1 hour or until doubled in bulk. Bake at 350° for 25 to 30 minutes or until top is lightly browned and loaf sounds hollow when tapped. Remove from dish; let cool slightly on a wire rack. Serve warm. Yield: 1 loaf.

Peachtree Bouquet
The Junior League of DeKalb County, Georgia

Cracked Pepper Bread

4¼ cups all-purpose flour, divided

2 tablespoons sugar

¾ teaspoon salt

2 teaspoons coarsely ground pepper

1 package dry yeast

1¼ cups milk

2 tablespoons butter or margarine

1 egg

1 egg yolk, beaten

Combine 2 cups flour, sugar, salt, pepper, and yeast in a large mixing bowl; stir well. Combine milk and butter in a saucepan; heat until butter melts, stirring occasionally. Cool to 120° to 130°.

Gradually add milk mixture to flour mixture, beating at high speed of an electric mixer. Add egg and ½ cup flour; beat 2 minutes at medium speed. Gradually stir in remaining 1¾ cups flour to make a soft dough. Turn dough out onto a lightly floured surface, and knead until smooth and elastic. Place in a well-greased bowl, turning to grease top. Cover and let rise in a warm place (85°), free from drafts, 1 hour or until doubled in bulk.

Punch dough down; let rest 10 minutes. Divide dough in half. Shape each half into a round, slightly flat loaf. Place loaves on a lightly greased baking sheet; brush with egg yolk. Make several diagonal slits about ¼-inch deep across the top of each loaf, using a sharp knife.

Cover and let rise in a warm place, free from drafts, 45 minutes or until doubled in bulk. Bake at 375° for 15 to 20 minutes or until loaves sound hollow when tapped. Remove from baking sheet immediately, and let cool on wire racks. Yield: 2 loaves.

Cooking in Clover II
The Jewish Hospital of St. Louis, Missouri

Herb-Parmesan Bread

2 packages dry yeast
2 cups warm water (105° to 115°)
½ cup grated Parmesan cheese
2 tablespoons sugar
2 tablespoons butter or margarine, melted

1 tablespoon plus 1½ teaspoons dried whole oregano
2 teaspoons salt
4¼ cups all-purpose flour
1 tablespoon grated Parmesan cheese

Dissolve yeast in warm water in a large mixing bowl; let stand 5 minutes. Add ½ cup Parmesan cheese, sugar, butter, oregano, salt, and 3 cups flour; beat at medium speed of an electric mixer 2 minutes. Gradually stir in remaining flour (dough will be sticky).

Place dough in a well-greased bowl, turning to grease top. Cover and let rise in a warm place (85°), free from drafts, 45 minutes or until doubled in bulk. Stir dough well. Place in a lightly greased 2-quart soufflé dish. Sprinkle 1 tablespoon Parmesan cheese over dough. Bake at 375° for 45 minutes or until golden. Remove from dish; let cool on a wire rack. Yield: 1 loaf.   Mavis Flemmer

A Rainbow of Recipes
The Education Department, Regional Treatment Center
Fergus Falls, Minnesota

Caraway Puffs

1 package dry yeast
2⅓ cups all-purpose flour, divided
¼ teaspoon baking soda
1 cup cottage cheese
¼ cup water
1 tablespoon butter or margarine

2 tablespoons sugar
1 teaspoon salt
1 egg
2 teaspoons caraway seeds
2 teaspoons grated onion

Combine yeast, 1⅓ cups flour, and baking soda; set aside.

Place cottage cheese in container of an electric blender or food processor; cover and process until smooth. Combine cottage cheese, water, butter, sugar, and salt in a saucepan; heat until butter melts, stirring occasionally. Cool to 120° to 130°. Add to dry ingredients, beating at low speed of an electric mixer until well blended. Add egg, caraway seeds, and grated onion, beating at medium speed 3 minutes. Stir in remaining 1 cup flour. Turn dough out onto a lightly floured surface, and knead 6 to 8 times. Place in a well-greased bowl, turning to grease top. Cover and let rise in a warm place (85°), free from drafts, 1½ hours or until doubled in bulk.

Punch dough down; turn out onto a lightly floured surface, and knead lightly 4 or 5 times. Divide dough into 12 equal pieces. Shape each piece into a ball, and place in greased muffin pans. Cover and let rise in a warm place, free from drafts, 30 minutes or until doubled in bulk. Bake at 400° for 12 to 15 minutes or until lightly browned. Yield: 1 dozen.

Hunt to Harbor
The Junior League of Baltimore, Maryland

Bread Sticks

1 package dry yeast
1½ cups warm water (105° to 115°)
1 tablespoon honey
1 teaspoon salt
4 to 4½ cups all-purpose flour

3 tablespoons butter or margarine, melted
1 tablespoon garlic salt (optional)

Dissolve yeast in warm water; let stand 5 minutes. Stir in honey and salt. Gradually stir in enough flour to make a soft dough.

Turn dough out onto a lightly floured surface, and knead until smooth and elastic (about 1 minute).

Divide dough into 24 equal pieces. Shape each piece into a 10-inch rope. (Cover dough while working to prevent drying.) Place ropes 2 inches apart on greased baking sheets. Brush tops with melted butter. Sprinkle with garlic salt, if desired. Cover and let rise in a warm place (85°), free from drafts, 30 minutes or until almost doubled in bulk. Bake at 400° for 12 to 15 minutes or until lightly browned. Yield: 2 dozen.   Karen Hansen

Parker's Blue Ribbon Recipes
The Parker Ward Relief Society
St. Anthony, Idaho

Easy Croissants

1 package dry yeast
1 cup warm water (105° to 115°)
5 cups all-purpose flour, divided
⅓ cup sugar
1½ teaspoons salt
¾ cup evaporated milk
1 egg
¼ cup butter, melted
1 cup butter
1 egg, beaten
1 tablespoon water

Dissolve yeast in warm water in a medium mixing bowl; let stand 5 minutes. Add 1 cup flour, sugar, salt, milk, and 1 egg, beating at low speed of an electric mixer until smooth. Stir in ¼ cup melted butter; set aside.

Place remaining 4 cups flour in a large mixing bowl; cut in 1 cup butter with a pastry blender until mixture resembles coarse meal. Fold yeast mixture into flour mixture just until dry ingredients are moistened. Cover and chill 2 hours.

Turn dough out onto a lightly floured surface, and knead lightly 6 to 8 times. Divide dough into 4 equal portions. Roll each portion to a 16-inch circle; cut into 8 wedges. Roll up each wedge, beginning at wide end, and seal points. Place rolls, point side down, on an ungreased baking sheet, and curve each roll into a half-moon shape. Cover and let rise in a warm place (85°), free from drafts, 1½ hours or until rolls are doubled in bulk.

Combine beaten egg and 1 tablespoon water; brush rolls with egg mixture. Bake at 400° for 10 minutes or until lightly browned. Yield: 32 croissants.

Cornsilk
The Junior League of Sioux City, Iowa

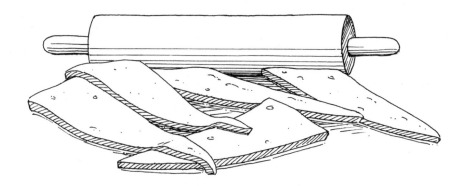

Hocus-Pocus Buns

1 package dry yeast
¼ cup warm water (105° to 115°)
¾ cup warm milk (105° to 115°)
¼ cup shortening
¼ cup sugar
1 egg

3¾ cups all-purpose flour
1 teaspoon salt
1 cup sugar
1 tablespoon ground cinnamon
24 large marshmallows
1 cup butter or margarine, melted

Dissolve yeast in warm water in a medium mixing bowl; let stand 5 minutes. Stir in warm milk; set aside.

Cream shortening in a large mixing bowl; gradually add ¼ cup sugar, beating at medium speed of an electric mixer until mixture is light and fluffy. Add egg, beating well. Combine flour and salt in a medium mixing bowl; add to creamed mixture alternately with milk mixture, beginning and ending with flour mixture. Mix well after each addition.

Turn dough out onto a lightly floured surface, and knead until smooth and elastic (about 5 minutes). Place in a well-greased bowl, turning to grease top. Cover and let rise in a warm place (85°), free from drafts, 1½ hours or until doubled in bulk.

Punch dough down. Let rest 5 minutes. Cover and let rise in a warm place, free from drafts, 30 minutes. Divide dough in half. Roll half of dough to ¼-inch thickness on a lightly floured surface. Cut dough into twelve 3½-inch circles. Repeat procedure with remaining half of dough.

Combine 1 cup sugar and cinnamon in a small shallow dish; stir well. Dip each marshmallow in melted butter, and roll in sugar mixture. Place a marshmallow in center of each dough circle. Wrap dough around marshmallows, pinching edges firmly to seal. Dip each round in melted butter, and roll in sugar mixture. Place in well-greased muffin pans. Bake at 375° for 25 to 30 minutes. Remove buns from pans, and serve immediately. Yield: 2 dozen.

Hilda Holmdahl Anderson, Gayle Anderson

Remembering Our Heritage
Herndon Covenant Church Women
Herndon, Kansas

Deluxe Blueberry Buns

3½ to 4 cups all-purpose
  flour, divided
1 package dry yeast
1⅓ cups evaporated milk
¼ cup plus 2 tablespoons
  butter or margarine
¼ cup sugar
1 teaspoon salt

1 egg
¼ cup butter or margarine,
  melted
½ cup sugar
1 teaspoon grated lemon rind
2 teaspoons ground cinnamon
2 cups fresh blueberries
Sugar Glaze

Combine 1½ cups flour and yeast in a large mixing bowl; stir well, and set aside.

Combine evaporated milk, ¼ cup plus 2 tablespoons butter, ¼ cup sugar, and salt in a small saucepan; heat until butter melts, stirring constantly. Cool to 120° to 130°. Add milk mixture and egg to flour mixture, beating at low speed of an electric mixer 3 minutes. Gradually stir in enough remaining flour to make a soft dough.

Place dough in a well-greased bowl, turning to grease top. Cover and let rise in a warm place (85°), free from drafts, 1 hour and 15 minutes or until doubled in bulk.

Punch dough down, and divide in half; cover and let rest 10 minutes. Roll each half to a 14- x 8-inch rectangle; brush with melted butter, leaving a ½-inch margin around edges. Combine ½ cup sugar, lemon rind, and cinnamon; sprinkle evenly over each rectangle of dough. Sprinkle blueberries evenly over dough. Roll up dough, jellyroll fashion, starting at long side; moisten and pinch edges to seal (do not seal ends). Cut each roll into 12 slices. Place slices, cut side down, in two ungreased 9-inch round cakepans.

Cover and let rise in a warm place, free from drafts, 1 hour or until doubled in bulk. Bake at 375° for 18 to 20 minutes. Drizzle Sugar Glaze over warm rolls. Yield: 2 dozen.

Sugar Glaze

1½ cups sifted powdered
  sugar

3 tablespoons milk
1½ teaspoons vanilla extract

Combine all ingredients in a medium mixing bowl, stirring until smooth. Yield: about ⅔ cup.

Sooner Sampler
The Junior League of Norman, Oklahoma

Overnight Caramel-Pecan Rolls

2 cups milk
⅓ cup sugar
⅓ cup shortening
2 packages dry yeast
½ cup warm water (105° to 115°)
1 egg
1 tablespoon baking powder
2 teaspoons salt
6½ to 7½ cups all-purpose flour

1 cup firmly packed brown sugar
½ cup butter or margarine
2 tablespoons light corn syrup
1 cup pecan halves
¼ cup butter or margarine, melted
½ cup sugar
1 tablespoon plus 1 teaspoon ground cinnamon

Combine milk, ⅓ cup sugar, and shortening in a saucepan; heat until shortening melts, stirring occasionally. Cool to 105° to 115°.

Dissolve yeast in warm water in a large mixing bowl; let stand 5 minutes. Stir in milk mixture, egg, baking powder, salt, and 3 cups flour, beating at medium speed of an electric mixer until smooth. Gradually stir in enough remaining flour to make a soft dough.

Turn dough out onto a floured surface, and knead until smooth and elastic (about 5 minutes). Place in a well-greased bowl, turning to grease top. Cover and let rise in a warm place (85°), free from drafts, 1 hour or until doubled in bulk.

Combine brown sugar and ½ cup butter in a saucepan. Cook over medium heat, stirring until sugar and butter melt. Remove from heat; stir in corn syrup. Spread mixture evenly in two greased 13- x 9- x 2-inch baking pans. Sprinkle each with ½ cup pecans; set aside.

Punch dough down, and divide in half. Roll each half to a 12- x 10-inch rectangle; brush each rectangle with melted butter. Combine ½ cup sugar and cinnamon; sprinkle mixture evenly over rectangles. Roll up jellyroll fashion, starting at long side. Pinch seams to seal (do not seal ends). Cut into 1-inch slices. Place slices, cut side down, in prepared pans. Cover and refrigerate at least 12 hours, or let rise in a warm place, free from drafts, 30 minutes or until doubled in bulk. Bake at 350° for 30 to 35 minutes or until golden brown. Immediately invert pans onto serving plates. Let stand 1 minute to allow caramel mixture to drizzle over rolls. Remove pans. Yield: 2 dozen.   Marcie Stoppel

Home at the Range
Chapter EX-P.E.O.
Oakley, Kansas

Rich Hot Cinnamon Rolls

¾ cup milk
½ cup sugar
1 teaspoon salt
½ cup butter or margarine
2 packages dry yeast
½ cup warm water (105° to 115°)

4½ cups all-purpose flour
2 eggs, beaten
½ cup butter or margarine, melted
1 cup sugar
1 tablespoon ground cinnamon

Combine milk, ½ cup sugar, salt, and ½ cup butter in a saucepan; heat until butter melts, stirring occasionally. Cool to 105° to 115°.

Dissolve yeast in warm water in a large mixing bowl; let stand 5 minutes. Stir in milk mixture, 1½ cups flour, and eggs; beat at medium speed of an electric mixer until smooth. Stir in remaining 3 cups flour to make a soft dough.

Turn dough out onto a lightly floured surface, and knead until smooth and elastic (about 10 minutes). Place in a well-greased bowl, turning to grease top. Cover and let rise in a warm place (85°), free from drafts, 1 hour (dough will not quite double in bulk).

Punch dough down; turn out onto a lightly floured surface. Divide dough in half. Roll each half of dough to a 16- x 10-inch rectangle. Brush each rectangle with melted butter.

Combine 1 cup sugar and cinnamon; sprinkle half of mixture evenly over each rectangle. Roll dough, jellyroll fashion, starting at long side. Pinch seams to seal (do not seal ends). Cut each roll into 1-inch slices; place slices, cut side down, in 9-inch square baking pans that have been greased and sprinkled with sugar.

Cover and let rise in a warm place, free from drafts, 40 minutes (rolls will not double in bulk). Bake at 375° for 20 to 25 minutes or until lightly browned. Yield: 32 rolls.

Finely Tuned Foods
The Symphony League
Leawood, Kansas

Cakes

This elaborate architectural valentine in Kennebunk, Maine, known as the Wedding Cake House, is an example of scroll-saw design. The "fanciful frosting" completely transforms this simple two-story house into an ornate showplace.

☆☆☆

Strawberry Crunch Cake

2 (10-ounce) packages frozen
  sliced strawberries, thawed
1 cup butter or margarine,
  softened
1¼ cups sugar
2 eggs
2 cups all-purpose flour
1 teaspoon baking powder
½ teaspoon baking soda

½ teaspoon salt
1 (8-ounce) carton
  commercial sour cream
⅓ cup firmly packed brown
  sugar
½ cup chopped pecans
1 teaspoon ground cinnamon
Glaze (recipe follows)
Whipped cream

Drain strawberries, reserving juice for glaze. Set strawberries and juice aside.

Cream butter; gradually add 1¼ cups sugar, beating well at medium speed of an electric mixer. Add eggs, one at a time, beating well after each addition.

Combine flour and next 3 ingredients; add to creamed mixture alternately with sour cream, beginning and ending with flour mixture. Mix after each addition.

Combine brown sugar, pecans, and cinnamon; set aside.

Pour half of batter into a lightly greased 13- x 9- x 2-inch baking pan. Spoon strawberries over batter; sprinkle with half of brown sugar mixture. Top with remaining batter, and sprinkle with remaining brown sugar mixture.

Bake at 350° for 40 to 45 minutes or until a wooden pick inserted in center of cake comes out clean. Let cake cool; cut into squares. Top each square with warm glaze and a dollop of whipped cream. Yield: 15 servings.

Glaze

Reserved strawberry juice
1 tablespoon plus 1 teaspoon
  cornstarch

2 teaspoons lemon juice

Combine strawberry juice and cornstarch in a small saucepan; cook over medium heat, stirring constantly, until mixture begins to boil. Boil 1 minute, stirring constantly. Remove from heat; stir in lemon juice. Yield: 1 cup.   Jennifer Flynn

... More Than Cookies!
The Northwest Georgia Girl Scout Council, Inc.
Atlanta, Georgia

O'Connor's Famous Gingerbread

½ cup butter or margarine,
  softened
1 cup sugar
2 eggs
1 cup buttermilk
1 teaspoon baking soda

¾ cup molasses
2 cups all-purpose flour
1 teaspoon ground ginger
Powdered sugar (optional)
Sweetened whipped cream
  (optional)

Cream butter; gradually add sugar, beating at medium speed of an electric mixer. Add eggs, one at a time, beating well after each addition. Combine buttermilk and soda; add to sugar mixture, mixing well. Add molasses to sugar mixture, mixing well.

Sift flour and ginger together. Add flour mixture to sugar mixture, mixing well. Pour batter into a greased and floured 13- x 9- x 2-inch baking pan. Bake at 350° for 45 minutes or until a wooden pick inserted in center comes out clean. If desired, serve gingerbread dusted with powdered sugar or topped with a dollop of whipped cream. Yield: 15 servings.   Sr. Mary Agnes Casey

Sinfully Good
The Catholic Library Association
Haverford, Pennsylvania

Chocolate-Zucchini Cake

1 tablespoon lemon juice
1 cup milk
½ cup butter or margarine,
  softened
½ cup vegetable oil
1¾ cups sugar
2 eggs
1 teaspoon vanilla extract
2½ cups all-purpose flour

¼ cup cocoa
1 teaspoon baking soda
½ teaspoon baking powder
½ teaspoon ground cinnamon
¼ teaspoon salt
2 cups peeled, shredded
  zucchini
½ cup semisweet chocolate
  morsels

Combine lemon juice and milk; let stand 5 minutes. Combine butter, oil, and sugar in a large mixing bowl; beat at medium speed of an electric mixer until well blended. Add milk mixture, eggs, and vanilla, mixing well. Combine flour and next 5 ingredients; add to egg mixture, mixing well. Stir in zucchini. Spoon batter into a lightly greased 13- x 9- x 2-inch baking pan. Sprinkle chocolate morsels over batter. Bake at 350° for 45 to 50 minutes or until a wooden pick inserted in center comes out clean. Let cool; cut into squares. Yield: 15 servings.   Sandy Kinsley, Paula Raiche

Na Zdrowie II
The Women's Auxiliary-Polish American Club of Agawam
Feeding Hills, Massachusetts

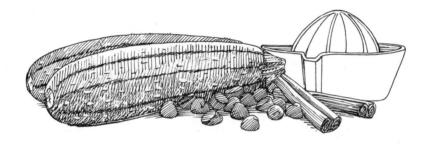

Macadamia Nut Fruitcake

1 (16-ounce) jar maraschino cherries, drained
1 pound candied pineapple, chopped
½ pound whole macadamia nuts
1 cup flaked coconut
½ cup all-purpose flour

3 eggs
½ cup sugar
2 teaspoons vanilla extract
¾ cup all-purpose flour
½ teaspoon baking soda
½ teaspoon salt
2 teaspoons grated lemon rind

Combine first 5 ingredients; toss gently. Set aside.

Combine eggs, sugar, and vanilla; beat at medium speed of an electric mixer until well blended. Combine ¾ cup flour, soda, salt, and lemon rind; gradually add to egg mixture, beating until smooth. Stir macadamia nut mixture into batter. Spoon batter into a greased and wax paper-lined 9- x 5- x 3-inch loafpan. Bake at 350° for 1 hour and 10 minutes or until a wooden pick inserted in center comes out clean. Cool in pan 10 minutes; remove from pan, and let cool completely on a wire rack. Yield: 1 loaf.   Audrey Berk

Another Taste of Palm Springs
Tiempo de Los Niños, an Auxiliary of Desert Hospital
Palm Springs, California

Praline Pound Cake

1 cup butter, softened
½ cup shortening
2 cups firmly packed brown sugar
1 cup sugar
5 eggs
3 cups all-purpose flour

½ teaspoon baking powder
¼ teaspoon salt
¾ cup milk
¼ cup praline liqueur
½ teaspoon vanilla extract
1 cup chopped pecans

Cream butter and shortening; add sugars, beating until light and fluffy. Add eggs, one at a time; beat after each addition. Combine flour, baking powder, and salt; add to creamed mixture alternately with milk and liqueur, beginning and ending with flour mixture. Mix after each addition. Stir in vanilla and pecans. Pour batter into a greased and floured 10-inch tube pan. Bake at 350° for 1½ hours or until cake tests done. Cool 15 minutes. Remove from pan; cool on a wire rack. Yield: one 10-inch cake.   Peggy Webb

Pot Luck
Village Green
Temple, New Hampshire

Yogurt Pound Cake

1 cup butter, softened
1½ cups sugar
3 eggs
2¼ cups all-purpose flour
½ teaspoon baking soda

½ teaspoon salt
1 teaspoon grated lemon rind
1 teaspoon vanilla extract
1 (8-ounce) carton orange or peach yogurt

Cream butter; add sugar, beating well. Add eggs, one at a time; beat after each addition. Combine flour, soda, and salt. Add to creamed mixture; mix just until blended. Add lemon rind, vanilla, and yogurt; mix well. Pour batter into a well-greased and floured 10-inch Bundt pan. Bake at 350° for 1 hour or until cake tests done. Cool 15 minutes; remove from pan, and cool on a wire rack. Yield: one 10-inch cake.

Boston Tea Parties
The Museum of Fine Arts
Boston, Massachusetts

German Chocolate Pound Cake

1 (4-ounce) package sweet baking chocolate	½ teaspoon baking soda
1 cup butter or margarine, softened	1 teaspoon salt
	¾ teaspoon cream of tartar
1¾ cups sugar	¼ teaspoon ground cinnamon
3 eggs	¾ cup milk
1 egg yolk	1 teaspoon vanilla extract
2¾ cups flour	Sweet Chocolate Glaze

Grease and flour a 10-inch tube pan. Line bottom of pan with wax paper. Set aside.

Place chocolate in top of a double boiler; bring water to a boil. Reduce heat to low; cook until chocolate melts. Let cool.

Cream butter; gradually add sugar, beating well at medium speed of an electric mixer. Add eggs and yolk, one at a time, beating well after each addition. Add chocolate, mixing well.

Combine flour and next 4 ingredients; add flour mixture to chocolate mixture alternately with milk, beginning and ending with flour mixture. Mix after each addition. Stir in vanilla. Pour batter into pan. Bake at 350° for 1 hour and 5 minutes or until a wooden pick inserted in center comes out clean. Cool in pan 15 minutes; remove from pan, and let cool on a wire rack. Pour Sweet Chocolate Glaze over top of cake. Yield: one 10-inch cake.

Sweet Chocolate Glaze

1 (4-ounce) package sweet baking chocolate	1 egg white
	1 cup sifted powdered sugar
1 tablespoon butter or margarine	1 to 2 tablespoons water

Combine chocolate and butter in top of a double boiler; bring water to a boil. Reduce heat to low; cook until chocolate melts. Cool.

Beat egg white (at room temperature) at high speed of an electric mixer 1 minute or until soft peaks form. Gradually add powdered sugar, beating until stiff peaks form and sugar dissolves (2 to 4 minutes). Fold chocolate mixture into egg whites. Add water, stirring until smooth. Yield: 1 cup.   Brandon Kincaid

Calling All Cooks Two
The Telephone Pioneers of America
Birmingham, Alabama

Sister Mayme's Delightful Golden Orange Chiffon Cake

1¾ cups plus 2 tablespoons
  all-purpose flour
1½ cups sugar
1 tablespoon baking powder
1 teaspoon salt
½ cup vegetable oil

5 eggs, separated
¾ cup water
1 tablespoon grated orange
  rind
3 egg whites
½ teaspoon cream of tartar

Sift together flour, sugar, baking powder, and salt in a large mixing bowl. Make a well in center of dry ingredients; add oil, egg yolks, water, and orange rind. Beat at medium speed of an electric mixer 2 minutes.

Beat 8 egg whites (at room temperature) in a large mixing bowl at high speed 1 minute or until foamy. Add cream of tartar, beating until stiff peaks form (2 to 4 minutes).

Pour egg yolk mixture in a thin, steady stream over entire surface of egg whites; gently fold whites into yolk mixture. Pour batter into an ungreased 10-inch tube pan, spreading evenly with a spatula. Bake at 350° for 55 minutes or until cake springs back when lightly touched. Remove from oven; invert pan, and let cool 40 minutes. Loosen cake from sides of pan, using a narrow metal spatula; remove from pan. Yield: one 10-inch cake.   Margaret Weimer

The Cove Cookery
St. John's Lutheran Church
Accident, Maryland

Sweet Potato-Nut Roll

3 eggs
1 cup sugar
⅔ cup cooked, mashed sweet
  potatoes
1 teaspoon lemon juice
¾ cup all-purpose flour
1 teaspoon baking powder
½ teaspoon salt

2 teaspoons ground cinnamon
1 teaspoon ground ginger
½ teaspoon ground nutmeg
1 cup chopped pecans
¼ cup sifted powdered sugar,
  divided
Filling (recipe follows)

Grease bottom and sides of a 15- x 10- x 1-inch jellyroll pan with vegetable oil; line with wax paper, and grease and flour wax paper. Set aside.

Beat eggs until foamy. Gradually add 1 cup sugar, beating until thick and lemon colored (5 to 6 minutes). Gradually add sweet potatoes and lemon juice, beating well after each addition.

Combine flour and next 5 ingredients; gradually fold into sweet potato mixture. Spread batter evenly in prepared pan. Sprinkle with pecans. Bake at 350° for 15 minutes or until a wooden pick inserted in center comes out clean.

Sift 2 tablespoons powdered sugar in a 15- x 10-inch rectangle on a linen towel. When cake is done, immediately loosen from sides of pan, and turn out onto sugared towel. Carefully peel off wax paper. Starting at narrow end, roll up cake and towel together; let cake cool completely on a wire rack, seam side down.

Unroll cake. Spread cake with filling, and carefully reroll cake, without towel. Chill. Place cake, seam side down, on a serving plate. Sift remaining 2 tablespoons powdered sugar over roll just before serving. Yield: 8 to 10 servings.

Filling

¼ cup butter or margarine,
  softened
2 (3-ounce) packages cream
  cheese, softened

1 cup sifted powdered sugar
½ teaspoon vanilla extract

Combine butter and cream cheese, beating at high speed of an electric mixer until light and fluffy. Add powdered sugar and vanilla, beating until smooth. Yield: about 1½ cups.

Unbearably Good!
The Junior Service League of Americus, Georgia

Almond-Crusted Torte

1⅔ cups all-purpose flour
1½ cups sugar
⅛ teaspoon salt
1 cup butter or margarine,
  melted

2 eggs, beaten
2 tablespoons almond extract
¾ cup sliced almonds

Combine flour, sugar, salt, butter, eggs, and almond extract in a large mixing bowl, stirring well. Pour batter into a lightly greased 10-inch pieplate. Sprinkle with sliced almonds.

Bake at 350° for 35 to 40 minutes or until torte is lightly browned. Yield: 10 to 12 servings.

Uptown Down South
The Junior League of Greenville, South Carolina

Almond-Lemon Torte

7 eggs, separated
¾ cup sugar
2 cups coarsely ground
  almonds

2 teaspoons grated lemon
  rind
Glaze (recipe follows)

Beat egg yolks until thick and lemon colored. Add sugar, stirring well. Stir in almonds and lemon rind. Set aside.

Beat egg whites (at room temperature) in a large mixing bowl at high speed of an electric mixer until stiff peaks form (2 to 4 minutes). Gently fold beaten egg whites into almond mixture. Pour batter into a greased and floured 10-inch springform pan. Bake at 350° for 1 hour or until a wooden pick inserted in center comes out clean. Cool in pan 10 minutes.

Prick surface of torte at 1-inch intervals, using a wooden pick. Pour warm glaze over torte in pan, and let stand 10 minutes. Remove torte from pan, and let cool completely on a wire rack. Yield: one 10-inch torte.

Glaze

½ cup sugar
½ cup lemon juice
1 egg yolk, beaten

2 teaspoons grated lemon
  rind
1 teaspoon butter

Combine sugar, lemon juice, egg yolk, and lemon rind in a small saucepan, stirring well. Cook over medium heat, stirring constantly, until mixture thickens slightly. Remove from heat; add butter, stirring until butter melts. Yield: ⅔ cup.   Susan Tober Andron

Pesach Potpourri
The Sinai Akiba Academy
Los Angeles, California

Poppy Seed Cake

1 cup vegetable oil
3 eggs
2¼ cups sugar
3 cups all-purpose flour
1½ teaspoons baking powder
1½ teaspoons salt

1½ cups milk
1½ teaspoons almond extract
1½ teaspoons butter flavoring
1 (2⅛-ounce) can poppy seeds
Glaze (recipe follows)

Combine oil, eggs, and sugar in a large mixing bowl; beat at medium speed of an electric mixer 2 minutes.

Combine flour, baking powder, and salt; add to egg mixture alternately with milk, beginning and ending with flour mixture. Mix after each addition. Stir in flavorings and poppy seeds.

Pour batter into a well-greased and floured 10-inch Bundt pan. Bake at 350° for 1 hour or until a wooden pick inserted in center comes out clean. Cool in pan 10 minutes; remove from pan, and place on a serving plate. While warm, prick cake surface at 1-inch intervals with a wooden pick; pour glaze over cake. Yield: one 10-inch cake.

Glaze

½ cup sugar
¼ cup orange juice
½ teaspoon almond extract

½ teaspoon butter flavoring
½ teaspoon vanilla extract

Combine all ingredients in a small mixing bowl; beat at medium speed of an electric mixer until well blended (mixture will be grainy). Yield: ½ cup.

Bound to Please
The Junior League of Boise, Idaho

Macaroon Marble Cake

½ cup shortening
¼ cup sugar
4 eggs, separated and
  divided
¼ cup cocoa
1 teaspoon instant coffee
  granules
¾ cup hot water
2 cups all-purpose flour
½ cup commercial sour
  cream

1 teaspoon vanilla extract
1 teaspoon baking soda
½ teaspoon salt
1 cup sugar, divided
1 teaspoon vanilla extract
1 (7-ounce) package flaked
  coconut
1 tablespoon all-purpose flour
Chocolate Glaze

Cream shortening; gradually add ¼ cup sugar, beating well at medium speed of an electric mixer. Add egg yolks, one at a time, beating well after each addition.

Dissolve cocoa and instant coffee granules in hot water; add half of cocoa mixture to egg yolk mixture alternately with 2 cups flour, beginning and ending with flour. Combine sour cream, 1 teaspoon vanilla, baking soda, and salt in a small mixing bowl, stirring well; add to batter with remaining half of cocoa mixture.

Beat 3 egg whites (at room temperature) in a large bowl at high speed of an electric mixer 1 minute or until soft peaks form. Gradually add ½ cup sugar, 1 tablespoon at a time, beating until stiff peaks form and sugar dissolves (2 to 4 minutes). Gently fold meringue mixture into batter.

Beat 1 egg white (at room temperature) in a medium bowl at high speed 1 minute or until soft peaks form. Gradually add remaining ½ cup sugar, 1 tablespoon at a time, beating until stiff peaks form and sugar dissolves. Gently stir in 1 teaspoon vanilla, coconut, and 1 tablespoon flour.

Spoon half of batter into a greased 10-inch tube pan. Sprinkle with coconut mixture. Top with remaining batter. Bake at 350° for 1 hour to 1 hour and 10 minutes. Cool in pan 10 minutes; remove from pan, and let cool completely on a wire rack. Drizzle Chocolate Glaze over top of cake. Yield: one 10-inch cake.

Chocolate Glaze

1 (6-ounce) package
  semisweet chocolate
  morsels

1 tablespoon shortening
½ teaspoon vanilla extract

Combine all ingredients in top of a double boiler; bring water to a boil. Reduce heat to low; cook until chocolate melts. Use immediately. Yield: ½ cup.

Ceil Wallace

250 Years of Cooking in Harwinton
Friends of the Harwinton Library
Harwinton, Connecticut

A Yankee's Blueberry Cake

¼ cup butter
1 cup sugar
1 egg
2½ cups all-purpose flour
1 tablespoon baking powder

¼ teaspoon ground nutmeg
1 cup milk
3 cups fresh or frozen
    blueberries, thawed
Cream Cheese Frosting

Cream butter; gradually add sugar, beating well at medium speed of an electric mixer. Add egg, and beat well.

Combine flour, baking powder, and nutmeg; add to creamed mixture alternately with milk, beginning and ending with flour mixture. Mix after each addition. Fold in blueberries.

Pour batter into a greased and floured 10-inch Bundt pan. Bake at 350° for 45 to 50 minutes or until a wooden pick inserted in center comes out clean. Cool in pan 5 minutes; remove from pan, and let cool completely on a wire rack. Spread Cream Cheese Frosting on top of cake. Yield: one 10-inch cake.

Cream Cheese Frosting

1 (8-ounce) package cream
    cheese, softened
½ cup sifted powdered sugar

1 tablespoon milk
½ teaspoon vanilla extract

Beat cream cheese at medium speed of an electric mixer until light and fluffy. Add powdered sugar and remaining ingredients; beat until smooth. Yield: 1 cup.

Kathy Gregg

Keeping the Feast
The Episcopal Church Women of St. Thomas Church
Abingdon, Virginia

Prune Cake

1 cup vegetable oil	1 teaspoon ground cinnamon
3 eggs	1 teaspoon ground nutmeg
1½ cups sugar	1 cup buttermilk
2 cups all-purpose flour	1 teaspoon vanilla extract
1 teaspoon baking soda	1 cup chopped prunes
1 teaspoon salt	1 cup chopped pecans
1 teaspoon ground allspice	Topping (recipe follows)

Combine oil, eggs, and sugar in a large mixing bowl; beat at medium speed of an electric mixer 2 minutes.

Combine flour, baking soda, salt, allspice, cinnamon, and nutmeg in a medium mixing bowl; add flour mixture to sugar mixture alternately with buttermilk, beginning and ending with flour mixture. Mix well after each addition. Stir in vanilla, chopped prunes, and chopped pecans.

Pour batter into a greased and floured 10-inch Bundt pan. Bake at 350° for 1 hour or until a wooden pick inserted in center comes out clean. Cool in pan 10 minutes; remove from pan, and place on a serving plate.

Prick warm cake surface at 1-inch intervals with a wooden pick. Pour one third of topping over cake, and let stand 5 minutes. Repeat procedure 2 more times with remaining topping. Store cake in refrigerator. Yield: one 10-inch cake.

Topping

½ cup butter or margarine	1 cup sugar
½ cup buttermilk	1 teaspoon vanilla extract
1 teaspoon dark corn syrup	

Combine butter, buttermilk, corn syrup, and sugar in a small saucepan. Cook over medium heat, stirring constantly, until butter and sugar melt. Remove mixture from heat, and stir in vanilla. Yield: 1⅔ cups.   Mary L. Phillips

Southern Secrets
SouthTrust Corporation
Birmingham, Alabama

Purple Ribbon Pumpkin Cake

2 cups all-purpose flour
2 teaspoons baking soda
½ teaspoon salt
2 teaspoons ground cinnamon
1 teaspoon ground cloves
½ teaspoon ground ginger
¼ teaspoon ground nutmeg

2 cups sugar
4 eggs
1 cup vegetable oil
1 (16-ounce) can pumpkin
Cream Cheese Frosting
Pecan halves

Combine first 7 ingredients; set aside. Combine sugar and eggs in a large bowl; beat at high speed of an electric mixer until light and fluffy. Add oil and pumpkin, beating well. Gradually add flour mixture, 1 cup at a time, beating at low speed just until blended.

Pour batter into an ungreased 9-inch tube pan. Bake at 350° for 1 hour or until cake springs back when lightly touched. Cool in pan 10 minutes; remove from pan, and let cool completely on a wire rack. Frost top and sides of cake with Cream Cheese Frosting, and garnish with pecan halves. Yield: one 9-inch cake.

Cream Cheese Frosting

2 (3-ounce) packages cream
cheese, softened

1 teaspoon vanilla extract
3 cups sifted powdered sugar

Combine cream cheese and vanilla, beating at medium speed of an electric mixer until smooth. Gradually add powdered sugar, 1 cup at a time, beating until mixture reaches spreading consistency. Yield: 1½ cups.

Melissa Chadwick

Home at the Range
Chapter EX-P.E.O.
Oakley, Kansas

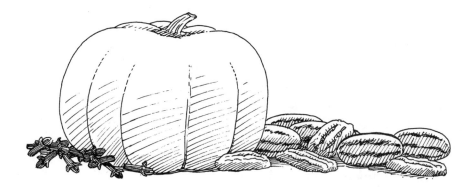

Real Lane Cake

1 cup butter or margarine,
  softened
1 cup sugar
3 cups all-purpose flour
1 tablespoon baking powder
1 teaspoon salt

1 cup milk
1 teaspoon vanilla extract
6 egg whites
1 cup sugar
Filling (recipe follows)
Frosting (recipe follows)

Cream butter; gradually add 1 cup sugar, beating well at medium speed of an electric mixer.

Combine flour, baking powder, and salt; add to creamed mixture alternately with milk, beginning and ending with flour mixture. Mix after each addition. Stir in vanilla.

Beat egg whites (at room temperature) at high speed of electric mixer 1 minute. Gradually add 1 cup sugar, 1 tablespoon at a time, beating until stiff peaks form and sugar dissolves (2 to 4 minutes). Gently fold meringue into cake batter.

Pour batter into 2 greased and floured 9-inch round cakepans. Bake at 375° for 35 minutes or until a wooden pick inserted in center comes out clean. Cool in pans 10 minutes; remove from pans, and let cool completely on wire racks.

Split cake layers in half horizontally to make 4 layers. Place one cake layer, cut side up, on a serving plate; spread with one third of filling. Repeat procedure with second and third layers. Place remaining layer, cut side down, on top of cake. Spread frosting on top and sides of cake. Yield: one 4-layer cake.

Filling

1 cup candied cherries,
  chopped
¾ cup golden raisins,
  chopped
⅓ cup bourbon

8 egg yolks
1¼ cups sugar
½ cup butter or margarine
1½ cups flaked coconut
1 cup chopped pecans

Combine cherries, raisins, and bourbon in a small bowl, stirring well. Cover and let stand at room temperature at least 8 hours.

Combine egg yolks, sugar, and butter in top of a large double boiler. Cook over medium heat, stirring constantly, 20 minutes or until mixture is thickened.

Remove from heat; stir in cherry mixture, coconut, and pecans. Let cool completely. Yield: 3½ cups.

Frosting

1⅓ cups sugar	½ teaspoon salt
⅓ cup water	2 egg whites
1 tablespoon light corn syrup	1 teaspoon vanilla extract

Combine all ingredients except vanilla in top of a large double boiler. Beat at low speed of an electric mixer 30 seconds or just until ingredients are blended. Bring water to a boil; beat mixture at high speed 7 minutes or until stiff peaks form. Remove from heat. Add vanilla; beat 2 minutes or until frosting reaches spreading consistency. Yield: 4 cups.

Hunt to Harbor
The Junior League of Baltimore, Maryland

Rum-Raisin Cheesecake

1¾ cups graham cracker or vanilla wafer crumbs	1½ cups sugar
2 tablespoons sugar	1 tablespoon vanilla extract
2 tablespoons butter or margarine, melted	6 eggs
	4 egg yolks
5 (8-ounce) packages cream cheese, softened	¾ to 1 cup dark rum
	⅓ cup half-and-half
	1 cup raisins

Combine crumbs, 2 tablespoons sugar, and butter, mixing well. Press firmly into bottom and ½ inch up the sides of a buttered 10-inch springform pan. Set aside.

Beat cream cheese at high speed of an electric mixer until light and fluffy. Add 1½ cups sugar and vanilla, beating well. Add eggs and egg yolks, one at a time, beating well after each addition. Add rum and half-and-half; mix well. Stir in raisins. Pour batter into prepared pan. Place in a large shallow pan. Pour water to a depth of 1½ inches into larger pan. Bake at 350° for 1½ hours or until cheesecake is set. Let cool to room temperature on a wire rack; chill at least 8 hours. To serve, carefully remove sides of springform pan. Yield: 12 to 14 servings.

Claudia Stone

State Hospital Cooks
Patient/Staff Advocacy Committee, Vermont State Hospital
Waterbury, Vermont

Amaretto Cheesecake

2 cups vanilla wafer crumbs
2 tablespoons sugar
½ cup butter or margarine, melted
4 (8-ounce) packages cream cheese, softened
1 cup sugar
2 eggs
¼ cup amaretto
1 (16-ounce) carton commercial sour cream
¾ cup sugar
2 tablespoons amaretto

Combine first 3 ingredients; mix well. Press firmly into bottom of a 10-inch springform pan. Bake at 350° for 5 minutes; set aside.

Beat cream cheese until light and fluffy; add 1 cup sugar, mixing well. Add eggs, one at a time, beating well after each addition. Stir in ¼ cup amaretto; pour batter into prepared pan. Bake at 350° for 30 to 40 minutes or until cheesecake is set.

Beat sour cream at medium speed of an electric mixer 2 minutes. Add remaining sugar and amaretto; beat 1 minute. Spread over cheesecake. Bake at 350° for 10 minutes. Let cool to room temperature on a wire rack; chill 8 hours. To serve, remove sides of springform pan. Yield: 10 to 12 servings.   Emily Carlisle

McComb's International Cuisine Affair
McComb Interdenominational Care Association
McComb, Mississippi

White Chocolate Mousse Cake

3 eggs
2 cups sugar
1¼ cups vegetable oil
1 tablespoon plus 1 teaspoon vanilla extract
1⅓ cups boiling water
1 cup cocoa
2½ cups all-purpose flour
1¼ teaspoons baking powder
1¼ teaspoons baking soda
¾ teaspoon salt
1 (18-ounce) jar strawberry preserves
White Chocolate Mousse Filling
Frosting (recipe follows)

Beat eggs until foamy. Gradually add sugar, beating until mixture is thick and lemon colored. Add oil and vanilla; beat 2 minutes. Combine water and cocoa, stirring until smooth. Combine flour, baking powder, soda, and salt; add flour mixture to egg mixture alternately with cocoa mixture, beginning and ending with flour mixture. Mix just until blended after each addition.

Pour batter into 3 greased and floured 9-inch round cakepans. Bake at 350° for 30 minutes or until a wooden pick inserted in center comes out clean. Cool in pans 5 minutes; remove from pans, and let cool completely on wire racks.

To assemble, split cake layers in half horizontally to make 6 layers. Place one cake layer on a serving plate. Spread ½ cup preserves over cake layer. Top with second cake layer. Top with half of White Chocolate Mousse Filling. Repeat layers once. Top with fifth cake layer, and spread with remaining ½ cup preserves. Top with remaining cake layer, cut side down. Spread frosting on top and sides of cake. Yield: one 6-layer cake.

White Chocolate Mousse Filling

½ **pound white chocolate, coarsely chopped**	2 **tablespoons water**
¼ **cup sugar**	2 **egg whites**
	1 **cup whipping cream**

Place white chocolate in top of a double boiler; bring water to a boil. Reduce heat to low; cook until chocolate melts, stirring occasionally. Remove from heat, and set aside.

Combine sugar and water in a small saucepan. Cook over medium heat until mixture reaches soft ball stage (234°). Beat egg whites (at room temperature) in a large bowl at high speed of an electric mixer 1 minute or until soft peaks form. Continue beating, slowly adding syrup mixture. Continue beating, slowly adding melted chocolate. Beat at high speed until very thick. Let cool to room temperature.

Beat whipping cream until stiff peaks form. Fold into cooled white chocolate mixture. Chill thoroughly. Yield: about 3 cups.

Frosting

1 **(16-ounce) package powdered sugar, sifted**	½ **cup cocoa**
½ **cup butter or margarine, softened**	½ **cup evaporated milk**
	1 **teaspoon vanilla extract**

Combine all ingredients; beat at high speed of an electric mixer until smooth and creamy. Yield: 3 cups.   Joyce Walker Mayo

A Dash of Down East
The Junior Guild of Rocky Mount, North Carolina

Austrian Chocolate Ecstasy Cake

4 (1-ounce) squares semisweet
  chocolate
¼ cup butter
2 eggs, beaten
2 cups sugar
1½ cups milk
1 teaspoon vanilla extract

1½ cups all-purpose flour
1 teaspoon baking powder
½ teaspoon salt
1 cup finely chopped pecans
Fudge Filling
Chocolate Cream

Combine chocolate and butter in top of a double boiler; cook over low heat until melted. Remove from heat. Gradually stir one-fourth of hot mixture into eggs; add to remaining hot mixture, stirring constantly. Add sugar, milk, and vanilla to chocolate mixture, beating until well blended. Combine flour, baking powder, and salt; add to chocolate mixture, beating 1 minute. Stir in pecans.

Grease two 9-inch round cakepans, and line with wax paper; grease wax paper. Pour batter into prepared pans; bake at 350° for 30 to 35 minutes or until a wooden pick inserted in center comes out clean. Cool in pans 5 minutes; remove from pans, and remove wax paper. Let cake layers cool completely on wire racks.

Spread Fudge Filling between layers; spread Chocolate Cream on top and sides of cake. Chill thoroughly. Yield: one 2-layer cake.

Fudge Filling

4 (1-ounce) squares semisweet
  chocolate
¼ cup butter

½ cup sifted powdered sugar
⅓ cup milk

Combine chocolate and butter in top of a double boiler; cook over low heat until melted. Remove from heat; add sugar, stirring until smooth. Stir in milk. Cover and chill 1½ hours or until filling is of spreading consistency. Yield: 1 cup.

Chocolate Cream

2 cups whipping cream
1 teaspoon vanilla extract

1 cup sifted powdered sugar
⅔ cup cocoa, sifted

Combine all ingredients; chill 30 minutes. Beat until stiff peaks form. Yield: 4 cups.   Mrs. J. Phillip Coyle

Southern Elegance
The Junior League of Gaston County, North Carolina

Perfect Chocolate Cake

1 cup cocoa	2 teaspoons baking soda
2 cups boiling water	½ teaspoon baking powder
1 cup butter or margarine,	½ teaspoon salt
softened	1½ teaspoons vanilla extract
2½ cups sugar	Filling (recipe follows)
4 eggs	Frosting (recipe follows)
2¾ cups all-purpose flour	Pecan halves (optional)

Combine cocoa and water; stir until smooth. Set aside.

Cream butter; gradually add sugar. Add eggs, one at a time, beating well after each addition. Combine flour, soda, baking powder, and salt; add to creamed mixture alternately with cocoa mixture, beginning and ending with flour mixture. Mix after each addition (do not overbeat). Stir in vanilla.

Grease three 9-inch round cakepans, and line with wax paper; grease wax paper. Pour batter into prepared pans. Bake at 350° for 25 to 30 minutes or until a wooden pick inserted in center comes out clean. Cool in pans 10 minutes; remove from pans, and remove wax paper. Cool completely on wire racks. Spread filling between layers; spread frosting on top and sides of cake. Garnish with pecan halves, if desired. Store in refrigerator. Yield: one 3-layer cake.

Filling

1 cup whipping cream	¼ cup sifted powdered sugar
1 teaspoon vanilla extract	

Beat whipping cream and vanilla until foamy; gradually add powdered sugar, beating until soft peaks form. Yield: 2 cups.

Frosting

1 cup semisweet chocolate	¾ cup butter or margarine
morsels	2½ cups sifted powdered
½ cup half-and-half	sugar

Combine first 3 ingredients in a saucepan; cook over medium heat, stirring until smooth. Remove from heat; blend in sugar. Place saucepan over ice; beat chocolate mixture until frosting is of spreading consistency. Yield: 2½ cups.   Deb Shealy

From the Hills
The Lutheran Church of Vestavia Hills, Alabama

Wellesley Fudge Cake

4 (1-ounce) squares
  unsweetened chocolate
½ cup water
1¾ cups sugar, divided
½ cup butter, softened
3 eggs
1⅔ cups all-purpose flour

1 teaspoon baking soda
1 teaspoon salt
¾ cup milk
1 teaspoon vanilla extract
Hungarian Chocolate Frosting
Chopped walnuts (optional)

Combine chocolate and water in a small saucepan; cook over low heat, stirring constantly, until chocolate melts. Add ½ cup sugar, and cook 2 minutes, stirring constantly. Remove from heat, and let mixture cool.

Cream butter; gradually add remaining 1¼ cups sugar, beating well at medium speed of an electric mixer. Add eggs, one at time, beating well after each addition.

Combine flour, soda, and salt; add to creamed mixture alternately with milk, beginning and ending with flour mixture. Mix after each addition. Stir in chocolate mixture and vanilla.

Pour batter into 2 greased and floured 9-inch round cakepans. Bake at 350° for 30 to 35 minutes or until a wooden pick inserted in center comes out clean. Cool in pans 10 minutes; remove from pans, and let cool completely on wire racks.

Spread Hungarian Chocolate Frosting between layers and on top and sides of cake. Garnish with chopped walnuts, if desired. Yield: one 2-layer cake.

Hungarian Chocolate Frosting

5 (1-ounce) squares
  unsweetened chocolate
½ cup butter or margarine

3 cups sifted powdered sugar
⅓ cup hot water
2 egg yolks

Combine chocolate and butter in a small saucepan. Place over low heat, and cook until chocolate and butter melt. Pour mixture into a medium mixing bowl. Add sugar, water, and egg yolks, beating at low speed of an electric mixer until well blended. Cool to spreading consistency. Yield: 2 cups.   Audrey Vargas

A Cook's Book of Recipes from the Pacific Northwest
The Rosehill Community Center
Mukilteo, Washington

Cookies & Candies

Looking from the pillars of Louisiana's Oak Alley Plantation house toward the levee, the full three hundred yards of the great arch of oak trees is an impressive sight. Each tree enclosing the alleyway has a spread of about 150 feet.

☆☆☆

Frosted Pumpkin Cookies

1 cup butter or margarine,
softened
½ cup sugar
½ cup firmly packed brown
sugar
1 egg
1 cup cooked, mashed
pumpkin
1 teaspoon vanilla extract
2 cups all-purpose flour
1 teaspoon baking
powder
1 teaspoon baking soda
½ teaspoon salt
2½ teaspoons ground
cinnamon
½ teaspoon ground nutmeg
¼ teaspoon ground ginger
½ cup chopped pecans or
walnuts
½ cup chopped raisins or
dates
½ cup firmly packed brown
sugar
¼ cup milk
1 tablespoon butter or
margarine
1 cup sifted powdered
sugar
¾ teaspoon vanilla extract

Cream 1 cup butter; gradually add ½ cup sugar and ½ cup brown sugar, beating well at medium speed of an electric mixer until mixture is light and fluffy. Add egg; beat well. Stir in pumpkin and 1 teaspoon vanilla.

Combine flour, baking powder, soda, salt, cinnamon, nutmeg, and ginger in a medium mixing bowl; gradually add to pumpkin mixture, mixing well. Stir in pecans and raisins.

Drop dough by rounded teaspoonfuls onto lightly greased cookie sheets. Bake at 375° for 10 minutes or until cookies are lightly browned. Cool slightly on cookie sheets; remove cookies to wire racks to cool completely.

Combine ½ cup brown sugar, milk, and 1 tablespoon butter in a small saucepan. Cook over low heat, stirring constantly, until butter melts and sugar dissolves. Remove from heat, and add powdered sugar and ¾ teaspoon vanilla, beating at low speed of electric mixer until mixture is smooth. Spread frosting over cookies. Yield: about 12 dozen.   L. M. Rush

The Brevillier Village Cookbook
The Brevillier Village Auxiliary
Erie, Pennsylvania

Coconut-Macadamia Cookies

½ cup butter or margarine, softened
½ cup sugar
½ cup firmly packed brown sugar
1 egg
1 teaspoon vanilla extract
1 cup all-purpose flour
½ teaspoon baking powder
½ teaspoon baking soda
½ teaspoon salt
½ cup quick-cooking oats, uncooked
½ cup chopped macadamia nuts
2 cups grated coconut, divided

Cream butter; gradually add sugars, beating well at medium speed of an electric mixer until light and fluffy. Add egg and vanilla, mixing well. Combine flour, baking powder, soda, and salt; add to creamed mixture, mixing well. Stir in oats, nuts, and 1⅓ cups coconut. Drop dough by rounded teaspoonfuls onto greased cookie sheets. Sprinkle with remaining ⅔ cup coconut. Bake at 375° for 8 to 10 minutes or until lightly browned. Cool slightly on cookie sheets; remove to wire racks to cool completely. Yield: 4 dozen.

South of the Fork
The Junior League of Dallas, Texas

Buffalo Chip Cookies

1 cup shortening
1 cup butter or margarine, softened
2 cups sugar
2 cups firmly packed brown sugar
4 eggs
2 teaspoons vanilla extract
4 cups all-purpose flour
2 teaspoons baking powder
2 teaspoons baking soda
2 cups regular oats, uncooked
2 cups corn flakes
1 cup chopped pecans
1 cup shredded coconut
1 (12-ounce) package semisweet chocolate morsels

Cream shortening and butter; gradually add sugars, beating well at medium speed of an electric mixer until light and fluffy. Add eggs and vanilla; beat well. Combine flour, baking powder, and soda; add to creamed mixture, mixing well. Add oats and remaining ingredients, one at a time, stirring well after each addition. Drop dough by tablespoonfuls 2 inches apart onto ungreased cookie sheets. Bake at 350° for 10 to 12 minutes or until lightly browned. Cool on wire racks. Yield: about 9½ dozen.   Roberta Byrd

The Great Entertainer Cookbook
The Buffalo Bill Historical Center
Cody, Wyoming

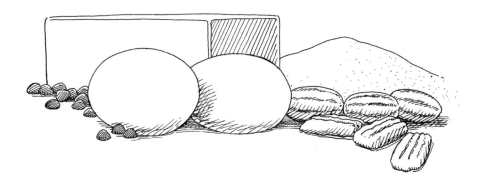

Chocolate Chip Meringues

2 egg whites
⅛ teaspoon cream of tartar
⅛ teaspoon salt
¾ cup sugar
1 cup semisweet chocolate
  morsels

½ cup chopped pecans or
  walnuts
½ teaspoon vanilla extract

Beat egg whites (at room temperature), cream of tartar, and salt at high speed of an electric mixer 1 minute. Gradually add sugar, 1 tablespoon at a time, beating until stiff peaks form and sugar dissolves (about 2 to 4 minutes). Stir in chocolate morsels, chopped pecans, and vanilla.

Drop meringue mixture by teaspoonfuls onto cookie sheets lined with aluminum foil. Bake at 300° for 25 minutes or until dry. Cool completely on cookie sheets; carefully peel cookies from foil. Yield: 5 dozen.   Helen Carr

Old Irving Park Association Cookbook
The Old Irving Park Association
Chicago, Illinois

Almond Refrigerator Cookies

1 cup butter or margarine, softened
1 cup sugar
1 egg
1 teaspoon almond extract
2¼ cups all-purpose flour
1½ teaspoons baking powder
½ teaspoon salt
1 cup slivered blanched almonds, finely chopped

Cream butter; gradually add sugar, beating well at medium speed of an electric mixer. Add egg and almond extract; beat well. Combine flour, baking powder, and salt; add to creamed mixture, beating well. Stir in almonds.

Chill dough 15 minutes. Shape dough into three 6-inch rolls; wrap in wax paper, and chill at least 3 hours. Unwrap rolls, and cut into ¼-inch slices; place on ungreased cookie sheets. Bake at 350° for 12 to 15 minutes or until lightly browned. Cool on wire racks. Yield: 6 dozen.   Norma Anderson

Remembering Our Heritage
Herndon Covenant Church Women
Herndon, Kansas

Praline Butter Cookies

1 cup butter, softened
1 cup sugar
2 egg yolks
½ teaspoon vanilla extract
2 tablespoons praline liqueur
2 cups all-purpose flour
1 teaspoon baking powder
¼ teaspoon salt
1 cup pecan halves

Cream butter; gradually add sugar, beating well at medium speed of an electric mixer. Add egg yolks, one at a time, beating after each addition. Stir in vanilla and praline liqueur.

Combine flour, baking powder, and salt; gradually add to creamed mixture, mixing well. Shape dough into 1-inch balls; place 2 inches apart on ungreased cookie sheets. Press a pecan half into center of each cookie. Bake at 300° for 20 minutes or until lightly browned. Cool on wire racks. Yield: 4 dozen.

Sounds Delicious!
The Volunteer Council of the Tulsa Philharmonic Society, Inc.
Tulsa, Oklahoma

Ginger Crinkles

1 cup sugar
⅔ cup vegetable oil
1 egg
¼ cup molasses
2 cups all-purpose flour

2 teaspoons baking soda
½ teaspoon salt
1 teaspoon ground ginger
1 teaspoon ground cinnamon

Combine sugar, oil, and egg, beating well at medium speed of an electric mixer. Add molasses, beating well. Combine flour and remaining ingredients; stir into sugar mixture.

Shape dough into 1-inch balls. Place on ungreased cookie sheets. Bake at 350° for 8 to 10 minutes. Let cookies cool on wire racks. Yield: about 4 dozen.   Marge Hehn

From the Hills
The Lutheran Church of Vestavia Hills, Alabama

Melt-In-Your-Mouth Sugar Cookies

1 cup butter or margarine,
   softened
1 cup vegetable oil
1 cup sugar
1 cup sifted powdered sugar
2 eggs

1 teaspoon vanilla extract
4½ cups all-purpose flour
1 teaspoon baking soda
1 teaspoon salt
1 teaspoon cream of tartar

Combine butter, oil, and sugars in a large mixing bowl; beat well at medium speed of an electric mixer. Add eggs, one at a time, beating after each addition; stir in vanilla. Combine flour, soda, salt, and cream of tartar in a medium mixing bowl; add to creamed mixture, beating well.

Shape dough into 1-inch balls; place on ungreased cookie sheets. Flatten with bottom of a glass dipped in sugar. Bake at 350° for 8 to 10 minutes. Cool on wire racks. Yield: 8 dozen.   Gail Wangen

Good Cooking Cookbook
United Lutheran Church
Langdon, North Dakota

Hawaiian Delight Cookies

1 cup butter or margarine,
  softened
1 (8-ounce) package cream
  cheese, softened
2½ cups all-purpose flour
1 cup chopped macadamia
  nuts, divided

3 eggs, beaten
1½ cups firmly packed brown
  sugar
½ cup shredded coconut
2 tablespoons all-purpose
  flour
1 teaspoon baking powder

Cream butter and cream cheese; gradually add 2½ cups flour, beating until well blended. Shape dough into 1-inch balls. Pat balls into greased muffin pans, shaping into shells. Sprinkle ½ cup chopped nuts evenly over shells.

Combine eggs and brown sugar in a medium bowl; mix well. Stir in remaining ½ cup chopped nuts, coconut, and remaining ingredients. Pour mixture evenly into shells, filling half full. Bake at 350° for 15 to 18 minutes. Reduce heat to 250°, and bake 10 minutes. Yield: 3 dozen.   Lorna Burger

We, The Women of Hawaii Cookbook
We, The Women of Hawaii
Waialua, Oahu

Chocolate-Filled Thimble Cookies

¾ cup butter or margarine,
  softened
½ cup firmly packed brown
  sugar
1 egg, separated
½ teaspoon vanilla extract

1½ cups all-purpose flour
¼ teaspoon salt
1 cup finely chopped pecans
  or walnuts
Chocolate Filling

Cream butter; gradually add sugar, beating well. Add egg yolk and vanilla; mix well. Combine flour and salt; add to creamed mixture; beat well. Shape dough into a ball; cover and chill 2 hours.

Shape dough into 1-inch balls. Slightly beat egg white; dip balls in egg white, and roll in pecans. Place 2 inches apart on ungreased cookie sheets. Press thumb in each ball of dough, leaving an indentation. Bake at 350° for 10 to 15 minutes or until lightly browned. Cool on wire racks. Spoon 1 teaspoon Chocolate Filling into each cookie indentation. Yield: 3 dozen.

Chocolate Filling

¾ cup semisweet chocolate morsels

1 tablespoon shortening

2 tablespoons light corn syrup

1 tablespoon water

1 teaspoon vanilla extract

Combine semisweet chocolate morsels and shortening in top of a double boiler; bring water to a boil. Reduce heat to low; cook until chocolate melts. Remove from heat, and stir in corn syrup, water, and vanilla. Yield: ¾ cup.   Kaye Sarby

Beyond the Village Gate
The Parmadale Children's Village
Parma, Ohio

Vienna Raspberry-Chocolate Bars

1 cup butter or margarine, softened

½ cup sugar

2 egg yolks

2½ cups all-purpose flour

1 (10-ounce) jar raspberry jam

1 cup semisweet chocolate morsels

4 egg whites

¼ teaspoon salt

1 cup sugar

2 cups finely chopped pecans or walnuts

Cream butter; gradually add ½ cup sugar, beating well at medium speed of an electric mixer. Add egg yolks, one at a time, beating well after each addition; stir in flour. Press mixture evenly into a lightly greased 15- x 10- x 1-inch jellyroll pan. Bake at 350° for 15 to 20 minutes or until lightly browned.

Spread raspberry jam over crust; sprinkle with chocolate morsels. Beat egg whites (at room temperature) and salt at high speed of electric mixer until foamy. Gradually add 1 cup sugar, 1 tablespoon at a time, beating until stiff peaks form and sugar dissolves (2 to 4 minutes). Gently fold in pecans.

Carefully spread meringue mixture over morsels, sealing to edge of crust. Bake at 350° for 25 minutes or until golden brown. Cut into bars immediately. Yield: 5 dozen.

Boston Tea Parties
The Museum of Fine Arts
Boston, Massachusetts

Layered Apricot Bars

1 (6-ounce) package dried
    apricots
½ cup butter or margarine,
    softened
¼ cup sugar
1 cup all-purpose flour
2 eggs
¾ cup firmly packed brown
    sugar

⅓ cup all-purpose flour
½ teaspoon baking powder
¼ teaspoon salt
½ cup walnuts, chopped
1 teaspoon vanilla extract
Powdered sugar

Combine apricots and water to cover in a small saucepan, and bring to a boil; reduce heat, and simmer, uncovered, 15 minutes or until tender. Drain well. Coarsely chop apricots, and set aside.

Cream butter; gradually add ¼ cup sugar, beating at medium speed of an electric mixer until light and fluffy. Stir in 1 cup flour. Press mixture into a greased 8-inch square baking pan. Bake at 350° for 15 to 20 minutes or until lightly browned.

Beat eggs at medium speed of electric mixer until thick and lemon colored. Gradually add brown sugar, beating well. Combine ⅓ cup flour, baking powder, and salt; add to creamed mixture, mixing well. Stir in apricots, walnuts, and vanilla.

Spread apricot mixture evenly over crust. Bake at 350° for 30 minutes. Let cool in pan. Dust lightly with powdered sugar, and cut into bars. Yield: 2 dozen.

Finely Tuned Foods
The Symphony League
Leawood, Kansas

Butter-Nut Squares

1 cup butter or margarine,
    softened
⅔ cup sugar
1 egg, separated

1⅔ cups all-purpose flour
½ teaspoon ground cinnamon
1 cup chopped walnuts,
    divided

Cream butter; gradually add sugar, beating at medium speed of an electric mixer until light and fluffy. Add egg yolk, beating until mixture is smooth.

Combine flour and cinnamon; add to creamed mixture, mixing well. Stir in ½ cup walnuts. Press mixture evenly into a lightly greased 15- x 10- x 1-inch jellyroll pan. Beat egg white until foamy, and brush over mixture.

Sprinkle remaining ½ cup walnuts over mixture in pan. Bake at 300° for 50 to 60 minutes or until lightly browned. Cut into squares immediately. Yield: 2 dozen. Elaine Weiser

I Must Have That Recipe
Albert Einstein College of Medicine, Yeshiva University
Bronx, New York

Pumpkin Pie Squares

1 cup all-purpose flour	2 eggs
½ cup quick-cooking oats, uncooked	1 teaspoon ground cinnamon
½ cup firmly packed brown sugar	½ teaspoon salt
	½ teaspoon ground ginger
½ cup butter or margarine	¼ teaspoon ground cloves
2 cups cooked, mashed pumpkin	½ cup firmly packed brown sugar
¾ cup sugar	2 tablespoons butter or margarine
1 (12-ounce) can evaporated milk	½ cup chopped pecans
	Whipped cream

Combine flour, oats, and ½ cup brown sugar in a medium bowl. Cut in ½ cup butter with a pastry blender until mixture resembles coarse meal. Press mixture evenly into an ungreased 13- x 9- x 2-inch baking pan. Bake at 350° for 15 minutes.

Combine pumpkin and next 7 ingredients, stirring well. Pour over baked crust. Bake at 350° for 20 minutes.

Place ½ cup brown sugar in a small bowl; cut in 2 tablespoons butter with a pastry blender until mixture resembles coarse meal. Stir in pecans. Sprinkle over pumpkin mixture. Bake an additional 20 minutes or until set. Cool and cut into squares. Serve with a dollop of whipped cream. Yield: 1 dozen. Lorraine Steel

Parker's Blue Ribbon Recipes
The Parker Ward Relief Society
St. Anthony, Idaho

Cream Cheese Brownies

1 (4-ounce) package sweet
baking chocolate
3 tablespoons butter or
margarine
2 tablespoons butter or
margarine, softened
1 (3-ounce) package cream
cheese, softened
¼ cup sugar
1 egg
1 tablespoon all-purpose flour

½ teaspoon vanilla extract
2 eggs
¾ cup sugar
½ cup all-purpose flour
½ teaspoon baking powder
¼ teaspoon salt
1 teaspoon vanilla extract
¼ teaspoon almond extract
½ cup chopped pecans or
walnuts

Combine chocolate and 3 tablespoons butter in top of a double boiler; bring water to a boil. Reduce heat to low; cook until chocolate melts. Set aside to cool.

Cream together 2 tablespoons butter and cream cheese; gradually add ¼ cup sugar, beating well at medium speed of an electric mixer until light and fluffy. Add 1 egg, 1 tablespoon flour, and ½ teaspoon vanilla; stir well, and set aside.

Beat 2 eggs at medium speed of electric mixer until thick and lemon colored. Gradually add ¾ cup sugar, beating well. Combine ½ cup flour, baking powder, and salt; add to egg mixture, mixing well. Stir in cooled chocolate mixture, flavorings, and pecans.

Pour half of batter into a greased 8-inch square baking pan. Spread with cream cheese mixture; top with remaining batter. Cut through mixture in pan with a knife to create a marbled effect. Bake at 350° for 35 to 40 minutes. Cool on a wire rack; cut into squares. Store in refrigerator. Yield: 16 brownies.   Ann Jones

Deep in the Heart
The Junior Forum of Dallas, Texas

Frosted Fudge Brownies

½ cup butter or margarine
2 (1-ounce) squares
unsweetened chocolate
1 cup sugar
2 eggs

1 teaspoon vanilla extract
½ cup all-purpose flour
Frosting (recipe follows)
1 (1-ounce) square
unsweetened chocolate

Combine butter and 2 squares chocolate in top of a double boiler; bring water to a boil. Reduce heat to low; cook until chocolate melts, stirring occasionally. Remove from heat.

Add sugar to melted chocolate mixture, stirring well. Add eggs and vanilla, stirring well. Add flour, and mix well.

Spread batter in a greased 8-inch square baking pan. Bake at 350° for 18 to 20 minutes. Let brownies cool in pan; chill at least 1 hour. Spread brownies with frosting, and chill 30 minutes or until frosting is set.

Place 1 square chocolate in top of a double boiler; bring water to a boil. Reduce heat to low; cook until chocolate melts, stirring occasionally. Quickly spread melted chocolate over frosted brownies. Chill 1 hour or until chocolate is set. Cut brownies into squares, and serve chilled. Store in refrigerator. Yield: 20 brownies.

Frosting

1 tablespoon butter or
  margarine, softened
½ cup sifted powdered
  sugar

¼ teaspoon peppermint
  extract
2 teaspoons milk

Combine butter, powdered sugar, and peppermint extract in a small mixing bowl, and mix well. Add milk, stirring until mixture reaches spreading consistency. Yield: enough for 20 brownies.

Helen Burton

As You Like It
St. Bernard's School
New York, New York

Honeycomb Candy

1 cup sugar	1 cup dark corn syrup
1 tablespoon vinegar	1 tablespoon baking soda
¼ teaspoon salt	

Combine sugar, vinegar, salt, and corn syrup in a large saucepan. Cook over medium heat, stirring gently, until sugar dissolves. Cover and cook 2 to 3 minutes to wash down sugar crystals from sides of pan. Uncover and cook, without stirring, until mixture reaches hard crack stage (300°).

Remove from heat, and stir in soda. Pour into a well-greased 9-inch metal baking pan. Let cool in pan on a wire rack. Break into pieces. Yield: about 1 pound.   Nita Scriven

Around the World, Around Our Town
Friends of the San Pedro Library
San Pedro, California

Aunt Mil's Great, Great Butter Crunch

1 cup butter	¼ cup finely chopped pecans or walnuts
1 cup sugar	
2 tablespoons water	½ cup semisweet chocolate morsels
1 tablespoon light corn syrup	

Melt butter in a saucepan over low heat; add sugar, stirring well. Bring mixture to a boil, stirring constantly. Stir in water and corn syrup. Cook over medium heat, stirring constantly, until mixture reaches soft crack stage (290°). Remove from heat, and stir in chopped pecans. Pour candy mixture into a buttered 15- x 10- x 1-inch jellyroll pan, spreading to ¼-inch thickness (do not spread to edges of pan). Let cool completely.

Place chocolate morsels in top of a double boiler; bring water to a boil. Reduce heat to low; cook until chocolate melts. Spread melted chocolate over candy layer. Chill candy until chocolate is set. Break candy into pieces, and store in refrigerator in an airtight container. Yield: 1 pound.   Dale Wells

Royle Round-Up of Recipes
Royle School Parent-Teacher Association
Darien, Connecticut

Peanut Brittle

2 cups sugar
1 cup light corn syrup
2¾ cups raw peanuts

1 teaspoon water
1 teaspoon vanilla extract
½ teaspoon baking soda

Combine sugar and corn syrup in a large Dutch oven. Cook over low heat to soft ball stage (240°), washing down sugar crystals from sides of pan. Add peanuts; continue cooking over low heat, stirring constantly, to hard crack stage (300°). Remove from heat. Stir in water, vanilla, and soda. Spread mixture evenly in a buttered 15- x 10- x 1-inch jellyroll pan. Let cool completely. Break into pieces. Yield: 2 pounds.

Stir Crazy!
The Junior Welfare League of Florence, South Carolina

Spiced Pecans

1 egg white
1 tablespoon water
3 cups pecan halves
½ cup sugar

1 teaspoon ground cinnamon
½ teaspoon salt
½ teaspoon ground nutmeg
½ teaspoon ground cloves

Beat egg white (at room temperature) and water at high speed of an electric mixer until foamy. Add pecans, stirring to coat. Combine sugar and remaining ingredients in a small bowl, and sprinkle over pecans; stir well. Spread pecans in a single layer on a lightly greased baking sheet. Bake at 350° for 30 minutes, stirring twice. Let cool. Yield: about 3 cups.   Earline Childers

The Bishop's Bounty
St. Mary's Training School for Retarded Children
Alexandria, Louisiana

Almond Truffles

3 tablespoons butter, softened
½ cup sifted powdered sugar
6 (1-ounce) squares semisweet
  chocolate, finely grated
1 egg yolk, lightly beaten
2 tablespoons white crème de
  cacao

24 whole blanched almonds,
  toasted
½ cup finely chopped
  blanched almonds, toasted

Cream butter; gradually add powdered sugar, beating well at medium speed of an electric mixer. Add grated chocolate, beaten egg yolk, and crème de cacao; beat until blended. Cover and chill mixture at least 1 hour.

Shape mixture into 1-inch balls, inserting one whole almond into center of each ball. Roll truffles in chopped almonds. Cover and chill 8 hours. Store in refrigerator. Yield: 2 dozen.

Hunt to Harbor
The Junior League of Baltimore, Maryland

Kentucky Bourbon Balls

½ cup butter, softened
1 (16-ounce) package
  powdered sugar, sifted
¼ cup bourbon
1 cup chopped pecans

4 (1-ounce) squares semisweet
  chocolate
4 (1-ounce) squares
  bittersweet chocolate

Cream butter; gradually add sugar, beating well at medium speed of an electric mixer. Stir in bourbon. Knead until mixture is blended and does not stick to hands; knead in pecans. Refrigerate 1 to 2 hours. Shape into 1-inch balls. Chill at least 8 hours.

Place semisweet and bittersweet chocolate in top of a double boiler; bring water to a boil. Reduce heat to low; cook until chocolate melts. Working quickly, dip each ball into melted chocolate. Place on wax paper to cool. Store in refrigerator. Yield: 4 dozen.

The Kentucky Derby Museum Cookbook
The Kentucky Derby Museum
Louisville, Kentucky

Desserts

Carefully restored old homes, such as this one on Eddy Street, are plentiful in San Francisco, California. These charmingly detailed homes are modern-day reminders of the now architecturally fashionable Victorian era.

☆☆☆

Pears Melba

3 cups water
1 (3-inch) stick cinnamon
1 teaspoon vanilla
   extract
1 tablespoon plus 1½
   teaspoons fresh lemon
   juice, divided
1 (3- x 1-inch) strip lemon
   rind

8 large pears
1 (10-ounce) package frozen
   raspberries, thawed
1 tablespoon cornstarch
1 cup low-fat cottage cheese
2 teaspoons sugar
Fresh mint sprigs

Combine water, cinnamon stick, vanilla, 1 tablespoon lemon juice, and lemon rind in a large skillet. Bring to a boil.

Peel pears and core just from the bottom, cutting to but not through the stem end. Cut pears in half lengthwise, cutting through stem. Add pears to liquid in skillet. Cover, reduce heat, and simmer 10 minutes. Remove from heat; let pears cool in cooking liquid.

Drain raspberries, reserving juice. Set raspberries aside.

Combine cornstarch and raspberry juice in a small saucepan. Bring to a boil over medium-low heat; cook 1 minute or until mixture thickens. Remove from heat, and gently stir in raspberries. Let cool.

Place cottage cheese, remaining 1½ teaspoons lemon juice, and sugar in container of an electric blender or food processor; cover and process until smooth.

Remove pear halves from liquid, using a slotted spoon, and drain pears well.

Spoon cottage cheese mixture evenly into cavities of half the pear halves, and top with matching halves. Stand pears upright on individual dessert plates. (Level pears, if necessary, by cutting a thin slice from bottom of each.) Spoon 2 tablespoons raspberry sauce over each serving. Garnish with mint sprigs. Yield: 8 servings.

Sounds Delicious!
The Volunteer Council of the Tulsa Philharmonic Society, Inc.
Tulsa, Oklahoma

Caramelized Pears

1 quart water
2 tablespoons lemon juice,
  divided
6 medium-size firm pears
2 tablespoons unsalted butter
  or margarine, melted

½ cup Riesling or other dry
  white wine
¼ cup superfine sugar
Whipped cream or
  commercial sour cream
  (optional)

Combine 1 quart water and 1 tablespoon lemon juice in a large bowl; stir well. Peel, core, and quarter pears, soaking pears in water mixture until all pears are prepared. Drain well, and pat dry with paper towels.

Sauté pears in butter in a large skillet 10 minutes or until golden brown. Add wine; bring to a boil, reduce heat, and simmer 5 minutes or until liquid is absorbed, stirring constantly. Sprinkle remaining 1 tablespoon lemon juice and sugar over pears. Cook over medium-high heat, stirring gently, until sugar melts and pears are lightly glazed. If desired, top each serving with a dollop of whipped cream. Serve warm. Yield: 6 servings.

The Finishing Touch
Temple Israel Sisterhood
Dayton, Ohio

Pineapple "No Ka Oi"

1 fresh pineapple
1½ cups sliced bananas
1½ cups sliced strawberries
2 kiwifruit, peeled and sliced

Italian Meringue
Crème Anglaise
Raspberry Sauce

Cut pineapple in half lengthwise. Scoop out pulp, leaving ½-inch-thick shells; set shells aside. Cut pineapple pulp into bite-size pieces, discarding core. Combine pineapple, bananas, strawberries, and kiwifruit; toss gently. Spoon fruit mixture into pineapple shells. Place filled pineapple shells on a baking sheet. Spread Italian Meringue over fruit, sealing to edges. Bake at 350° for 12 to 15 minutes or until meringue is golden brown.

To serve, divide Crème Anglaise evenly among individual dessert plates. Drizzle Raspberry Sauce around edge of Crème Anglaise.

Spoon meringue-topped fruit from shells into center of Crème Anglaise. Yield: 6 to 8 servings.

Italian Meringue

1 cup sugar
½ cup water

¼ teaspoon cream of tartar
3 egg whites

Combine sugar, water, and cream of tartar in a heavy saucepan. Cook over low heat, stirring constantly, until sugar dissolves. Cover and cook until mixture reaches soft ball stage (238°).

Beat egg whites (at room temperature) at high speed of an electric mixer until soft peaks form. Slowly add syrup mixture, and continue beating until stiff peaks form. Yield: 5 cups.

Crème Anglaise

1¼ cups milk
¼ cup sugar
3 egg yolks

Pinch of salt
1 teaspoon vanilla extract

Place milk in top of a double boiler; bring water to a boil. Cook until milk is thoroughly heated. Set aside.

Combine sugar, egg yolks, and salt in a medium mixing bowl; beat at high speed of an electric mixer 5 minutes or until mixture is thickened. Gradually stir about one-fourth of hot milk into yolk mixture; add to remaining hot milk in double boiler, stirring constantly. Cook in top of double boiler over low heat, stirring constantly, until mixture thickens and coats the back of a metal spoon. Remove from heat, and stir in vanilla. Let mixture cool to room temperature. Yield: 1⅓ cups.

Raspberry Sauce

1 (10-ounce) package frozen
raspberries, thawed

1 teaspoon fresh lemon juice

Combine raspberries and lemon juice in container of an electric blender or food processor; cover and process until mixture is smooth. Press raspberry mixture through a sieve, and discard seeds. Yield: 1 cup.

The Gathering
The Blue Bird Circle
Houston, Texas

Frozen Lemon Cream in Orange Cups

1 cup milk
1 cup whipping cream
1 cup sugar
⅛ teaspoon salt
2 tablespoons grated lemon
  rind

⅔ cup fresh lemon juice
½ teaspoon lemon extract
3 medium-size oranges
6 lemon slices (optional)

Combine milk, whipping cream, sugar, and salt in a heavy saucepan; cook over medium heat, stirring constantly, until sugar dissolves. Pour mixture into a freezer tray, and freeze until firm. Spoon frozen mixture into a large mixing bowl, and beat at medium speed of an electric mixer until smooth and creamy. Add lemon rind, juice, and extract, and mix well. Return mixture to freezer tray, and freeze until slushy.

Cut oranges in half crosswise. Clip membranes, and remove pulp, reserving pulp for other uses. Fill orange cups with lemon mixture, freeze until firm. Garnish each orange cup with a lemon slice, if desired. Yield: 6 servings.

Stir Crazy!
The Junior Welfare League of Florence, South Carolina

Coffee Tortoni

2 tablespoons instant coffee
  granules
2 egg whites
¾ cup sugar, divided
2 cups whipping cream
2 teaspoons vanilla extract
¼ teaspoon almond extract

¼ cup sliced blanched
  almonds, toasted
¼ cup flaked coconut, toasted
Additional sliced blanched
  almonds, toasted
Maraschino cherries

Sprinkle coffee granules over egg whites; let stand 10 minutes. Beat egg whites at high speed of an electric mixer until soft peaks form. Add ¼ cup sugar, 1 tablespoon at a time, beating until stiff peaks form and sugar dissolves (2 to 4 minutes).

Combine whipping cream and vanilla and almond flavorings; beat at high speed of electric mixer until foamy. Gradually add remaining ½ cup sugar, beating until stiff peaks form. Fold whipped cream into egg white mixture. Fold in ¼ cup toasted almonds and coconut. Spoon mixture into paper-lined muffin pans. Cover and freeze until firm. Top with additional toasted almonds and maraschino cherries. Yield: 1 dozen.

Finely Tuned Foods
The Symphony League
Leawood, Kansas

Frozen Mint Desserts

1 cup butter
2 cups sifted powdered
  sugar
4 (1-ounce) squares
  unsweetened chocolate,
  melted and cooled
4 eggs

2 teaspoons vanilla extract
1 teaspoon peppermint
  extract
1 to 2 tablespoons graham
  cracker crumbs (optional)
Whipped cream (optional)

Combine butter and powdered sugar in a large mixing bowl; beat at high speed of an electric mixer until mixture is light and fluffy. Add cooled chocolate, eggs, and vanilla and peppermint flavorings; beat at medium speed of an electric mixer until well blended.

Spoon mixture into a pastry bag fitted with a No. 4 star tip. Pipe into paper-lined miniature (1¾-inch) muffin pans. Sprinkle with graham cracker crumbs, if desired. Freeze at least 5 hours.

To serve, remove from freezer and, if desired, pipe whipped cream on top of desserts. Yield: 5 dozen.   Mrs. Joe Hyche

Kitchen Sampler
The Junior Service League of Bessemer, Alabama

Frozen Halva Dessert

6 eggs, separated
⅔ cup sugar
2 cups whipping cream
½ pound halva (sesame-honey candy), flaked

Commercial chocolate sauce (optional)
Additional flaked halva (optional)

Beat egg yolks at medium speed of an electric mixer until thick and lemon colored. Gradually add sugar, beating well.

Beat whipping cream until stiff peaks form; fold into egg yolk mixture. Beat egg whites (at room temperature) at high speed of electric mixer until stiff peaks form. Fold into egg yolk mixture. Sprinkle halva over egg yolk mixture, and fold in gently. Pour into a lightly oiled 12-cup mold; cover and freeze at least 8 hours.

Unmold dessert onto a serving plate. If desired, drizzle chocolate sauce over dessert, and sprinkle with additional halva. Yield: 10 to 12 servings.   Maureen Berkman

I Must Have That Recipe
Albert Einstein College of Medicine, Yeshiva University
Bronx, New York

Frozen Chocolate-Almond Mousse

⅔ cup chopped almonds, toasted and divided
½ cup graham cracker crumbs
3 tablespoons sugar, divided
3 tablespoons butter or margarine, melted
1 pint chocolate chip ice cream, softened

1 (6-ounce) package semisweet chocolate morsels
2 eggs, separated
½ cup whipping cream
3 tablespoons dark rum
Whipped cream

Combine ⅓ cup almonds, graham cracker crumbs, 1 tablespoon sugar, and melted butter; mix well. Firmly press crumb mixture into the bottom of an 8-inch springform pan. Bake crust at 350° for 10 minutes; let cool.

Spread softened ice cream over crust; freeze until firm.

Place chocolate morsels in top of a double boiler; bring water to a boil. Reduce heat to low; cook until chocolate melts.

Beat egg whites (at room temperature) at high speed of an electric mixer until foamy. Gradually add remaining 2 tablespoons sugar, 1 tablespoon at a time, beating until soft peaks form.

Beat ½ cup whipping cream at high speed of electric mixer until soft peaks form.

Beat egg yolks at medium speed of electric mixer until thick and lemon colored. Add melted chocolate and rum, beating well. Fold in beaten egg whites and whipped cream. Reserve 2 tablespoons almonds; fold remaining almonds into chocolate mixture.

Spread chocolate mixture over ice cream layer; sprinkle with reserved almonds. Cover and freeze 8 hours or until ice cream is firm. Garnish with additional whipped cream. Yield: 8 servings.

Simply Sensational
TWIGS, The Auxiliary of the Children's Medical Center
Dayton, Ohio

Almond Mousse

2 eggs, separated
⅓ cup sugar
1 tablespoon water
1 teaspoon vanilla extract
1 teaspoon almond extract

1 cup whipping cream, whipped
12 crisp almond macaroon cookies, crushed

Beat egg yolks at medium speed of an electric mixer until thick and lemon colored. Combine yolks, sugar, and water in top of a double boiler, stirring well; bring water to a boil. Reduce heat to low; cook, stirring constantly, until sugar dissolves. Remove from heat, and let cool. Stir in flavorings. Beat egg whites (at room temperature) at high speed of electric mixer until stiff peaks form. Fold egg whites and whipped cream into yolk mixture.

Sprinkle half the macaroon crumbs in the bottom of a 9- x 5- x 3-inch loafpan. Top with mousse mixture, and sprinkle with remaining crumbs. Freeze until firm. To serve, remove from pan, and place on a serving plate. Cut into 1-inch slices. Yield: 8 servings.

Steeped in Tradition
The Junior Service League of DeLand, Florida

Upper Crust Blackberry Sorbet

1 cup sugar
1 cup water
2 (16-ounce) packages frozen
  blackberries, thawed
3 large Granny Smith apples,
  peeled, cored, and chopped

2 tablespoons applejack
  brandy or blackberry-
  flavored liqueur
¼ cup orange juice

Combine sugar and water in a saucepan; cook over medium heat until sugar dissolves. Chill. Place blackberries and apples in container of an electric blender; cover and process until smooth. Press puree through a sieve to remove seeds; discard seeds. Add puree, brandy, and orange juice to sugar mixture, stirring well. Pour mixture into freezer can of a 1-gallon hand-turned or electric ice cream freezer. Freeze according to manufacturer's instructions. Let ripen 1 hour before serving. Yield: 1½ quarts.

Upper Crust: A Slice of the South
The Junior League of Johnson City, Tennessee

Strawberry-Champagne Sorbet

1 cup whipping cream
½ cup sugar
1 (10-ounce) package frozen
  strawberries, thawed and
  mashed

1½ cups champagne
2 egg whites
¼ cup sugar
Fresh strawberries (optional)
Fresh mint sprigs (optional)

Combine whipping cream and ½ cup sugar in a saucepan; cook over low heat, stirring constantly, until sugar dissolves. Cool to room temperature. Stir in mashed strawberries and champagne.

Beat egg whites (at room temperature) at high speed of an electric mixer until soft peaks form. Gradually add ¼ cup sugar, 1 tablespoon at a time, beating until stiff peaks form and sugar dissolves (2 to 4 minutes). Fold egg whites into strawberry mixture. Pour mixture into freezer can of a 1-gallon hand-turned or electric freezer. Freeze according to manufacturer's instructions. If desired, garnish with fresh strawberries and mint sprigs. Yield: 1 quart.

California Heritage Continues
The Junior League of Pasadena, California

Banana-Walnut Ice Cream

2 (16-ounce) cartons
  commercial sour cream
4 (14-ounce) cans sweetened
  condensed milk

8 cups half-and-half
4 cups mashed bananas
1 cup chopped walnuts

Combine all ingredients. Pour into freezer can of a 1½-gallon hand-turned or electric freezer. Freeze according to manufacturer's instructions. Let ripen 1 hour before serving. Yield: 1½ gallons.

Very Innovative Parties
The Loma Linda University School of Dentistry Auxiliary
Loma Linda, California

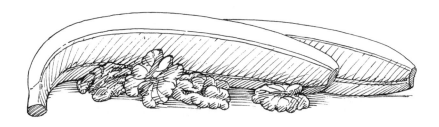

White Chocolate Ice Cream

1 cup water
¾ cup sugar
6 egg yolks
1 teaspoon vanilla extract

10 ounces white chocolate,
  melted
2 cups whipping cream
Fresh raspberries (optional)

Combine water and sugar in a heavy saucepan. Cook over low heat, stirring until sugar dissolves. Cook over medium heat, stirring occasionally, until mixture comes to a boil. Boil 5 minutes.

Combine egg yolks and vanilla; beat 7 minutes or until thick and lemon colored. Pour hot sugar mixture in a thin, steady stream over egg yolk mixture; beat until thickened and cooled (about 10 minutes). Gradually add white chocolate; continue beating 7 minutes. Stir in cream. Cover and freeze 8 hours or until firm. Garnish with raspberries, if desired. Yield: 5 cups.   Connie Monsma

Some Enchanted Eating
Friends of the West Shore Symphony Orchestra
Muskegon, Michigan

Best Homemade Vanilla Ice Cream

4 eggs, beaten
3 cups milk
2 cups sugar
½ teaspoon salt

1 (12-ounce) can evaporated
milk, chilled
1 tablespoon vanilla extract

Combine eggs, 3 cups milk, and sugar in a large heavy saucepan; cook over low heat until mixture thickens, stirring constantly. Remove from heat; cool.

Stir salt and remaining ingredients into egg mixture. Pour mixture into freezer can of a 1-gallon hand-turned or electric freezer. Freeze according to manufacturer's instructions. Let ripen at least 1 hour before serving. Yield: about 3 quarts.

Necessities and Temptations
The Junior League of Austin, Texas

Chock-Full-of-Chocolate Ice Cream

3 (1-ounce) squares
unsweetened chocolate
¼ cup unsalted butter
1 (14-ounce) can sweetened
condensed milk
1½ teaspoons vanilla extract
3 egg yolks
2 (1-ounce) squares semisweet
chocolate
½ cup strong brewed coffee

½ cup half-and-half
¾ cup sugar
2 tablespoons white crème de
cacao
1½ teaspoons dark rum
2 cups whipping cream
2 (1-ounce) squares
unsweetened chocolate,
grated
¼ teaspoon salt

Combine 3 squares unsweetened chocolate and butter in top of a double boiler; bring water to a boil. Reduce heat to low; cook until chocolate and butter melt. Stir in sweetened condensed milk. Remove from heat, and stir in vanilla. Beat egg yolks at medium speed of an electric mixer until thick and lemon colored; gradually add melted chocolate mixture, beating well. Set aside.

Combine 2 squares semisweet chocolate, coffee, half-and-half, and sugar in top of a double boiler; bring water to a boil. Reduce heat to low, and cook, stirring constantly, until mixture is smooth. Remove from heat; stir in crème de cacao and rum. Add coffee mixture, cream, grated chocolate, and salt to egg yolk mixture, stirring well. Pour into freezer can of a 1-gallon hand-turned or electric freezer. Freeze according to manufacturer's instructions. Let ripen at least one hour before serving. Yield: 1½ quarts.

Purple Sage and Other Pleasures
The Junior League of Tucson, Arizona

Frozen Mocha Torte

1 cup crisp macaroon cookie crumbs (about 10 macaroons)
2 tablespoons butter or margarine, melted
3 cups chocolate ice cream, softened
Hot Fudge Sauce, divided
3 cups coffee ice cream, softened
4 ounces English toffee-flavored candy bars, coarsely crushed

Combine crumbs and butter; mix well. Press crumb mixture into the bottom of a 9-inch springform pan. Bake at 350° for 8 minutes. Let cool on a wire rack. Spread chocolate ice cream over crust; top with ¼ cup Hot Fudge Sauce. Freeze until firm. Spread coffee ice cream over fudge sauce layer. Sprinkle crushed candy over coffee ice cream layer; drizzle ¼ cup Hot Fudge Sauce over top. Cover and freeze 8 hours or until ice cream is firm. Serve with remaining Hot Fudge Sauce. Yield: 10 servings.

Hot Fudge Sauce

6 (1-ounce) squares unsweetened chocolate
¼ cup butter or margarine
2 cups sugar
1 cup half-and-half
1 (14-ounce) can sweetened condensed milk
3 tablespoons brandy (optional)

Combine chocolate and butter in a saucepan. Cook over medium heat, stirring until chocolate melts. Add sugar and half-and-half; cook, stirring constantly, until thickened. Gradually add milk; cook 20 minutes, stirring occasionally. Remove from heat; stir in brandy, if desired. Let cool. Yield: 4 cups.

Crème de Colorado
The Junior League of Denver, Colorado

Mocha-Amaretto Mousse

1 (6-ounce) package
semisweet chocolate
morsels
3 tablespoons apricot nectar
2 tablespoons amaretto
2 eggs
2 egg yolks
1 tablespoon plus 1½
teaspoons instant coffee
granules

¼ cup sugar
¾ teaspoon almond extract
½ teaspoon vanilla extract
2 cups whipping cream,
divided
2 tablespoons powdered sugar
⅛ teaspoon amaretto
⅛ teaspoon almond extract
Chocolate curls

Combine chocolate morsels, apricot nectar, and 2 tablespoons amaretto in top of a double boiler; bring water to a boil. Reduce heat to low; cook until chocolate melts. Let cool.

Combine eggs and next 5 ingredients in container of an electric blender. Add 1 cup whipping cream; cover and process until well blended. Add chocolate mixture, and blend until smooth. Pour mixture into individual serving dishes; chill until set.

Beat remaining 1 cup whipping cream until foamy; gradually add powdered sugar, ⅛ teaspoon amaretto, and ⅛ teaspoon almond extract, beating until soft peaks form. Top each serving with sweetened whipped cream and chocolate curls. Yield: 8 servings.

Biscayne Bights and Breezes
The Villagers, Inc.
Coral Gables, Florida

Chocolate Chip Mousse Supreme

1 (8½-ounce) package
chocolate wafer cookies,
crushed (about 2 cups)
½ cup butter or margarine,
melted
¼ cup sugar
1 (12-ounce) package
semisweet chocolate
mini-morsels
3 tablespoons water

6 egg yolks
¼ cup sugar
4 cups whipping cream,
whipped
1 cup semisweet chocolate
mini-morsels
Additional whipped cream
(optional)
Chocolate leaves (optional)

Butter sides of a 10-inch springform pan; line bottom of pan with wax paper. Combine crushed wafer cookies, butter, and ¼ cup sugar; stir well. Press mixture firmly in bottom and 2 inches up sides of prepared pan. Chill 15 minutes.

Combine 12-ounce package of mini-morsels and water in a medium saucepan. Cook over low heat, stirring constantly, until chocolate melts and mixture is smooth. Remove from heat, and let cool.

Combine egg yolks and ¼ cup sugar in a large mixing bowl. Beat at medium speed of an electric mixer until thick and lemon colored.

Combine melted chocolate and egg mixture; stir well. Fold whipped cream and 1 cup mini-morsels into chocolate mixture. Pour mixture into crust; chill at least 6 hours or until firm. Remove sides of pan. If desired, garnish with additional whipped cream and chocolate leaves. Yield: 10 to 12 servings.

Crème de LA Coast
Small World Guild-Childrens Hospital of Orange County, California

French Silk Supreme

1 (8-ounce) package unsweetened chocolate	8 eggs
2 cups butter, softened	24 ladyfingers
3 cups sugar	Whipped cream
1 tablespoon plus 1 teaspoon vanilla extract	Chocolate shavings

Place unsweetened chocolate in top of a double boiler; bring water to a boil. Reduce heat to low; cook until chocolate melts. Set aside.

Cream butter with a large heavy-duty mixer. Add sugar; beat until light and fluffy. Beat in cooled chocolate and vanilla. Add eggs, one at a time, beating 5 to 7 minutes after each addition.

Split ladyfingers in half lengthwise. Line bottom and sides of a 10-inch springform pan with ladyfingers. Pour filling into prepared pan; cover and chill at least 4 hours or until set. Remove sides of pan. Garnish with whipped cream and chocolate shavings. Yield: 10 to 12 servings.

Winning at the Table
The Junior League of Las Vegas, Nevada

Chocolate Decadence with Crème Anglaise and Raspberry Puree

1 pound bar bittersweet
    chocolate
½ cup plus 2 tablespoons
    butter
4 eggs
1 tablespoon sugar
1 tablespoon all-purpose flour

2 cups whipping cream
1 tablespoon powdered sugar
1 teaspoon vanilla extract
Crème Anglaise
1 (10-ounce) package frozen
    raspberries, thawed, pureed,
    and strained

Combine chocolate and butter in top of a double boiler; bring water to a boil. Reduce heat to low; cook until chocolate and butter melt. Remove from heat; set aside.

Combine eggs and 1 tablespoon sugar in top of double boiler; bring water to a boil. Reduce heat to low; cook, stirring constantly, 2 to 3 minutes or until sugar dissolves. Remove from heat; pour into a large mixing bowl. Beat at high speed of an electric mixer 5 to 10 minutes or until eggs have tripled in volume. Fold flour into egg mixture. Stir one-third of flour mixture into chocolate mixture; fold chocolate mixture into remaining flour mixture.

Spoon mixture into an 8-inch springform pan that has been lined with parchment paper. Bake at 425° for 15 minutes. Let cool completely in pan on a wire rack. Cover and freeze at least 8 hours.

Beat whipping cream until foamy; gradually add powdered sugar and vanilla, beating until stiff peaks form.

Carefully remove sides of springform pan. Invert cake onto a serving plate; remove parchment. Spread two-thirds of whipped cream over top of cake. Spoon remaining whipped cream into a pastry bag fitted with star tip No. 132. Pipe rosettes on top and around bottom of cake. Chill.

Spoon Crème Anglaise onto individual dessert plates. Top with a slice of cake; drizzle with raspberry puree. Yield: 8 to 10 servings.

Crème Anglaise

1 cup milk
1 cup whipping cream
5 egg yolks
½ cup sugar

1 tablespoon Grand Marnier
    or other orange-flavored
    liqueur

Combine milk and whipping cream in a small saucepan; bring just to a boil over medium-low heat. Set aside.

Combine egg yolks and sugar in a large mixing bowl; beat at high speed of an electric mixer 4 minutes or until thick and lemon colored. Gradually add milk mixture to egg mixture, stirring with a wire whisk.

Pour mixture into top of a double boiler; bring water to a boil. Reduce heat to low; cook, stirring constantly, 8 to 10 minutes or until thickened. Pour into a mixing bowl; set bowl in cold water. Stir occasionally until cool. Stir in Grand Marnier. Cover with plastic wrap, gently pressing wrap directly onto surface of custard; chill at least 3 hours. Yield: 2¾ cups.

Palette to Palate
The Junior League of St. Joseph and Albrecht Art Museum
St. Joseph, Missouri

Chilled Lemon Soufflé

2 envelopes unflavored
  gelatin
½ cup water
5 eggs, separated
1¼ cups sugar
1 tablespoon grated lemon
  rind

⅔ cup fresh lemon juice
2 cups whipping cream
¼ teaspoon cream of tartar
2 cups fresh blueberries or
  raspberries

Sprinkle gelatin over water in a small saucepan; let stand 1 minute. Cook over low heat, stirring until gelatin dissolves. Set aside.

Beat egg yolks at medium speed of an electric mixer until thick and lemon colored; gradually add sugar, beating well. Gradually add lemon rind and juice, beating well.

Beat whipping cream until soft peaks form (do not overbeat); fold whipped cream into egg yolk mixture. Add gelatin, and stir until mixture begins to thicken.

Beat egg whites (at room temperature) and cream of tartar at high speed of electric mixer 1 minute or until soft peaks form. Fold beaten egg whites into whipped cream mixture. Spoon mixture into a 2-quart soufflé dish; cover and chill until firm. Serve with fresh blueberries. Yield: 6 to 8 servings.

Delicious Decisions
The Junior League of San Diego, California

Pineapple Cream Delight

1 (16-ounce) can pineapple
   slices in heavy syrup,
   undrained
¼ cup unsalted butter or
   margarine, softened
½ cup sugar
4 egg yolks

3 cups whipping cream,
   divided
½ cup ground blanched
   almonds
2 teaspoons light rum
36 ladyfingers
¼ cup sugar

Drain pineapple, reserving juice. Set juice aside. Finely chop pineapple; set aside.

Cream butter; gradually add ½ cup sugar, beating at medium speed of an electric mixer until well blended. Add egg yolks, one at a time, beating well after each addition. Beat 1 cup whipping cream until soft peaks form; fold into butter mixture. Add reserved pineapple, almonds, and rum, stirring gently.

Line bottom of a lightly greased 10-inch springform pan with 12 ladyfingers; drizzle with ⅓ cup reserved pineapple juice. Top with half of almond mixture. Repeat layers. Top with 12 ladyfingers, and drizzle with remaining pineapple juice. Cover and chill 3 hours.

Beat remaining 2 cups whipping cream at high speed of electric mixer until foamy; gradually add ¼ cup sugar, beating until soft peaks form. Spread over dessert; chill. Carefully remove sides of pan before serving. Yield: 10 to 12 servings.

Peachtree Bouquet
The Junior League of DeKalb County, Georgia

Pumpkin Mousse

1½ cups cooked, mashed
   pumpkin
1 cup sugar
¼ teaspoon salt
1 tablespoon minced
   crystallized ginger
1 teaspoon ground cinnamon

1 teaspoon ground nutmeg
½ teaspoon ground cloves
½ cup cognac
1 teaspoon vanilla extract
2 cups whipping cream,
   whipped

Combine first 7 ingredients in a large bowl; stir well. Stir in cognac and vanilla. Fold in whipped cream; pour mixture into a lightly

oiled 6-cup mold. Cover and chill until firm. Unmold onto a serving
plate. Yield: 12 servings.   Louise Brown

Favorite Recipes from Friends
The Town Hill School
Lakeville, Connecticut

Appleway Pudding

½ cup raisins
½ cup chopped dates
2 cups peeled, diced cooking
  apples
½ cup chopped walnuts or
  pecans
1¼ cups all-purpose flour
1 cup sugar
1 teaspoon baking soda

¼ teaspoon salt
1 teaspoon ground cinnamon
1 egg, beaten
½ cup cold brewed coffee
½ cup butter or margarine,
  melted
1 teaspoon vanilla extract
Lemon Sauce

Combine raisins, dates, apple, and walnuts; toss well. Set aside.
Combine flour and next 4 ingredients; add apple mixture, stirring
well. Add egg, coffee, butter, and vanilla to flour mixture; stir well.
Pour batter into a well-greased 8-inch square baking pan. Bake at
350° for 1 hour. Serve with Lemon Sauce. Yield: 6 to 8 servings.

Lemon Sauce

½ cup sugar
1 tablespoon cornstarch
1 cup water
2 tablespoons plus 1½
  teaspoons butter or
  margarine

½ teaspoon grated lemon
  rind
1 tablespoon plus 1½
  teaspoons lemon juice
⅛ teaspoon salt

Combine sugar, cornstarch, and water in top of a double boiler;
bring water to a boil. Reduce heat to low; cook until mixture
thickens, stirring frequently. Remove from heat; add butter and
remaining ingredients, stirring until butter melts. Yield: 1¼ cups.

Rave Revues
Lakewood Center Associates, Lakewood Center for the Arts
Lake Oswego, Oregon

Perfect Banana Pudding

2 tablespoons self-rising
  flour
⅔ cup sugar
⅛ teaspoon salt
2 eggs, separated
2 cups milk

1 teaspoon vanilla extract
1 (12-ounce) package vanilla
  wafers
3 large bananas
2 tablespoons sugar

Combine flour, ⅔ cup sugar, and salt in a heavy saucepan, stirring well. Set aside.

Beat egg yolks in a large mixing bowl at high speed of an electric mixer until foamy; combine beaten yolks and milk, mixing well. Stir egg yolk mixture into flour mixture; cook over medium heat, stirring constantly, until mixture is thickened and smooth. Remove from heat, and stir in vanilla.

Layer half the vanilla wafers in a 1½-quart baking dish. Slice 1½ bananas, and layer over wafers. Pour half the custard mixture over bananas. Repeat layers.

Beat egg whites (at room temperature) at high speed of electric mixer 1 minute. Gradually add 2 tablespoons sugar, 1 tablespoon at a time, beating until stiff peaks form and sugar dissolves (2 to 4 minutes). Spread meringue over custard, sealing to edge of dish. Bake at 400° for 6 to 8 minutes or until meringue is golden brown. Yield: 6 servings.   Verlan Harden

Calling All Cooks Two
The Telephone Pioneers of America
Birmingham, Alabama

Eggs & Cheese

A dairy farm with guernsey cows is as typical of Wisconsin's pastoral countryside as are her lakes and streams. Wisconsin supplies the country with a high percentage of the nation's dairy products, producing more cheese than any other state.

☆☆☆

French Scrambled Eggs

12 eggs
¼ teaspoon salt
⅛ teaspoon pepper

2 tablespoons butter
2 tablespoons whipping
cream

Combine eggs, salt, and pepper; stir briskly with a fork until blended. Melt butter in a large skillet, rotating skillet to coat bottom; add egg mixture. Cook over medium-low heat, stirring constantly, until eggs are firm, but still moist. Remove from heat; stir in cream. Serve immediately. Yield: 6 to 8 servings.   Connie Gibbons

Southern Elegance
The Junior League of Gaston County, North Carolina

Elegant Eggs

1 (10-ounce) package frozen
patty shells
1 cup sliced fresh
mushrooms
2 tablespoons butter or
margarine
2 tablespoons all-purpose
flour
1 cup milk
½ teaspoon salt

2 tablespoons Chablis or
other dry white wine
8 eggs, lightly beaten
½ cup commercial sour
cream
¼ cup chopped fresh chives
½ teaspoon salt
¼ teaspoon pepper
¼ cup butter or margarine

Bake patty shells according to package directions; set aside.
Sauté mushrooms in 2 tablespoons butter 3 minutes. Add flour; stir until smooth. Cook 1 minute, stirring constantly. Gradually add milk; cook over medium heat, stirring until thickened and bubbly. Stir in ½ teaspoon salt and wine. Set aside; keep warm.
Combine eggs and next 4 ingredients; mix well. Melt ¼ cup butter in a large skillet; pour in egg mixture. Cook, without stirring, until mixture begins to set on bottom. Draw a spatula across bottom of pan to form large curds. Continue until eggs are thickened, but still moist. Spoon egg mixture into patty shells; top with mushroom sauce. Serve immediately. Yield: 6 servings.

Cooking in Clover II
The Jewish Hospital of St. Louis, Missouri

Apple-Cheese Omelet

1 (3-ounce) package cream
cheese, softened
1 ounce Gorgonzola cheese or
blue cheese, crumbled
1 cooking apple, peeled,
cored, and chopped

3 tablespoons butter or
margarine, divided
1 teaspoon sugar
4 eggs
1 tablespoon plus 1 teaspoon
water

Combine cream cheese and Gorgonzola cheese in a small bowl; mix well, and set aside.

Sauté apple in 1 tablespoon butter in a skillet until tender. Add sugar; cook over low heat, stirring constantly, until sugar melts and turns a light golden brown. Remove from heat, and set aside.

Combine eggs and water, stirring with a wire whisk just until blended. Heat a 6-inch omelet pan or heavy skillet over medium heat until hot enough to sizzle a drop of water. Add 1 tablespoon butter, and rotate pan to coat bottom.

Pour in half of egg mixture. As mixture starts to cook, gently lift edges of omelet with a spatula, and tilt pan so that uncooked portion flows underneath. When egg mixture is set, spoon half of apples over half of omelet; top with half of cheese mixture. Fold omelet in half, and transfer to a serving plate.

Repeat procedure with remaining butter, egg mixture, apples, and cheese mixture. Yield: 2 servings.   Elaine Henzler

Favorite Recipes from Friends
The Town Hill School
Lakeville, Connecticut

Breakfast Pudding

⅓ cup butter or margarine,
melted
3 eggs
1½ cups milk
1⅓ cups all-purpose
flour

½ teaspoon salt
1 (8-ounce) package
brown-and-serve sausage
links, cut into ¼-inch slices
Maple syrup

Pour melted butter into a 13- x 9- x 2-inch baking dish. Set aside. Combine eggs, milk, flour, and salt in a large bowl; beat at medium speed of an electric mixer until well blended. Pour egg mixture into prepared baking dish. Arrange sausage slices over egg mixture. Bake at 400° for 30 to 35 minutes. Serve immediately with warm maple syrup. Yield: 6 to 8 servings.   Pat Donoho

As You Like It
St. Bernard's School
New York, New York

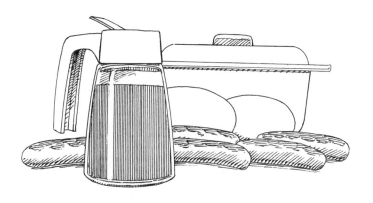

Sausage and Eggs

1 pound bulk pork sausage	2 cups milk
6 eggs	6 slices white bread
1 teaspoon salt	1 cup (4 ounces) shredded
1 teaspoon dry mustard	Cheddar cheese

Cook sausage in a large skillet over medium heat until browned, stirring to crumble; drain well. Place sausage in a greased 8-inch square baking pan. Set aside.

Combine eggs and next 3 ingredients in a large bowl; beat at medium speed of an electric mixer until foamy. Remove crust from bread; cut bread into 1-inch cubes. Stir bread cubes and cheese into egg mixture.

Pour egg mixture over sausage. Bake at 350° for 45 minutes or until set. Yield: 6 servings.   Tama Erickson

Remembering Our Heritage
Herndon Covenant Church Women
Herndon, Kansas

Scrumptious Eggs

6 cups (1½ pounds) shredded
  Monterey Jack cheese
¾ pound fresh mushrooms,
  sliced
1 small onion, chopped
¼ cup butter or margarine,
  melted

1 cup cubed cooked ham
7 eggs, beaten
1¾ cups milk
½ cup all-purpose flour
1 tablespoon seasoned salt
1 tablespoon chopped fresh
  parsley

Place half of cheese in a buttered 13- x 9- x 2-inch baking dish. Sauté mushrooms and onion in ¼ cup butter in a large skillet until tender; spoon vegetable mixture over cheese. Sprinkle ham over vegetable mixture; top with remaining cheese. Combine eggs, milk, flour, seasoned salt, and chopped parsley; beat well. Pour egg mixture evenly over cheese. Bake at 350° for 45 minutes or until set. Yield: 10 to 12 servings.

Finely Tuned Foods
The Symphony League
Leawood, Kansas

Cheese and Mushroom Ramequin

3 tablespoons plus 1½
  teaspoons butter or
  margarine
½ cup all-purpose flour
½ cup milk
½ teaspoon salt
⅛ teaspoon nutmeg

⅛ teaspoon pepper
4 eggs
1½ cups (6 ounces) shredded
  Swiss cheese, divided
Filling (recipe follows)
1 tablespoon butter or
  margarine

Melt 3 tablespoons plus 1½ teaspoons butter in a heavy saucepan over low heat; add flour, stirring until smooth. Cook 1 minute, stirring constantly. Gradually add milk; cook over medium heat, stirring constantly, until mixture is thickened and bubbly. Remove from heat; stir in salt, nutmeg, and pepper. Add eggs, one at a time, beating well after each addition. Stir in 1 cup cheese. Pour half of egg mixture into a greased 9-inch square baking dish; layer filling over egg mixture, and top filling with remaining egg mixture. Sprinkle remaining ½ cup cheese over egg mixture, and dot with 1 tablespoon butter. Bake at 400° for 25 minutes or until set. Serve immediately. Yield: 6 servings.

Filling

1 cup finely chopped fresh mushrooms	1 teaspoon vegetable oil
1 tablespoon chopped green onions	1 tablespoon all-purpose flour
1 tablespoon butter or margarine, melted	¼ cup whipping cream
	½ teaspoon salt
	½ teaspoon pepper

Sauté mushrooms and green onions in butter and hot oil in a skillet over medium heat 5 minutes or until tender, stirring frequently. Add flour, stirring until smooth. Cook 1 minute, stirring constantly. Gradually add cream; cook until thickened, stirring constantly. Stir in salt and pepper. Yield: about ½ cup.

Make It Miami
The Guild of the Museum of Science, Inc.
Miami, Florida

Puffed Eggs Monterey

6 eggs	¾ cup (3 ounces) shredded Monterey Jack cheese
½ cup milk	2 tablespoons butter or margarine, softened
1 teaspoon salt	4 slices white bread
½ teaspoon pepper	
2 tablespoons chopped green chiles	

Combine first 4 ingredients; stir until blended. Stir in chiles and cheese. Spread butter over one side of each bread slice; cut each slice into 4 triangles. Arrange half of the bread triangles, buttered side out and cut side down, around the edge of a 9-inch pieplate. Arrange remaining bread triangles, buttered side down, in bottom of pieplate. Pour egg mixture over bread. Bake at 350° for 30 minutes or until set. Yield: 6 servings.   Cynthia O'Rourke

Another Taste of Palm Springs
Tiempo de Los Niños, an Auxiliary of Desert Hospital
Palm Springs, California

Three-Cheese Brunch

9 eggs, beaten
1½ teaspoons sugar
1½ teaspoons salt
⅛ teaspoon ground red
  pepper
3 (8-ounce) packages
  Monterey Jack cheese,
  cubed
18 ounces cream cheese,
  cubed

1 (12-ounce) carton
  small-curd cottage cheese
1 tablespoon butter or
  margarine, cut into small
  pieces
¾ cup all-purpose flour
1½ teaspoons baking powder
1 (4-ounce) can chopped
  green chiles, drained
  (optional)

Combine eggs, sugar, salt, and pepper in a medium bowl; stir well.
Combine cheeses in a large bowl, stirring well. Stir butter into
cheese mixture.

Combine flour and baking powder in a small bowl; stir well. Add
flour and egg mixtures to cheese mixture, stirring gently. Stir in
green chiles, if desired.

Pour egg mixture into a greased 13- x 9- x 2-inch baking dish.
Bake at 350° for 45 to 50 minutes or until set. Let stand 5 to 10
minutes before serving. Yield: 15 to 18 servings.

Bound to Please
The Junior League of Boise, Idaho

Cheese Strata

1 (10-ounce) package frozen
  chopped broccoli
12 slices white bread
4 cups (16 ounces) shredded
  Cheddar cheese, divided
2 cups diced cooked ham

6 eggs, lightly beaten
3½ cups milk
2 tablespoons instant minced
  onion
½ teaspoon salt
¼ teaspoon dry mustard

Cook broccoli according to package directions. Drain broccoli
well, pressing between paper towels to remove moisture; set cooked
broccoli aside.

Remove crust from bread. Cut 6 slices of bread into small cubes,
and place in a greased 13- x 9- x 2-inch baking dish. Sprinkle with 3
cups Cheddar cheese; top with diced ham. Arrange remaining 6

slices of bread over ham. Combine eggs, milk, onion, salt, and mustard in a small mixing bowl; beat well. Pour egg mixture over bread slices. Cover and chill at least 6 hours. Bake, uncovered, at 325° for 1 hour and 10 minutes. Remove from oven, and top with remaining 1 cup Cheddar cheese. Bake an additional 5 minutes or until cheese melts. Let stand 10 minutes; cut into squares, and serve immediately. Yield: 10 to 12 servings.

Upper Crust: A Slice of the South
The Junior League of Johnson City, Tennessee

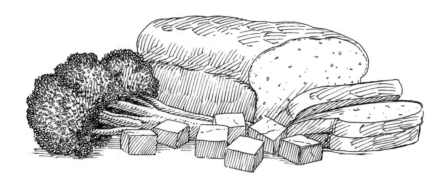

Dutch Baby

1 cup all-purpose flour
½ teaspoon salt
6 eggs, beaten
1 cup milk
2 tablespoons butter or
   margarine, melted
2 tablespoons shortening
Honey

Combine first 5 ingredients in container of an electric blender or food processor; cover and process 30 seconds. Scrape down sides of container with rubber spatula, if necessary, and process 30 seconds or until smooth. Chill batter at least 1 hour.

Grease two 9-inch round cakepans with shortening. Heat cakepans at 450° for 5 minutes. Remove pans from oven; pour batter evenly into pans. Bake at 450° for 20 minutes. Reduce heat to 350°, and bake 5 to 10 minutes or until lightly browned. Serve immediately with honey. Yield: 8 servings.   Barbara Schmidlapp

The Great Entertainer Cookbook
The Buffalo Bill Historical Center
Cody, Wyoming

Perfect Cheese Soufflé

¼ cup butter or margarine
¼ cup plus 2 tablespoons
  all-purpose flour
1 cup evaporated milk
6 eggs, separated

1 cup (4 ounces) shredded
  Cheddar cheese
1 teaspoon salt
⅛ teaspoon cream of tartar

Cut a piece of aluminum foil long enough to fit around a 2-quart soufflé dish, allowing a 1-inch overlap; fold foil lengthwise into thirds. Lightly oil one side of foil and bottom of dish. Wrap foil around outside of dish, oiled side against dish, allowing it to extend 1½ inches above rim to form a collar; secure with string. Set aside.

Melt butter in a heavy saucepan over low heat; add flour, stirring until smooth. Cook 1 minute, stirring constantly. Gradually add milk; cook over medium heat, stirring constantly, until thickened and bubbly. Beat egg yolks until thick and lemon colored. Add beaten egg yolks, cheese, and salt to milk mixture, stirring until cheese melts; remove from heat, and let cool 30 minutes.

Beat egg whites (at room temperature) at high speed of an electric mixer until foamy. Add cream of tartar, and beat until stiff peaks form. Fold one-third of egg whites into cheese mixture; carefully fold in remaining egg whites.

Pour mixture into prepared soufflé dish. Bake at 350° for 25 to 30 minutes or until soufflé is puffed and golden brown. Remove collar, and serve immediately. Yield: 8 servings.

The Market Place
The Junior Woman's Club of Augusta, Georgia

Blue Cheese Soufflé

6 eggs
½ cup whipping cream
⅛ teaspoon salt
¼ teaspoon pepper
1 teaspoon Worcestershire
  sauce

⅛ teaspoon hot sauce
1 (4-ounce) package blue
  cheese, crumbled
11 ounces cream cheese,
  softened and cut into 1-inch
  pieces

Lightly butter the bottom of a 1½-quart soufflé dish; set aside. Combine eggs, whipping cream, salt, pepper, Worcestershire sauce, and hot sauce in the container of an electric blender or food processor; cover and process 30 seconds or until mixture is smooth. Add blue cheese and cream cheese; cover and process 10 seconds or until smooth.

Pour mixture into prepared soufflé dish. Bake at 375° for 50 minutes or until soufflé is puffed and golden brown. Serve immediately. Yield: 6 servings.

Palm Country Cuisine
The Junior League of Greater Lakeland, Florida

Tomato Quiche

Pastry for one 10-inch pie
3 tablespoons butter or margarine
4 medium tomatoes, peeled and chopped
3 large green onions, chopped
1 tablespoon chopped fresh basil
1 teaspoon salt
¼ teaspoon ground white pepper
1 (8-ounce) package Swiss cheese, diced
3 eggs
1 cup half-and-half

Line a 10-inch quiche dish with pastry. Trim excess pastry around edges. Bake at 400° for 5 minutes; remove from oven, and prick with a fork. Bake an additional 5 minutes.

Melt butter in a large saucepan over medium heat. Add tomato, green onions, basil, salt, and white pepper, and stir well. Cook 10 minutes or until mixture is reduced by half. Drain and discard excess liquid. Let tomato mixture cool.

Layer diced Swiss cheese in baked pastry shell; spread cooled tomato mixture over cheese.

Combine eggs and half-and-half; beat at medium speed of an electric mixer until well blended. Pour egg mixture over tomato mixture. Bake at 425° for 10 minutes; reduce heat to 375°, and bake 30 to 35 minutes or until set. Let stand 10 minutes before serving. Yield: one 10-inch quiche.   Marilyn Wilkes

I Must Have That Recipe
Albert Einstein College of Medicine, Yeshiva University
Bronx, New York

Italian-Zucchini Quiche

Pastry for one 10-inch pie
4 cups thinly sliced zucchini
1 cup chopped onion
½ cup butter or margarine,
  melted
½ cup chopped fresh parsley
½ teaspoon salt
¼ teaspoon garlic powder
¼ teaspoon dried whole basil
¼ teaspoon dried whole
  oregano
2 eggs, beaten
2 cups (8 ounces) shredded
  Muenster cheese
2 teaspoons Dijon mustard

Line a 10-inch quiche dish with pastry. Trim excess pastry around edges. Prick bottom and sides of pastry with a fork. Bake at 400° for 3 minutes; remove from oven, and prick pastry again with fork. Bake an additional 5 minutes.

Sauté zucchini and onion in butter in a large skillet until tender. Stir in parsley, salt, garlic powder, basil, and oregano. Combine eggs and cheese; stir into vegetable mixture.

Spread pastry with mustard. Pour vegetable mixture into pastry shell. Bake at 375° for 20 minutes or until set. Let stand 10 minutes before serving. Yield: one 10-inch quiche.   Ruth Patrick

. . . More Than Cookies!
The Northwest Georgia Girl Scout Council, Inc.
Atlanta, Georgia

Turkey Quiche

Pastry for one 9-inch pie
½ cup chopped celery
¼ cup chopped onion
1 tablespoon butter or
  margarine, melted
1 cup diced cooked turkey
2 tablespoons diced pimiento
3 eggs, beaten
1 cup milk
¼ cup mayonnaise
2 tablespoons prepared
  mustard
½ teaspoon salt
1 cup (4 ounces) shredded
  Cheddar cheese
Paprika

Line a 9-inch quiche dish with pastry. Trim excess pastry around edges. Prick bottom and sides of pastry with a fork. Bake at 375° for 5 minutes; remove from oven, and prick pastry again with fork. Bake an additional 5 minutes.

Sauté chopped celery and onion in butter in a skillet over medium heat until tender. Stir in diced turkey and pimiento. Remove from heat, and set aside.

Combine eggs, milk, mayonnaise, mustard, and salt in a large bowl; mix thoroughly. Add turkey mixture to egg mixture, and pour into pastry shell. Top with cheese, and sprinkle with paprika. Bake at 375° for 45 to 55 minutes or until set. Let stand 10 minutes before serving. Yield: one 9-inch quiche.   Leota Fenchel

Truly Golden Recipes
Golden Congregational Church
Ryan, Iowa

Baked Eggs and Bacon with Herb Sauce

¼ cup butter or margarine
¼ cup all-purpose flour
1 cup milk
1 cup whipping cream
4 cups (16 ounces) shredded sharp Cheddar cheese
½ cup chopped fresh parsley
2 tablespoons chopped fresh basil
1 small clove garlic, minced
½ teaspoon dried whole marjoram
⅛ teaspoon salt
18 hard-cooked eggs, sliced
1 pound sliced bacon, cooked and crumbled
1 cup buttered soft breadcrumbs
Fresh parsley sprigs (optional)

Melt butter in a heavy saucepan over low heat; add flour, stirring until smooth. Cook 1 minute, stirring constantly. Gradually add milk; cook over medium heat, stirring constantly, until thickened and bubbly. Stir in whipping cream and next 6 ingredients; cook over low heat, stirring until cheese melts.

Layer half each of egg slices, crumbled bacon, and sauce in a 13- x 9- x 2-inch baking dish. Repeat layers with remaining egg slices, bacon, and sauce. Top with breadcrumbs. Bake, uncovered, at 350° for 20 to 30 minutes. Garnish with parsley sprigs, if desired. Yield: 10 to 12 servings.

Delicious Decisions
The Junior League of San Diego, California

Pesto Cheesecake

¼ cup fine, dry breadcrumbs
¼ cup grated Parmesan
cheese
2½ cups loosely packed fresh
basil leaves
½ cup fresh parsley sprigs
¼ cup olive oil
½ teaspoon salt
1 large clove garlic

1 (16-ounce) carton ricotta
cheese
2 (8-ounce) packages cream
cheese, softened
1 (8-ounce) can grated
Parmesan cheese
4 eggs
½ cup pine nuts, toasted

Butter bottom and sides of a 9-inch springform pan. Combine breadcrumbs and ¼ cup Parmesan cheese in a small bowl, and stir well. Coat bottom and sides of buttered pan with breadcrumb mixture. Chill 15 minutes.

Combine fresh basil leaves, parsley sprigs, olive oil, salt, and garlic in container of an electric blender or food processor; cover and process 2 minutes or until mixture is smooth, scraping sides of bowl occasionally with a rubber spatula. Transfer basil mixture to a medium bowl, and set aside.

Combine ricotta cheese, cream cheese, and 8 ounces Parmesan cheese in container of electric blender or food processor; cover and process until mixture is smooth. Add eggs and basil mixture to cheese mixture; cover and process until smooth. Pour basil mixture into prepared pan. Sprinkle top with toasted pine nuts.

Place springform pan in a 15- x 10- x 1-inch jellyroll pan. Bake at 325° for 1 hour and 15 minutes. Turn oven off, partially open oven door, and let cheesecake cool 1 hour. Transfer to a wire rack. Remove sides of springform pan. Serve at room temperature. Yield: one 9-inch cheesecake.

Taste of Today
BUNWC, North Shore Illinois Chapter
Northfield, Illinois

Fish & Shellfish

A lighthouse stands alone on the rocky coast of Maine to guide fishermen safely back to harbor with their catches. A variety of fresh fish and shellfish are essential ingredients in New England Cuisine.

☆☆☆

Cajun Catfish

3 tablespoons dried parsley
  flakes
1 teaspoon garlic powder
1 teaspoon onion salt
1 teaspoon lemon-pepper
  seasoning
½ teaspoon celery salt
½ teaspoon paprika
Salt and pepper to taste
1 (8-ounce) can tomato sauce
2 tablespoons vegetable oil
1 tablespoon vinegar
8 (4-ounce) farm-raised
  catfish fillets
1 tablespoon grated Parmesan
  cheese

Combine first 10 ingredients. Place catfish in a 13- x 9- x 2-inch baking dish. Brush fillets with tomato sauce mixture; sprinkle with cheese. Bake at 350° for 40 minutes or until fish flakes easily when tested with a fork. Broil fillets 4 inches from heat 3 minutes or until lightly browned. Yield: 8 servings.   Martha Cox

Temptations
Presbyterian Day School
Cleveland, Mississippi

Sweet-and-Sour Fish Fillets

4 (4-ounce) cod or other fish
  fillets
¼ cup cornstarch
Vegetable oil
4 green onions, thinly sliced
2 cloves garlic, crushed
1 teaspoon grated fresh
  gingerroot
2 tablespoons vegetable oil
¼ cup soy sauce
2 tablespoons Chablis or
  other dry white wine
2 tablespoons vinegar
2 tablespoons sugar
⅛ teaspoon freshly ground
  pepper
Hot cooked rice

Dredge fillets in cornstarch. Fry in hot oil over medium heat 3 minutes on each side or until lightly browned. Sauté onions, garlic, and gingerroot in 2 tablespoons oil until onions are tender. Stir in soy sauce and remaining ingredients except rice; bring mixture comes to a boil. Pour sauce over fillets. Serve over rice. Yield: 4 servings.

Parishables
St. Paul's Episcopal Church
Cleveland Heights, Ohio

Herb-Baked Fillets

4 (8-ounce) flounder or other
  fish fillets
½ teaspoon salt
¼ teaspoon pepper
¼ cup chopped green onions
2 tablespoons chopped fresh
  parsley
½ cup olive oil
2 tablespoons lemon juice
¼ cup Dijon mustard
½ cup soft breadcrumbs

1 teaspoon minced fresh
  tarragon
1 teaspoon minced fresh
  thyme
1 teaspoon minced fresh
  rosemary
2 tablespoons butter or
  margarine
½ cup (2 ounces) shredded
  Gruyère or Swiss cheese

Place fillets in a large shallow dish, and sprinkle evenly with salt and pepper. Combine green onions, parsley, olive oil, and lemon juice, stirring well. Pour marinade over fillets. Cover and marinate in refrigerator 4 hours, turning occasionally.

Remove fillets from marinade, discarding marinade. Spread Dijon mustard over fillets, and place in a lightly greased 13- x 9- x 2-inch baking dish. Combine breadcrumbs, tarragon, thyme, and rosemary; sprinkle over fillets. Dot with butter; top with cheese. Bake, uncovered, at 400° for 15 to 20 minutes or until fish flakes easily when tested with a fork. Yield: 4 to 6 servings.

Simply Sensational
TWIGS, The Auxiliary of the Children's Medical Center
Dayton, Ohio

Savory Baked Fish

½ cup chopped celery
1½ pounds flounder or sole
  fillets
½ teaspoon salt
¼ teaspoon ground white
  pepper
¼ teaspoon dried whole
  rosemary, crushed

¼ teaspoon paprika
1 large tomato, sliced
½ cup chopped green
  onions
¼ cup Chablis or other dry
  white wine

Arrange celery evenly in the bottom of a 13- x 9- x 2-inch baking dish. Arrange fillets on top of celery. Sprinkle fillets evenly with salt, pepper, rosemary, and paprika. Place tomato slices over fillets; top with green onions. Pour wine into baking dish. Bake at 350° for 25 minutes or until fish flakes easily when tested with a fork. Yield: 4 to 6 servings.

The Market Place
The Junior Woman's Club of Augusta, Georgia

Fish Fillets with Basil Sauce

2 tablespoons butter or margarine
2 tablespoons all-purpose flour
½ cup canned diluted chicken broth
½ cup dry sherry
2 tablespoons chopped fresh chives

½ teaspoon dried whole basil
½ teaspoon dried whole thyme
8 (4-ounce) orange roughy or sole fillets
½ teaspoon salt
¼ teaspoon pepper
3 medium tomatoes, peeled and sliced

Melt butter in a heavy saucepan over low heat; add flour, stirring until smooth. Cook 1 minute, stirring constantly. Gradually add broth and sherry; cook over medium heat, stirring constantly, until mixture is thickened and bubbly. Stir in chives, basil, and thyme. Set aside. Place fillets in a lightly greased 13- x 9- x 2-inch baking dish; sprinkle with salt and pepper. Arrange tomato slices over fillets. Spoon sauce over tomatoes and fillets. Bake, uncovered, at 300° for 30 to 40 minutes or until fish flakes easily when tested with a fork. Serve immediately. Yield: 6 to 8 servings.

Finely Tuned Foods
The Symphony League
Leawood, Kansas

Broiled Fish Puff

1½ pounds sole fillets
¼ teaspoon salt
¼ teaspoon pepper
½ cup (2 ounces) shredded
  Cheddar cheese
½ cup mayonnaise
⅛ teaspoon ground red
  pepper
1 egg white
Lemon wedges (optional)
Fresh parsley sprigs
  (optional)

Sprinkle fillets evenly with salt and ¼ teaspoon pepper; place on a lightly greased broiler rack of broiler pan. Broil 4 inches from heat 6 to 8 minutes or until fish flakes easily when tested with a fork.

Combine cheese, mayonnaise, and red pepper; stir well. Beat egg white (at room temperature) at high speed of an electric mixer until stiff peaks form; fold egg white into cheese mixture. Spread cheese mixture over fillets; broil 3 to 4 minutes or until tops are puffed and golden brown. If desired, garnish with lemon and parsley. Serve immediately. Yield: 6 servings.   Susan Rubin

Some Enchanted Eating
Friends of the West Shore Symphony Orchestra
Muskegon, Michigan

Walnut-Crusted Sole

⅓ cup all-purpose flour
½ teaspoon salt
¼ teaspoon pepper
1 cup finely chopped walnuts
¼ cup cracker crumbs
4 (4-ounce) sole or flounder
  fillets
2 egg whites, lightly beaten
¼ cup clarified butter
1 to 2 tablespoons vegetable
  oil
Lemon wedges

Combine flour, salt, and pepper; set aside. Combine walnuts and cracker crumbs; set aside. Dredge fillets in flour mixture. Dip floured fillets in egg whites, and dredge in walnut mixture. Fry in butter and hot oil 3 minutes on each side or until golden brown. Serve with lemon wedges. Yield: 4 servings.   Arden Poole

A Visual Feast
The Founders Society, Detroit Institute of Arts
Detroit, Michigan

Sole Casserole

8 (4-ounce) sole fillets
½ cup butter or margarine,
  melted
¾ cup fine, dry breadcrumbs
1 tablespoon plus 1 teaspoon
  chopped fresh parsley
1 tablespoon plus 1 teaspoon
  chopped fresh dillweed

2 teaspoons Dijon mustard
1 teaspoon salt
½ teaspoon pepper
½ cup Chablis or other dry
  white wine
1 cup whipping cream
1 cup (4 ounces) shredded
  Cheddar cheese

Dip fillets in butter; coat with breadcrumbs. Sprinkle ½ teaspoon parsley and ½ teaspoon dillweed over each fillet; roll up, enclosing herbs. Place fillets, seam side down, in a 12- x 8- x 2-inch baking dish. Spread ¼ teaspoon mustard over each; sprinkle with salt and pepper. Combine wine and cream, stirring well; pour over rolls. Sprinkle with cheese. Cover and bake at 350° for 30 minutes; uncover and bake 10 minutes or until fish flakes easily when tested with a fork. Yield: 4 servings. Eileen McKay

Favorite Recipes from Friends
The Town Hill School
Lakeville, Connecticut

Grilled Salmon Steaks

6 (8-ounce) salmon steaks
  (about 1-inch thick)
½ cup olive oil
¼ cup chopped fresh dillweed
3 tablespoons minced green
  onions

3 tablespoons lime juice
1 tablespoon champagne
  mustard
½ teaspoon salt
¼ teaspoon pepper

Place salmon steaks in a shallow dish. Combine oil and remaining ingredients, stirring well. Pour marinade over steaks. Cover and marinate in refrigerator 1 hour. Remove salmon from marinade, reserving marinade. Grill salmon over hot coals 7 minutes on each side or until fish flakes easily when tested with a fork, basting frequently with marinade. Yield: 6 servings.

Dining In
The Young Woman's League of Westport, Connecticut

New Orleans Crabmeat

2 (9-ounce) packages frozen
  artichoke hearts
¼ cup butter or margarine
¼ cup minced green onions
2 tablespoons minced fresh
  parsley
1½ tablespoons all-purpose
  flour
1 cup half-and-half
1 cup (4 ounces) grated
  Gruyère cheese
3 tablespoons dry sherry

½ teaspoon salt
⅛ teaspoon ground red
  pepper
¼ teaspoon hot sauce
1 pound fresh lump
  crabmeat, drained and
  flaked
2 tablespoons fine, dry
  breadcrumbs
1 tablespoon butter or
  margarine, melted

Cook artichoke hearts according to package directions; drain. Arrange artichoke hearts in a greased 3-quart casserole; set aside.

Melt ¼ cup butter in a saucepan over low heat. Add onions and parsley, and sauté until onions are tender. Add flour, stirring until smooth. Gradually add half-and-half; cook over medium heat, stirring constantly, until thickened and bubbly. Add cheese, stirring until cheese melts. Add sherry and next 3 ingredients, stirring well. Remove from heat; stir in crabmeat. Spoon crabmeat mixture over artichoke hearts. Combine breadcrumbs and 1 tablespoon butter; sprinkle evenly over crabmeat mixture. Bake at 350° for 30 to 40 minutes. Yield: 6 servings.

Artist's Palate Cookbook
New Orleans Museum of Art-Women's Volunteer Committee
New Orleans, Louisiana

Herb-Baked Oysters

1½ cups fine, dry breadcrumbs
3 tablespoons minced fresh
  parsley
1½ teaspoons dried whole
  oregano
½ teaspoon salt
½ teaspoon dried whole
  thyme

1 clove garlic, crushed
¼ cup plus 1 tablespoon dry
  sherry
⅓ cup butter or margarine,
  melted
2 (12-ounce) containers fresh
  Standard oysters, undrained
Lemon wedges

Combine first 8 ingredients, stirring well. Drain oysters, reserving liquor. Place oysters in a lightly greased 10- x 6- x 2-inch baking dish; add ½ to ¾ cup reserved liquor. Sprinkle with breadcrumb mixture. Bake at 425° for 15 minutes or until lightly browned. Serve warm with lemon wedges. Yield: 8 servings.   Linda L. Unger

From the Hills
The Lutheran Church of Vestavia Hills, Alabama

Coquilles Saint Jacques

1 cup water
1 teaspoon lemon juice
½ teaspoon salt
2 pounds fresh sea scallops,
  rinsed and drained
¼ cup butter or margarine
¼ pound fresh mushrooms,
  sliced
¼ cup finely chopped onion
⅓ cup all-purpose flour
⅛ teaspoon pepper
1 cup half-and-half

½ cup milk
1 cup (4 ounces) shredded
  Gruyère cheese
½ cup Chablis or other dry
  white wine
1 tablespoon chopped fresh
  parsley
1 tablespoon lemon juice
½ cup fine, dry breadcrumbs
2 tablespoons butter or
  margarine, melted

Combine water, 1 teaspoon lemon juice, and salt in a medium saucepan; bring to a boil. Add scallops. Reduce heat, cover, and simmer 5 to 6 minutes. Drain and set aside.

Melt ¼ cup butter in a saucepan. Add mushrooms and onion; sauté until tender. Stir in flour and pepper. Cook, stirring constantly, 1 minute. Gradually stir in half-and-half and milk; cook over medium heat, stirring constantly, until thickened and bubbly. Add cheese; stir until cheese melts. Remove from heat; add wine, parsley, and 1 tablespoon lemon juice. Stir in scallops. Spoon mixture into 8 greased individual baking dishes or scallop shells. Combine breadcrumbs and 2 tablespoons butter, stirring well; sprinkle over scallop mixture. Broil 4 inches from heat 1 minute or until golden brown and thoroughly heated. Yield: 8 servings.   Arlene Ullman

Angel Fare
St. Michael and All Angels Episcopal Church
Portland, Oregon

Scallops Primavera

1 pound fresh sea scallops
1 cup uncooked long-grain
  rice
1 tablespoon oyster
  sauce
2 tablespoons soy sauce
1½ teaspoons minced fresh
  gingerroot, divided
¼ teaspoon sugar
2 tablespoons butter or
  margarine
2 tablespoons peanut oil
1 clove garlic, minced
2 cups broccoli flowerets
1 small sweet red pepper, cut
  into thin strips
½ cup thinly sliced
  carrots
¼ pound fresh snow pea
  pods, trimmed
½ cup sliced green onions
½ pint cherry tomatoes,
  halved
½ pound asparagus spears,
  cut into 1-inch pieces
1 tablespoon lemon juice
2 teaspoons Dijon mustard
½ teaspoon paprika
¼ teaspoon dried whole
  dillweed
¼ teaspoon pepper

Cut scallops in half crosswise. Rinse scallops in cold water; drain and set aside.

Prepare rice according to package directions, omitting salt. Combine rice, oyster sauce, soy sauce, ½ teaspoon gingerroot, and sugar; stir well. Set aside, and keep warm.

Heat butter and peanut oil in a wok or large skillet over high heat. Add minced garlic and remaining 1 teaspoon gingerroot; stir-fry 15 seconds. Add broccoli flowerets, sweet red pepper strips, and sliced carrot; stir-fry 3 to 5 minutes. Add snow peas and green onions; stir-fry 1 minute. Add cherry tomato halves and asparagus; stir-fry 1 minute or until vegetables are crisp-tender. Remove vegetables with a slotted spoon, and set aside.

Combine lemon juice, mustard, paprika, dillweed, and pepper in a small bowl; stir well. Set aside.

Sauté scallops in wok 2 to 3 minutes or until done. Stir in vegetables and lemon juice mixture. Cook until thoroughly heated. Serve over reserved cooked rice. Yield: 6 servings.

The Mystic Seaport All Seasons Cookbook
Mystic Seaport Museum Stores
Mystic, Connecticut

Coconut Shrimp

1¼ pounds unpeeled large
  fresh shrimp
1⅓ cups all-purpose
  flour
1 teaspoon salt
¼ teaspoon pepper

⅛ teaspoon paprika
1¼ cups beer
2 cups shredded coconut
Vegetable oil
Orange Mustard Sauce

Peel and devein shrimp, leaving tails intact.

Combine flour, salt, pepper, and paprika in a medium bowl, stirring well; make a well in center of flour mixture. Gradually add beer, stirring until batter is smooth.

Dip shrimp in batter, and dredge in shredded coconut. Fry shrimp in hot oil (350°) until lightly browned. Drain on paper towels. Serve with Orange Mustard Sauce. Yield: 6 servings.

Orange Mustard Sauce

¼ cup plus 2 tablespoons
  orange marmalade
¼ cup plus 2 tablespoons
  orange juice

2 tablespoons Dijon
  mustard

Combine orange marmalade, orange juice, and Dijon mustard in a small bowl, stirring well. Yield: about 1 cup.

Make It Miami
The Guild of the Museum of Science, Inc.
Miami, Florida

Garlic-Broiled Shrimp

2 pounds unpeeled large
  fresh shrimp
½ cup butter or margarine,
  melted
½ cup olive oil
¼ cup chopped fresh parsley
1 tablespoon chopped green
  onions

3 cloves garlic, minced
1 tablespoon plus 1½
  teaspoons fresh lemon
  juice
Freshly ground pepper
Hot cooked rice

Peel and devein shrimp. Set aside.

Combine butter and next 5 ingredients in a large shallow dish. Add shrimp, tossing to coat well. Cover and marinate in refrigerator at least 30 minutes, stirring occasionally.

Arrange shrimp in a single layer in a large, shallow baking dish; brush marinade over shrimp. Broil shrimp 4 inches from heat 3 minutes. Turn shrimp, and broil an additional 3 minutes or until shrimp turn pink. Sprinkle with pepper. Serve with pan drippings over hot cooked rice. Yield: 4 to 6 servings.

Off the Hook
The Junior League of Stamford-Norwalk
Darien, Connecticut

Fiery Cajun Shrimp

1 cup butter, melted
1 cup margarine, melted
⅓ cup Worcestershire sauce
¼ cup pepper
2 teaspoons salt
1 teaspoon dried whole
  rosemary

2 teaspoons hot sauce
3 cloves garlic, minced
6 lemons
6 pounds unpeeled large
  fresh shrimp

Combine butter, margarine, Worcestershire sauce, pepper, salt, rosemary, hot sauce, and minced garlic in a medium bowl; stir well. Squeeze juice of 2 lemons into butter mixture. Thinly slice remaining 4 lemons.

Pour ½ cup butter mixture into a 13- x 9- x 2-inch baking dish; layer shrimp and lemon slices over butter mixture to fill baking dish.

Repeat procedure with remaining ingredients in a second baking dish. Pour remaining butter mixture over top. Bake at 350° for 30 minutes or until shrimp turn pink, basting frequently with pan juices. Yield: 8 to 10 servings.   Rowena Brocato

The Bishop's Bounty
St. Mary's Training School for Retarded Children
Alexandria, Louisiana

Fireworks Shrimp

1 pound unpeeled medium-size fresh shrimp
3 cloves garlic, minced
½ teaspoon minced fresh gingerroot
1 tablespoon Chinese chile paste with garlic
3 tablespoons tomato sauce
2 tablespoons dry sherry
1 tablespoon oyster sauce
1 tablespoon light soy sauce
1 teaspoon red wine vinegar
1 teaspoon sesame oil
½ teaspoon sugar
2 tablespoons peanut oil, divided
4 stalks bok choy, sliced diagonally into 1½-inch pieces
¼ pound fresh snow pea pods, trimmed
3 green onions, sliced diagonally into 3-inch pieces
2 teaspoons cornstarch
3 tablespoons cold water

Peel and devein shrimp; cut shrimp in half lengthwise. Set aside.

Combine garlic, gingerroot, and chile paste; stir well. Combine tomato sauce, sherry, oyster sauce, soy sauce, vinegar, sesame oil, and sugar; stir well. Set aside.

Heat electric wok or skillet at 375° for 2 minutes. Add 1 tablespoon peanut oil around top of wok. Add shrimp, and stir-fry 2 to 3 minutes. Remove shrimp from wok; cover and set aside. Add remaining 1 tablespoon peanut oil to wok. Add chili paste mixture, bok choy, snow peas, and green onions; stir-fry 2 to 3 minutes or until vegetables are crisp-tender. Add tomato sauce mixture and shrimp. Combine cornstarch and water, stirring well. Add to wok. Stir-fry just until shrimp and vegetables are coated and sauce is thickened. Serve immediately. Yield: 4 servings.

California Treasure
The Junior League of Fresno, California

Shrimp Stuffed with Crabmeat

18 unpeeled jumbo fresh
  shrimp
¼ teaspoon salt
6 ounces fresh lump
  crabmeat, drained and
  flaked
2 hard-cooked eggs, finely
  chopped
1½ cups soft breadcrumbs
¼ cup plus 2 tablespoons
  butter or margarine,
  softened

3 tablespoons mayonnaise
1 tablespoon plus 1½
  teaspoons chopped fresh
  parsley
1 tablespoon chopped
  pimiento
¼ teaspoon Worcestershire
  sauce
2 tablespoons mayonnaise
1 tablespoon plus 1 teaspoon
  milk
Paprika

Peel and devein shrimp, leaving tails intact. Butterfly shrimp.
Place shrimp in a buttered 13- x 9- x 2-inch baking dish. Sprinkle
with salt. Combine crabmeat and next 7 ingredients; stir well. Top
each shrimp with 2 tablespoons crabmeat mixture. Combine 2
tablespoons mayonnaise and milk; drizzle over shrimp. Sprinkle
with paprika.

Bake at 325° for 20 minutes or until stuffing is golden brown and
shrimp turn pink. Yield: 4 to 6 servings.   Merry Robin Bachetti

VIP Cookbook, Volume VI
The American Cancer Society, Virginia Division
Vienna, Virginia

Seafood Terrine with Salmon

½ pound fresh sea scallops
½ pound sole fillets, cut into
  1-inch pieces
2 egg whites
1 egg
1 teaspoon salt, divided
¼ teaspoon ground white
  pepper
⅛ teaspoon ground red pepper
3 tablespoons butter or
  margarine, divided

4 shallots, minced
4 ounces fresh mushrooms
2 cups whipping cream
2 (10- x 5-inch) skinned
  ¾-inch-thick salmon fillets
  (about 2½ pounds)
¼ teaspoon pepper
2 tablespoons minced fresh
  dillweed, divided
2 ounces red caviar
Crème Fraîche Sauce

Position knife blade in food processor bowl; add scallops and sole. Cover and pulse 3 or 4 times until coarsely chopped. Add egg whites, egg, ½ teaspoon salt, white pepper, and red pepper; process 20 seconds or until mixture is smooth. Cover and chill 1 hour.

Melt 2 tablespoons butter in a medium skillet over medium heat. Add shallots, and sauté until tender.

Remove stems from mushrooms, and reserve for other uses. Thinly slice mushroom caps. Add sliced mushrooms to shallots in skillet, and sauté 4 minutes. Transfer mixture to a bowl. Cover and chill 30 minutes.

Process chilled scallop mixture, slowly adding whipping cream through food chute of processor bowl, scraping sides of processor bowl occasionally. Cover and chill 30 minutes.

Sprinkle salmon fillets with remaining ½ teaspoon salt, ¼ teaspoon pepper, and 1 teaspoon dillweed. Spoon ¾ cup scallop mixture over one fillet, leaving a ¼-inch border along sides. Cover with second fillet, dillweed side down. Press edges together gently.

Combine remaining scallop mixture, remaining 1 tablespoon plus 2 teaspoons dillweed, chilled mushroom mixture, and caviar in a medium bowl, stirring gently.

Butter a 3-quart terrine with remaining 1 tablespoon butter; fill one-fourth full with scallop mixture. Place layered salmon fillets in center of terrine, leaving a ½-inch border on sides and ends of terrine. Cover salmon with remaining scallop mixture, filling in sides and ends of terrine; smooth top with spatula. Cover loosely with greased aluminum foil.

Place terrine in a large baking pan; pour hot water into pan to a depth of 1 inch. Bake at 350° for 1 hour and 15 minutes or until a wooden pick inserted in center of terrine comes out clean. Let cool. Cover and chill at least 8 hours. Unmold onto a serving platter. Serve with Crème Fraîche Sauce. Yield: 6 to 8 servings.

Crème Fraîche Sauce

1½ cups crème fraîche	**¼ teaspoon salt**
2 tablespoons minced fresh	**¼ teaspoon hot sauce**
chives	**Ground white pepper to taste**

Combine all ingredients in a small bowl; stir well to combine. Yield: 1⅓ cups.

Libretto
The Opera Society of Fort Lauderdale, Florida

Seafood Strudel

3 tablespoons butter or
margarine
3 tablespoons all-purpose
flour
½ teaspoon Dijon mustard
¼ teaspoon salt
⅛ teaspoon ground red
pepper
¾ cup milk
2 tablespoons whipping
cream
1 cup soft breadcrumbs
¼ cup grated Parmesan
cheese
¼ teaspoon dry mustard
11 sheets commercial frozen
phyllo pastry, thawed
¾ cup butter or margarine,
melted
⅓ pound fresh lump
crabmeat, drained and flaked

⅓ pound cooked, peeled
shrimp (about ⅔ pound
unpeeled fresh shrimp),
coarsely chopped
⅓ pound cooked fresh bay
scallops, coarsely chopped
2 hard-cooked eggs, chopped
½ cup (2 ounces) shredded
Swiss cheese
¼ cup chopped fresh parsley
¼ cup chopped shallots
2 tablespoons chopped fresh
chives
1 large clove garlic, minced
¾ cup commercial sour
cream
2 tablespoons grated
Parmesan cheese
2 tablespoons chopped fresh
parsley

Melt 3 tablespoons butter in a saucepan over low heat; add flour, stirring until smooth. Cook 1 minute, stirring constantly. Stir in Dijon mustard, salt, and red pepper. Gradually add milk; cook over medium heat, stirring constantly, until thickened and bubbly. Remove from heat; stir in cream. Cover and chill 2 hours.

Combine breadcrumbs, ¼ cup Parmesan cheese, and dry mustard. Place one sheet of phyllo on a damp towel (keeping remaining phyllo covered). Lightly brush phyllo with melted butter. Sprinkle 1 tablespoon breadcrumb mixture over phyllo. Layer remaining sheets phyllo on first sheet, brushing each sheet with butter and sprinkling with 1 tablespoon breadcrumb mixture.

Combine seafood, and arrange on layered phyllo in a lengthwise roll along one long side, leaving a 2-inch margin from edge. Top seafood with remaining breadcrumb mixture. Sprinkle chopped egg, Swiss cheese, ¼ cup parsley, shallots, chives, and garlic over seafood mixture. Dollop chilled white sauce and sour cream evenly over seafood mixture. Fold short ends of layered phyllo in one inch. Fold long ends of layered phyllo in one inch. Roll phyllo, jellyroll fashion, starting with long side closest to seafood mixture. Brush with remaining melted butter. Bake on a lightly greased baking sheet at 375° for 12 minutes. Remove from oven, and slice diagonally into 8 slices; reshape roll. Return to oven; bake an additional 30 to 40 minutes or until golden brown. Transfer to a serving platter; top with 2 tablespoons Parmesan cheese and 2 tablespoons parsley. Yield: 6 to 8 servings.   Elsa Freeman McDowell

Charleston Receipts Repeats
The Junior League of Charleston, South Carolina

Millionaire's Seafood Extraordinaire

2 quarts water
3 or 4 (8-ounce) lobster tails
1½ quarts water
1½ to 2 pounds unpeeled medium-size fresh shrimp
½ cup plus 2 tablespoons butter or margarine
⅔ cup all-purpose flour
1 teaspoon salt
½ teaspoon paprika
3 to 3½ cups half-and-half
2 (6-ounce) packages frozen crabmeat, thawed and drained
1½ cups Chablis or other dry white wine
Hot cooked rice

Bring 2 quarts water to a boil; add lobster tails. Cover, reduce heat, and simmer 12 minutes. Drain. Rinse with cold water. Split and clean tails. Cut lobster tail meat into ½-inch pieces; set aside.

Bring 1½ quarts water to a boil; add shrimp, and cook 3 to 5 minutes. Drain well; rinse with cold water. Chill. Peel and devein shrimp; set aside.

Melt butter in a large skillet; add flour, salt, and paprika, stirring until smooth. Cook 1 minute, stirring constantly. Gradually add half-and-half; cook over medium heat, stirring constantly, until mixture is thickened and bubbly. Place lobster, shrimp, and crabmeat in a large Dutch oven; add white sauce and wine, stirring gently. Cook over medium heat just until thoroughly heated. Serve over rice. Yield: 8 to 10 servings.   Mary Sims

Beyond the Village Gate
The Parmadale Children's Village
Parma, Ohio

Poor Man's Paella

12 mussels
12 cherrystone clams
1 tablespoon cornmeal
¼ cup olive oil
1 (4-pound) broiler-fryer, cut up
¼ cup all-purpose flour
1 pound Italian sausage links
3 cloves garlic, minced
1 cup chopped onion
1 medium-size green pepper, chopped
6 cups canned diluted chicken broth
1 cup Chablis or other dry white wine
2 tablespoons tomato paste
2 large bay leaves
1 tablespoon dried whole oregano
¼ teaspoon hot sauce
½ teaspoon ground saffron
2½ cups uncooked long-grain rice
½ teaspoon salt
¼ teaspoon pepper
Chopped fresh parsley

Remove beards on mussels. Scrub mussel and clam shells with a brush; cover with cold water. Sprinkle with cornmeal, and set aside for 30 minutes; drain.

Heat oil in a large paella pan over medium heat. Dredge chicken in flour, and place in oil. Cover and cook chicken 25 minutes or until golden brown, turning occasionally. Add sausage, and cook until brown; prick sausage with a fork, and continue cooking, uncovered, 15 minutes. Remove chicken and sausage to a warm platter.

Pour off all but 2 tablespoons drippings. Sauté garlic, onion, and green pepper in pan drippings until tender. Stir in chicken broth and next 5 ingredients. Add saffron and rice; bring to a boil. Cover and cook 15 minutes or until rice is tender. Return chicken and sausage to paella pan; sprinkle with salt and pepper. Add mussels and clams; cover and cook until mussels and clams open. Remove and discard bay leaves. Sprinkle with chopped fresh parsley. Serve in paella pan. Yield: 8 servings.   Robert Simmons

The Cooks' Book
The Nightingale-Bamford School
New York, New York

Meats

The Navajo National Monument, established in 1909 in northern Arizona, is comprised of six hundred acres that protect the priceless remains of cliff-dwelling Pueblo Indians. This twelfth-century dwelling named Keet Seel, Navajo for "broken pottery," has 160 rooms and is the largest cliff dwelling in Arizona.

☆☆☆

Pot Roast Caribe

1 (3-pound) boneless chuck
  roast
2 tablespoons vegetable oil
2 cloves garlic, crushed
1 cup chopped onion
1 teaspoon salt
2 (8-ounce) cans tomato sauce
1 (4-ounce) can chopped
  green chiles, undrained
2 tablespoons sugar
1 tablespoon all-purpose
  flour
1 tablespoon cocoa
1 tablespoon chili powder
1 teaspoon dried whole
  oregano

1 teaspoon ground cumin
1 teaspoon ground coriander
¼ teaspoon ground cinnamon
1 teaspoon grated orange
  rind
½ cup ground blanched
  almonds
8 boiling onions, peeled
3 medium-size yellow squash,
  cut into 1-inch pieces
¼ cup slivered almonds,
  toasted
Fresh parsley sprigs
  (optional)
Cherry tomatoes (optional)

Brown roast on all sides in hot oil in a large Dutch oven; remove
roast, reserving drippings. Set aside.

Sauté garlic and chopped onion in pan drippings 5 minutes or
until onion is tender. Add salt, tomato sauce, and chopped green
chiles, stirring well.

Combine sugar, flour, cocoa, chili powder, oregano, cumin, coriander, and cinnamon in a small bowl; stir well.

Add sugar mixture, orange rind, and ground almonds to tomato
mixture in Dutch oven; stir well.

Return roast to Dutch oven; cover, reduce heat to low, and cook 2
hours or until meat is tender.

Add boiling onions and squash to Dutch oven; cook an additional
20 minutes or until vegetables are tender.

Remove roast to a serving platter; spoon sauce over roast. Arrange vegetables around roast, and sprinkle with slivered almonds.
If desired, garnish with parsley sprigs and cherry tomatoes. Yield: 6
to 8 servings.

Parishables
St. Paul's Episcopal Church
Cleveland Heights, Ohio

Marinated Sirloin Roast

1 (3- to 3½-pound) boneless
   sirloin tip roast, 2½ to 3
   inches thick
1 large onion, coarsely
   chopped
2 cloves garlic, minced
½ cup firmly packed brown
   sugar
1½ cups water
½ cup plus 2 tablespoons soy
   sauce
½ cup catsup

¼ cup bourbon
2 tablespoons vinegar
2 tablespoons Worcestershire
   sauce
1 tablespoon lemon juice
1 teaspoon salt
½ teaspoon chili powder
½ teaspoon coarsely ground
   pepper
½ teaspoon prepared mustard
⅛ teaspoon ground red
   pepper

Pierce roast with a fork in several places, and place in a 3-quart casserole; set aside.

Combine onion and remaining ingredients in container of an electric blender or food processor; cover and process until smooth. Pour marinade over roast. Cover and marinate in refrigerator at least 8 hours, turning occasionally. Remove meat from marinade, reserving marinade. Grill meat 6 inches from medium-low coals 30 minutes on each side or until a meat thermometer registers 140° (rare) or 150° (medium rare), basting frequently with reserved marinade. Yield: 6 to 8 servings.   Sallie Wingeleth

Compliments to the Cook
The YWCA of Salt Lake City, Utah

Beef Bourguignon

4 medium onions, sliced
2 tablespoons bacon
   drippings
1 (2-pound) top round roast,
   cut into 1-inch cubes
2 tablespoons all-purpose
   flour
½ teaspoon salt
½ teaspoon dried whole
   marjoram

½ teaspoon dried whole
   thyme
¼ teaspoon pepper
1 cup canned diluted beef
   broth
1 cup Burgundy or other dry
   red wine
1 pound fresh mushrooms,
   sliced
Hot cooked rice

Sauté onion in bacon drippings in a large skillet until tender. Transfer sautéed onion to a large Dutch oven, reserving drippings in skillet. Brown meat in drippings; drain well.

Place meat in Dutch oven; sprinkle with flour, salt, marjoram, thyme, and pepper. Add beef broth and wine; cover and bake at 325° for 1½ to 2 hours or until meat is tender, stirring occasionally. Stir in sliced mushrooms. Cover and chill meat and vegetables at least 8 hours.

Bake at 325° for 1 hour or until thoroughly heated. Serve over rice. Yield: 6 servings.

The Kentucky Derby Museum Cookbook
The Kentucky Derby Museum
Louisville, Kentucky

Saucy Barbecued Beef

1 (1½- to 2-pound) chuck roast
1¼ cups canned diluted beef broth
1 (8-ounce) can tomato sauce
1 cup catsup
1 large onion, chopped
⅓ cup orange juice
¼ cup cider vinegar
¼ cup lemon juice
¼ cup chili sauce
¼ cup orange marmalade
2 tablespoons chopped fresh parsley
1 tablespoon Worcestershire sauce
2 teaspoons chili powder
2 teaspoons paprika
½ teaspoon hot sauce
¼ teaspoon ground oregano
1 clove garlic, minced

Place roast in a large Dutch oven; add water to cover. Cover and simmer 1 hour. Uncover and cook an additional hour.

Remove and discard fat and bone from roast. Chop meat, and set meat aside.

Combine beef broth and remaining ingredients in Dutch oven; bring to a boil. Stir in chopped meat; reduce heat, and simmer 1 to 1½ hours. Yield: 6 servings.

Purple Sage and Other Pleasures
The Junior League of Tucson, Arizona

Bul-Ko-Ki

5 green onions, cut into very
   thin strips
1 small onion, thinly sliced
1 small carrot, scraped and
   shredded
1 clove garlic, minced
1 tablespoon sugar
3 tablespoons soy sauce
3 tablespoons olive oil
2 tablespoons Burgundy or
   other dry red wine
1 teaspoon sesame seeds
1 teaspoon hot sauce
½ teaspoon salt
Dash of pepper
1 (2-pound) top round roast,
   thinly sliced into 2-inch
   strips
Vegetable cooking spray

Combine green onions, onion, carrot, garlic, sugar, soy sauce, oil, wine, sesame seeds, hot sauce, salt, and pepper in a large shallow dish; stir well. Add meat, tossing gently. Cover and marinate in refrigerator 12 hours.

Remove meat from marinade, and discard marinade. Place meat on a broiler rack coated with cooking spray. Arrange vegetables on top of meat. Place rack in broiler pan. Broil 3 inches from heat 4 to 5 minutes; turn meat and broil 4 to 5 minutes or to desired degree of doneness. Yield: 8 servings.   Mala Puri

Academic Apron
The Middlesex School
Concord, Massachusetts

Holiday Beef Curry

2 pounds beef tenderloin
   steak or round steak, cut
   into ½-inch cubes
⅓ cup butter or margarine,
   melted
½ cup chopped celery
½ cup chopped onion
⅓ cup all-purpose flour
1 teaspoon salt
½ teaspoon curry powder
¼ teaspoon pepper
1 (10½-ounce) can beef
   bouillon
½ cup slivered almonds
2 (2½-ounce) jars sliced
   mushrooms, drained
Holiday Rice
Slivered toasted almonds
Fresh parsley sprigs

Brown beef in melted butter in a large Dutch oven over medium heat. Stir in chopped celery and chopped onion; cook 5 minutes. Add flour, salt, curry powder, and pepper, and stir well. Slowly add beef bouillon, stirring constantly. Stir in ½ cup slivered almonds and sliced mushrooms; cover and simmer mixture 45 minutes or until meat is tender.

Spoon meat mixture into center of rice ring. Garnish with toasted almonds and fresh parsley sprigs. Yield: 8 servings.

Holiday Rice

½ cup chopped onion
½ cup chopped celery
1 medium-size green pepper, chopped
½ cup butter or margarine, melted
3 cups cooked medium-grain rice

2 teaspoons salt
¼ cup chopped cooked broccoli
2 tablespoons chopped fresh parsley

Sauté onion, celery, and green pepper in butter in a skillet over medium heat 10 minutes or until tender. Remove from heat. Add rice, salt, broccoli, and chopped parsley; stir well. Spoon into a buttered 6-cup ring mold; immediately invert rice ring onto a serving platter. Yield: 8 servings.   Dot Stewart

Down Home In High Style
The Houston Academy
Dothan, Alabama

Chicken Fried Steak and Cream Gravy

2 pounds boneless round
  steak
1 cup all-purpose flour
1 teaspoon salt
1 teaspoon pepper

½ teaspoon garlic salt
2 eggs
¼ cup milk
Vegetable oil
Cream Gravy

Trim excess fat from steak; pound steak to ¼-inch thickness, using a meat mallet. Cut into serving size pieces. Combine flour, salt, pepper, and garlic salt. Combine eggs and milk; beat well. Dredge steak in flour mixture; dip in egg mixture, and dredge in flour mixture. Lightly pound steak. Heat 1 inch of oil in a skillet to 375°. Fry steak in hot oil until browned, turning steak once. Drain steak on paper towels. Reserve ¼ cup pan drippings for gravy. Serve steak with Cream Gravy. Yield: 6 to 8 servings.

Cream Gravy

¼ cup all-purpose flour
¼ cup pan drippings
2 to 3 cups milk

½ teaspoon salt
¼ teaspoon pepper

Add flour to pan drippings; cook over medium heat until bubbly, stirring constantly. Gradually add milk; cook until thickened and bubbly, stirring constantly. Stir in salt and pepper. Yield: 2¾ cups.

Diamonds in the Desert
The Woman's League of Ozona, Texas

Steak Diane

2 tablespoons all-purpose
  flour
½ teaspoon salt
⅛ teaspoon pepper
4 (6-ounce) beef tenderloin
  steaks
¼ cup butter or margarine,
  divided
1 tablespoon plus 1½
  teaspoons Dijon mustard

2 teaspoons Worcestershire
  sauce
2 cups sliced fresh
  mushrooms
2 tablespoons minced onion
½ cup canned beef broth,
  undiluted
¼ cup brandy

Combine flour, salt, and pepper. Dredge steaks in flour mixture. Melt 2 tablespoons butter in a large skillet over medium heat. Add steaks, and brown on both sides. Remove steaks from skillet. Set aside, and keep warm. Stir mustard and Worcestershire sauce into pan drippings in skillet. Add remaining 2 tablespoons butter, mushrooms, and onion. Sauté vegetables until tender. Stir in beef broth and brandy. Return steaks to skillet. Simmer 15 minutes or to desired degree of doneness. Yield: 4 servings.   Judy Tewell

Lone Star Legacy II
The Junior Forum of Austin, Texas

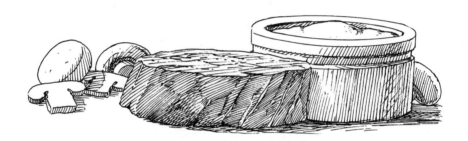

Peppercorn Steak

¼ **cup cracked pepper**
4 **(4- to 5-ounce) beef tenderloin steaks**
1 **cup chopped green onions**
1 **pound fresh mushrooms, sliced**
¼ **cup butter or margarine, melted**

1 **pound bacon, cooked and crumbled**
3 **tablespoons Chablis or other dry white wine**
Vegetable cooking spray

Pound pepper into both sides of steaks, using a meat mallet; set steaks aside. Sauté onions and mushrooms in butter in a skillet until tender. Add bacon and wine; set aside, and keep warm. Place steaks on a broiler rack coated with cooking spray; place rack in broiler pan. Broil 4 to 6 inches from heat 8 to 10 minutes on each side or to desired degree of doneness. Remove steaks to a platter, and top with mushroom mixture. Yield: 4 servings.   Chuck Lee

A Cook's Book of Recipes from the Pacific Northwest
The Rosehill Community Center
Mukilteo, Washington

Steak Adobe

½ cup chopped onion
1 tablespoon olive oil
2 (4-ounce) cans chopped green chiles, undrained
½ cup loosely packed fresh cilantro leaves
1 jalapeño pepper, seeded
2 teaspoons red currant jelly
1 teaspoon chicken-flavored bouillon granules

1 teaspoon Worcestershire sauce
½ teaspoon seasoned salt
¼ teaspoon dried whole oregano
1 small clove garlic
4 (8-ounce) boneless beef top loin steaks
4 (1-ounce) slices panela or Monterey Jack cheese

Sauté chopped onion in hot olive oil in a large saucepan.

Transfer onion mixture to container of an electric blender or food processor. Add green chiles, cilantro, jalapeño pepper, jelly, bouillon granules, Worcestershire sauce, seasoned salt, oregano, and garlic clove; cover and process until mixture is smooth.

Return chile mixture to saucepan; bring to a boil. Reduce heat, and simmer 10 minutes; keep sauce warm.

Grill steaks over medium coals 8 to 12 minutes. Turn steaks, and top with cheese slices; grill steaks an additional 8 to 12 minutes or to desired degree of doneness. Serve steaks immediately with warm sauce. Yield: 8 servings.

South of the Fork
The Junior League of Dallas, Texas

Pepper Steak

1½ pounds boneless sirloin steak
1 tablespoon shortening, melted
2 medium onions, chopped
½ teaspoon salt
1 cup canned diluted beef broth
3 tablespoons soy sauce

1 clove garlic, minced
2 green peppers, cut into 1-inch pieces
¼ cup cold water
2 tablespoons cornstarch
1 (10-ounce) can stewed tomatoes, undrained
Hot cooked rice

Trim excess fat from steak; cut steak into 1-inch pieces. Brown steak in shortening in a skillet. Add onion and salt; sauté until onion is tender. Stir in broth, soy sauce, and garlic. Cover, reduce heat, and simmer 10 minutes or until meat is tender. Add green pepper; cover and simmer 5 minutes. Combine water and cornstarch; stir well. Gradually stir cornstarch mixture into steak mixture; cook, stirring constantly, until mixture thickens. Add tomatoes; cook, stirring constantly, until thoroughly heated. Serve over rice. Yield: 4 to 6 servings.   Paulette Kilpatrick

The Share-Cropper
The Central Delta Academy Parent-Teacher Organization
Inverness, Mississippi

Empress Beef

½ **pound boneless sirloin steak**
3 **tablespoons vegetable oil**
¼ **teaspoon salt**
¼ **pound fresh snow pea pods, trimmed**
3 **celery stalks, chopped**
1 **(4-ounce) can sliced mushrooms, drained**
1 **large onion, sliced and separated into rings**

½ **cup water chestnuts, chopped**
½ **cup water**
¼ **cup plus 1 tablespoon soy sauce**
1 **tablespoon cornstarch**
1½ **teaspoons sugar**
Hot cooked rice

Partially freeze steak; slice steak diagonally across grain into 2- x ¼-inch strips.

Pour oil into wok or a heavy skillet; heat at high for 1 minute. Add steak and salt; stir-fry 5 minutes. Add snow peas, celery, mushrooms, onion, and water chestnuts; stir-fry 3 minutes. Cover, reduce heat, and simmer 3 minutes. Combine water, soy sauce, cornstarch, and sugar; stir well. Add cornstarch mixture to beef mixture, and cook until thickened, stirring constantly. Serve over rice. Yield: 2 to 4 servings.   Bernice Olson

Good Cooking Cookbook
United Lutheran Church
Langdon, North Dakota

Stuffed Flank Steak

¼ cup vegetable oil
3 tablespoons butter or margarine
3 cups (½-inch-thick) bread cubes
1 pound lean ground beef
1 cup finely chopped onion
¼ cup finely chopped celery
1 egg, beaten
2 cloves garlic, minced
1 tablespoon minced fresh parsley
1½ teaspoons salt
¼ teaspoon dried whole thyme
¼ teaspoon freshly ground pepper
1 (1¾-pound) flank steak
2 tablespoons butter or margarine
1 tablespoon vegetable oil
Salt and pepper to taste
2 bay leaves
1 carrot, scraped and thinly sliced
1 onion, finely chopped
1 large tomato, coarsely chopped
1 teaspoon dried whole thyme
2 cups canned diluted beef broth
1 cup Burgundy or other dry red wine
¼ cup cold water
2 tablespoons cornstarch

Heat ¼ cup oil and 3 tablespoons butter in a large skillet over medium heat. Add bread cubes, and sauté until browned on all sides. Remove from heat.

Combine ground beef and next 8 ingredients in a large bowl; mix well. Gently stir in sautéed bread cubes.

Cut a large pocket lengthwise in flank steak, using a sharp knife or shears. Stuff steak with ground beef mixture. Secure with string at 2-inch intervals.

Melt 2 tablespoons butter with 1 tablespoon oil in a large Dutch oven over medium-high heat. Sprinkle steak with salt and pepper to taste; brown meat in Dutch oven. Add bay leaves, carrot, onion, tomato, and thyme; cook, uncovered, 5 minutes over medium heat. Add beef broth and wine; bring to a boil. Reduce heat, cover, and simmer 1 hour and 15 minutes.

Transfer meat to a serving platter; remove string, and keep warm. Combine water and cornstarch, stirring well. Add cornstarch mixture to mixture in Dutch oven, stirring well. Cook over medium heat, stirring constantly, until gravy is thickened. Remove and discard bay leaves. Serve steak with gravy. Yield: 6 servings.

California Treasure
The Junior League of Fresno, California

Shredded Beef

1 (¾-pound) flank steak
1 tablespoon water chestnut
  powder
1 tablespoon dry sherry
2 teaspoons soy sauce
1 egg white, beaten
3 tablespoons peanut oil
1 clove garlic, sliced
2 teaspoons minced fresh
  gingerroot
½ cup shredded carrot

½ cup chopped sweet red
  pepper
1 hot red pepper, seeded and
  cut into very thin strips
1 cup fresh snow pea pods,
  trimmed and cut into very
  thin strips
4 green onions, cut into very
  thin strips
1 tablespoon peanut oil
Seasoning Sauce

Place steak in a large shallow dish. Combine water chestnut powder, sherry, soy sauce, and egg white, stirring well. Pour marinade over steak; cover and marinate in refrigerator 8 hours, turning occasionally. Drain steak, discarding marinade. Cut steak with the grain into thin shreds; set aside.

Pour 3 tablespoons peanut oil around top of preheated wok, coating sides; heat at medium high (325°) for 1 minute. Add garlic and gingerroot, and stir-fry 30 seconds.

Add shredded carrot, and stir-fry 1 minute. Add chopped sweet red pepper and next 3 ingredients, and stir-fry 2 minutes. Remove vegetables from wok, and set aside. Add 1 tablespoon peanut oil to wok; heat at high (375°) for 30 seconds. Add shredded meat, and stir-fry 4 minutes or to desired degree of doneness. Add Seasoning Sauce and vegetables to wok, and stir-fry just until mixture is thoroughly heated. Yield: 4 servings.

Seasoning Sauce

2 tablespoons plum sauce
1 tablespoon dry sherry
1 tablespoon red rice wine
  vinegar
1 tablespoon hoisin sauce

1 tablespoon bean sauce
1 teaspoon water chestnut
  powder
2 teaspoons hot sauce

Combine all ingredients in a small mixing bowl, stirring well. Yield: about ½ cup.   Millie Mesaku

We, The Women of Hawaii Cookbook
We, The Women of Hawaii
Waialua, Oahu

Flank Steak Teriyaki

1 (2-pound) flank steak
¾ cup vegetable oil
¼ cup soy sauce
3 tablespoons honey
2 tablespoons vinegar

1½ teaspoons grated fresh
  gingerroot
1 clove garlic, crushed
Vegetable cooking spray

Score meat diagonally across grain at ¾-inch intervals. Place meat in a 12- x 8- x 2-inch baking dish. Combine oil and next 5 ingredients, stirring well. Pour marinade over steak; cover and marinate in refrigerator 6 to 8 hours, turning occasionally.

Remove meat from marinade; discard marinade. Place meat on a broiler rack that has been coated with cooking spray; place rack in broiler pan. Broil 3 inches from heat 5 to 6 minutes on each side or to desired degree of doneness.

To serve, slice steak diagonally across grain into thin slices. Yield: 6 to 8 servings.   Nan Thorne Fogle

The Great Entertainer Cookbook
The Buffalo Bill Historical Center
Cody, Wyoming

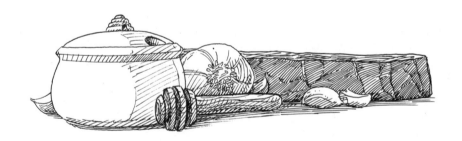

Beef Short Ribs Supreme

3 to 4 pounds beef short ribs
2 tablespoons vegetable oil
4 stalks celery, chopped
3 medium carrots, scraped
  and chopped
1 (6-ounce) can tomato paste
½ cup firmly packed brown
  sugar

½ cup chopped onion
½ cup water
½ cup red wine vinegar
2 tablespoons Dijon mustard
2 teaspoons salt
1 clove garlic, minced
1 bay leaf

Brown short ribs on all sides in hot oil in a Dutch oven. Cover and bake at 350° for 1 hour. Drain; return meat to Dutch oven. Add celery and carrot. Combine tomato paste and remaining ingredients; stir well. Pour over meat and vegetables in Dutch oven; cover and bake 1½ hours or until meat and vegetables are tender. Remove and discard bay leaf. Yield: 4 to 6 servings. Mary Stoddard

Favorite Recipes from Friends
The Town Hill School
Lakeville, Connecticut

Sweet-and-Sour Stuffed Cabbage

20 large cabbage leaves
  (about 2 large cabbages)
1 pound ground beef
1 egg
½ cup fine, dry breadcrumbs
¼ cup grated Parmesan
  cheese

¼ cup dried parsley flakes
¼ cup water
2 tablespoons grated onion
2 cloves garlic, minced
½ teaspoon salt
¼ teaspoon pepper
Sauce (recipe follows)

Cook cabbage in boiling water to cover 5 minutes or until tender; drain. Combine beef and next 9 ingredients; mix well. Place 2 tablespoons meat mixture in center of each cabbage leaf. Fold ends of leaves over; secure with wooden picks. Place in a Dutch oven. Pour sauce over cabbage. Cook over medium heat, partially covered, 30 minutes or until done. Yield: 8 servings.

Sauce

2 cups chopped onion
¼ cup vegetable oil
2 (15-ounce) cans tomato
  sauce

¼ cup sugar
¼ cup vinegar
¼ cup water

Sauté onion in hot oil in a saucepan until tender; add tomato sauce. Cook over medium heat 10 minutes; stir occasionally. Add sugar, vinegar, and water to tomato mixture; stir well. Yield: 5 cups.

Artist's Palate Cookbook
New Orleans Museum of Art-Women's Volunteer Committee
New Orleans, Louisiana

Suzie's Sweet-and-Sour Meat Loaf

2 pounds ground beef
2 (8-ounce) cans tomato
   sauce, divided
1¼ cups Italian-seasoned
   breadcrumbs
1 egg, beaten
1 medium onion, chopped
½ teaspoon salt

¼ teaspoon pepper
2 beef bouillon cubes
2 cups boiling water
¼ cup firmly packed brown
   sugar
¼ cup red wine vinegar
¼ cup prepared mustard

Combine ground beef, 1 can tomato sauce, breadcrumbs, beaten egg, chopped onion, salt, and pepper in a large bowl; mix well. Shape ground beef mixture into a 9-inch loaf, and place in a 13- x 9- x 2-inch baking dish. Bake meat loaf at 350° for 45 minutes. Drain off excess fat.

Dissolve bouillon cubes in boiling water in a large bowl. Add remaining can tomato sauce, brown sugar, vinegar, and mustard, stirring well. Pour tomato sauce mixture over meat loaf, and bake an additional 45 minutes. Yield: 8 servings.

Taste of Today
BUNWC, North Shore Illinois Chapter
Northfield, Illinois

Pizza with Meat Crust

1 pound ground beef
1 medium onion, minced
⅓ cup soft breadcrumbs
¼ cup canned diluted beef
   broth
1 clove garlic, minced
½ teaspoon salt
½ teaspoon pepper
¾ cup chopped tomato

4 ounces thinly sliced
   mozzarella cheese
3 tablespoons grated
   Parmesan cheese
1 tablespoon dried whole
   oregano
1 tablespoon minced fresh
   parsley

Combine ground beef, onion, breadcrumbs, beef broth, garlic, salt, and pepper in a large bowl; mix well.

Press meat mixture into a 9-inch pieplate, forming a shell. Bake at 375° for 20 to 25 minutes (meat crust will shrink in pan). Drain carefully. Sprinkle chopped tomato over meat crust. Top with mozzarella cheese slices. Sprinkle with Parmesan cheese, oregano, and parsley. Bake at 375° for 15 minutes or until cheese melts. Yield: 4 to 6 servings.   Cassy Quintal

Royle Round-Up of Recipes
Royle School Parent-Teacher Association
Darien, Connecticut

Veal Scallops with Mushrooms

⅓ cup all-purpose flour
½ teaspoon salt
⅛ teaspoon pepper
⅛ teaspoon ground red pepper
3 tablespoons butter or margarine
2 tablespoons vegetable oil
1 clove garlic, halved
1 pound (¼-inch-thick) veal scallops

1¼ cups sliced fresh mushrooms
½ cup canned diluted chicken broth
¼ cup dry white vermouth
1 tablespoon lemon juice
1 tablespoon finely chopped fresh parsley (optional)

Combine flour, salt, pepper, and red pepper in a shallow dish. Place butter, oil, and garlic in a large skillet over medium-high heat; cook until butter melts.

Dredge veal in flour mixture, and sauté in butter mixture in skillet 2 to 3 minutes on each side. Remove from heat. Place meat in a 12- x 8- x 2-inch baking dish, and set aside.

Remove and discard garlic from skillet, reserving drippings in skillet; sauté mushrooms in pan drippings over medium heat until tender. Arrange mushrooms over veal.

Combine chicken broth, vermouth, and lemon juice. Stir into pan drippings in skillet, and bring to a boil. Pour broth mixture over veal. Bake at 325° for 30 minutes. Garnish with fresh parsley, if desired. Yield: 4 servings.

Sounds Delicious!
The Volunteer Council of the Tulsa Philharmonic Society, Inc.
Tulsa, Oklahoma

Sautéed Veal Scallops with Tarragon

1 pound (¼-inch-thick) veal scallops
¼ cup butter or margarine, divided
1½ teaspoons vegetable oil
1 cup sliced fresh mushrooms
1 tablespoon chopped green onions
1 cup whipping cream
¼ cup dry vermouth
¼ cup canned diluted beef broth
1½ teaspoons dried whole tarragon
1½ teaspoons cornstarch
1 tablespoon cold water
¼ teaspoon salt
¼ teaspoon pepper
Chopped fresh parsley (optional)

Cook veal in 1 tablespoon plus 1½ teaspoons butter and oil in a large skillet over medium-high heat 4 minutes on each side. Remove veal, and keep warm, reserving 1 tablespoon drippings in skillet.

Sauté mushrooms in 1 tablespoon plus 1½ teaspoons butter in a small skillet 5 minutes or until tender; remove from heat, and set aside. Add green onions to 1 tablespoon reserved drippings, and sauté 1 minute. Stir in whipping cream, vermouth, beef broth, and tarragon; boil rapidly to reduce liquid to about ⅔ cup.

Combine cornstarch and water, stirring until blended; add to green onion mixture. Add mushrooms, and simmer, stirring constantly. Sprinkle salt and pepper over veal, and add to sauce; simmer until thoroughly heated. Remove from heat, and place in a warm serving dish. Melt remaining 1 tablespoon butter; pour over veal. Garnish with fresh parsley, if desired. Serve immediately. Yield: 4 servings.   Mary Woodruff Patterson

A Dash of Down East
The Junior Guild of Rocky Mount, North Carolina

Osso Buco (Braised Veal Shanks)

1½ cups finely chopped
  onion
½ cup finely chopped
  carrots
½ cup finely chopped celery
1 clove garlic, minced
¼ cup butter or margarine,
  melted
7 pounds (2-inch-thick)
  cross-cut veal shanks
½ teaspoon salt
½ teaspoon freshly ground
  pepper
1 cup all-purpose flour
½ cup olive oil

1 cup Chablis or other dry
  white wine
3 cups coarsely chopped
  tomato
¾ cup canned diluted
  chicken broth
6 sprigs fresh parsley
2 bay leaves
½ teaspoon dried whole basil
½ teaspoon dried whole
  thyme
Grated lemon rind (optional)
Chopped fresh parsley
  (optional)

Sauté onion, carrot, celery, and garlic in butter in a large Dutch oven until vegetables are tender. Set aside.

Sprinkle veal with salt and pepper; dredge in flour. Heat oil in a large skillet; add veal, and cook until golden brown. Place veal in Dutch oven with sautéed vegetables. Discard oil.

Add wine to skillet, cook over medium heat until reduced to ½ cup. Stir in chopped tomato, chicken broth, parsley sprigs, bay leaves, basil, and thyme; bring wine mixture to a boil, and pour over veal in Dutch oven. Cover and bake at 350° for 1½ hours or until veal is tender.

Remove veal and vegetables to a serving platter, using a slotted spoon. Remove and discard bay leaves. If desired, garnish veal and vegetables with grated lemon rind and chopped fresh parsley. Yield: 6 to 8 servings.

Biscayne Bights and Breezes
The Villagers, Inc.
Coral Gables, Florida

Kalbgulasch (Veal Goulash)

2 pounds lean veal, cut into
1½-inch pieces
1 teaspoon salt
½ teaspoon pepper
¼ cup butter or margarine,
melted
2 medium onions, sliced
2 large tomatoes, peeled and
quartered
1 tablespoon plus 1½
teaspoons all-purpose flour

⅔ cup Chablis or other dry
white wine
¼ cup canned beef broth,
undiluted
2 tablespoons lemon juice
1 to 2 teaspoons caraway
seeds
2 teaspoons paprika
Hot cooked noodles

Sprinkle veal with salt and pepper. Brown veal in butter over medium heat (do not overcook). Add onion and tomato; cook, uncovered, 30 minutes, stirring frequently. Stir in flour, and cook 1 minute. Stir in wine and next 4 ingredients; cover, reduce heat, and simmer 45 minutes or until veal is tender. Serve with noodles. Yield: 4 to 6 servings.   Dr. John P. Haas

Old Irving Park Association Cookbook
The Old Irving Park Association
Chicago, Illinois

Grilled Ginger Lamb

1 (5- to 7-pound) leg of lamb,
butterflied
½ cup Burgundy or other dry
red wine
½ cup vegetable oil
⅓ cup grated fresh
gingerroot
¼ cup soy sauce
¼ cup minced onion
2 cloves garlic, minced

Juice of 1 lemon
1 tablespoon plus 1½
teaspoons honey
1½ teaspoons salt
½ teaspoon pepper
⅛ teaspoon ground red
pepper
1 cup canned diluted beef
broth

Trim all visible fat from lamb. Place lamb in a large shallow dish, and set aside.
Combine Burgundy and remaining ingredients except broth in container of an electric blender; cover and process until smooth.

Pour marinade over lamb; cover and marinate in refrigerator 8 hours, turning occasionally.

Remove lamb from marinade, reserving marinade.

Grill lamb over medium coals 15 to 20 minutes on each side or until meat thermometer registers 140° (rare) or 150° (medium rare), basting frequently with reserved marinade.

Combine ¾ cup remaining marinade and beef broth in a medium saucepan; cook over medium heat, stirring constantly, until mixture comes to a boil. Boil 1 minute. Serve with lamb. Yield: 10 servings.

Gatherings
The Junior League of Milwaukee, Wisconsin

Broiled Lamb Chops

4 (1-inch-thick) lamb loin chops
½ cup cold strong coffee
¼ cup firmly packed brown sugar
2 tablespoons lemon juice
1 tablespoon prepared mustard

1 clove garlic, crushed
½ teaspoon Worcestershire sauce
⅛ teaspoon hot sauce
Chopped fresh parsley (optional)

Trim fat from lamb chops, reserving one piece of fat. Score fat at 1-inch intervals; set aside. Place chops in a shallow dish.

Combine coffee and next 6 ingredients in a small bowl; stir well. Pour marinade over chops. Cover and marinate in refrigerator 4 to 6 hours, turning occasionally.

Place reserved fat in a skillet, and cook over medium heat 1 minute. Remove and discard fat, leaving drippings in skillet.

Remove chops from marinade, reserving marinade. Place chops in pan drippings in skillet, and cook over medium-high heat 4 minutes on each side or to desired degree of doneness. Transfer chops to a serving platter, and keep warm.

Bring marinade to a boil in a small saucepan over medium heat, and cook 4 to 5 minutes or until reduced to one-third cup. Pour over chops. Garnish with fresh parsley, if desired. Yield: 2 to 4 servings.

Con Mucho Gusto
The Desert Club of Mesa, Arizona

Skillet Moussaka

1 medium eggplant
2 tablespoons all-purpose
  flour
1 pound ground lamb or
  ground beef
½ cup chopped onion
1 clove garlic, crushed
1 (8-ounce) can tomato sauce
½ teaspoon dried whole
  oregano
¼ teaspoon salt

¼ teaspoon pepper
2 tablespoons butter or
  margarine
2 tablespoons all-purpose
  flour
1 egg yolk
1 cup milk
1 cup (4 ounces) shredded
  Monterey Jack cheese
Chopped fresh parsley
  (optional)

Peel eggplant, and cut into ½-inch pieces. Coat with 2 tablespoons flour; set aside. Cook lamb, onion, and garlic in a skillet over medium heat until meat is browned, stirring to crumble meat; drain. Return meat mixture to skillet. Add eggplant; cook 6 to 8 minutes or until tender. Stir in tomato sauce and seasonings; simmer 5 minutes.

Melt butter in a saucepan; stir in 2 tablespoons flour. Combine egg yolk and milk; add to butter mixture, and cook over low heat until slightly thickened, stirring constantly. Pour sauce over meat mixture; top with cheese. Cover and cook over medium heat until cheese melts. Garnish with chopped fresh parsley, if desired. Yield: 4 to 6 servings.

Noel W. Hinners

Out of This World Cookbook II
The Woman's Club of Cocoa Beach, Florida

Egyptian Lamb Delight with Mint Sauce

1 pound ground lamb
½ cup fine, dry breadcrumbs
2 teaspoons salt
2 teaspoons dried whole
  marjoram
1 teaspoon dried whole thyme
¼ cup plain yogurt
1 tablespoon Worcestershire
  sauce

1 medium-size green pepper,
  finely chopped
6 cloves garlic, minced
1 medium onion, minced
2 eggs, beaten
2 tablespoons vegetable oil
2 cups hot cooked rice
Mint Sauce

Combine first 10 ingredients in a large bowl; mix well. Shape mixture into 48 (1-inch) balls; dip in beaten egg, and sauté in hot oil in a large skillet until lightly browned. Arrange meatballs over rice on a serving platter. Serve with Mint Sauce. Yield: 6 servings.

Mint Sauce

2 teaspoons cornstarch
2 teaspoons water
2 cups plain yogurt

2 teaspoons mint flakes
½ teaspoon garlic powder

Combine cornstarch and water in a small saucepan, and stir well. Add yogurt; bring to a boil over low heat. Cook until mixture is slightly thickened, stirring gently. Stir in mint flakes and garlic powder. Yield: 1¾ cups.   Lutisha Tesarek

The True Essentials of a Feast
The Library of Congress/LC Cooking Club
Washington, DC

Pork Roast and Apples

1 teaspoon salt
1 teaspoon ground ginger
½ teaspoon ground nutmeg
½ teaspoon ground cinnamon
⅛ teaspoon pepper
1 (4- to 5-pound) center pork
  loin roast
¼ cup honey

½ cup water
1 tablespoon lemon juice
¼ teaspoon ground ginger
¼ teaspoon ground nutmeg
¼ teaspoon ground cinnamon
2 medium-size cooking
  apples, peeled, cored, and
  sliced

Combine first 5 ingredients; rub on roast. Place roast, fat side up, on a rack in a roasting pan. Insert meat thermometer into thickest part of roast, making sure it does not touch fat or bone. Bake at 325° for 30 minutes or until thermometer registers 170°.

Combine honey and next 5 ingredients in a saucepan; stir well. Bring to a boil. Add apple; cover and simmer 8 minutes or until tender, stirring occasionally. Transfer roast to a platter; spoon apple mixture over roast. Yield: 10 to 12 servings.

Cornsilk
The Junior League of Sioux City, Iowa

Pork Loin with Grapes

1 (4-pound) rolled boneless pork loin roast
¼ cup plus 2 tablespoons Chablis or other dry white wine
3 tablespoons olive oil
5 juniper berries, crushed
2 whole cloves, crushed
1 clove garlic, crushed
½ teaspoon salt
¼ teaspoon pepper
1⅓ cups cold water
2 tablespoons butter or margarine

1 pound seedless green grapes, halved
⅔ cup unsweetened white grape juice
⅔ cup Chablis or other dry white wine
2 tablespoons butter or margarine, melted
2 tablespoons all-purpose flour
3 tablespoons gin
Small clusters of seedless green grapes

Place roast in a large shallow dish. Combine ¼ cup plus 2 tablespoons wine and next 4 ingredients, stirring well. Pour marinade over roast; cover and marinate in refrigerator 8 hours, turning occasionally.

Drain roast; reserve marinade. Place roast in a shallow roasting pan. Sprinkle with salt and pepper. Pour water in pan around roast. Insert meat thermometer into thickest part of roast, making sure it does not touch fat. Bake at 350° for 1 hour and 45 minutes or until meat thermometer registers 160°. Transfer roast to an ovenproof platter; keep warm.

Melt 2 tablespoons butter in a skillet. Add halved grapes, and cook over medium heat until thoroughly heated; set aside.

Add reserved marinade, grape juice, and ⅔ cup wine to roasting pan. Bring to a boil; reduce heat, and simmer 2 minutes.

Combine 2 tablespoons melted butter and flour; stir until smooth. Gradually add to grape juice mixture in roasting pan, stirring constantly. Cook until mixture thickens. Strain sauce, and add to reserved grape mixture; cook until thoroughly heated.

Place gin in a small long-handled saucepan; heat just until warm (do not boil). Remove from heat. Ignite with a long match, and pour over roast. Slice roast when flames die down. Serve with grape sauce. Garnish with grape clusters. Yield: 8 to 10 servings.

Treasured Recipes from Camargo to Indian Hill
The Indian Hill Historical Society
Cincinnati, Ohio

Pork Barbecue, North Carolina Style

1 (4- to 5-pound) Boston butt
  roast, trimmed
1 large onion, chopped
1½ cups water
1 cup vinegar
½ cup catsup
½ cup Worcestershire sauce

3 tablespoons brown sugar
2 tablespoons dry mustard
1 teaspoon salt
¼ teaspoon ground red
  pepper
¼ teaspoon pepper

Place roast in a roasting pan. Combine remaining ingredients in a medium bowl; stir well. Pour mixture over roast. Cover and bake at 325° for 5 to 6 hours or until meat is very tender. Remove from oven; let cool.

Skim fat from surface of sauce. Remove roast from sauce. Remove meat from bone, and chop meat. Return chopped meat to sauce in pan, and stir well. Cover and bake at 325° for 15 minutes or until thoroughly heated. Yield: 8 servings.

Palm Country Cuisine
The Junior League of Greater Lakeland, Florida

Sauerkraut and Country-Style Ribs Casserole

1 (16-ounce) jar sauerkraut,
  drained
1 medium onion, chopped
1 (16-ounce) can whole
  tomatoes, undrained

3 pounds country-style pork
  ribs
¾ cup firmly packed brown
  sugar

Spread sauerkraut evenly in a 13- x 9- x 2-inch baking dish. Top with onion, tomatoes, and ribs. Sprinkle with brown sugar. Cover and bake at 325° for 2 hours and 15 minutes. Uncover and bake an additional 45 minutes or until meat is tender. Serve with a slotted spoon. Yield: 4 servings.
Helen Marica

Firehouse Favorites
The Women's Auxiliary-Haddam Volunteer Fire Department
Higganum, Connecticut

Marinated Pork Chops with Dijon

1½ cups Chablis or other dry
   white wine
½ teaspoon salt
½ teaspoon dried whole basil
½ teaspoon dried whole
   oregano
½ teaspoon dried whole
   thyme
¼ teaspoon pepper

6 (1-inch-thick) pork loin
   chops
¼ cup all-purpose flour
3 tablespoons clarified butter
¼ cup chopped shallots
Juice of 1 small lemon
1 teaspoon Dijon mustard
¼ cup whipping cream

Combine wine, salt, basil, oregano, thyme, and pepper in a large shallow dish. Add pork chops. Cover and marinate in refrigerator 1 hour, turning chops after 30 minutes. Remove chops from marinade, reserving marinade.

Dust chops with flour. Sauté chops in clarified butter in a large skillet until browned on all sides. Add shallots, and sauté 6 minutes or until shallots are tender. Pour reserved marinade over chops in skillet. Add lemon juice, and simmer 10 minutes or until meat is tender, turning chops after 5 minutes. Transfer chops to a serving platter, and keep warm.

Add mustard to skillet, and cook until liquid is reduced by half. Add whipping cream, stirring until sauce is thickened. Spoon sauce over chops. Yield: 6 servings.

A Pinch of Salt Lake
The Junior League of Salt Lake City, Utah

Savory Ham Roll

¼ cup unsalted butter or
   margarine
½ cup all-purpose
   flour
2 cups milk
½ teaspoon salt

⅛ teaspoon ground white
   pepper
5 eggs, separated
¼ teaspoon hot sauce
Ham-Vegetable Filling

Lightly grease bottom and sides of a 15- x 10- x 1-inch jellyroll pan; line greased pan with wax paper, and lightly grease paper. Set jellyroll pan aside.

Melt butter in a heavy saucepan over low heat; add flour, stirring until smooth. Cook 1 minute, stirring constantly. Gradually add milk; cook over medium heat, stirring constantly, until mixture is thickened and bubbly. Stir in salt and pepper.

Beat egg yolks and hot sauce until thick and lemon colored. Gradually stir about one-fourth of hot white sauce into yolks; add to remaining hot white sauce, stirring constantly. Cook over medium heat 1 minute. Remove from heat, and let cool to room temperature, stirring occasionally.

Beat egg whites (at room temperature) at high speed of an electric mixer until stiff peaks form. Fold about one-fourth of egg whites into batter. Fold in remaining egg whites. Spread batter evenly in prepared pan. Bake at 400° for 25 to 30 minutes or until puffy and firm in center.

Immediately loosen roll from sides of pan, and turn out onto a kitchen towel. Peel off wax paper. Spread with Ham-Vegetable Filling. Roll up jellyroll fashion, starting at short end. Immediately place roll, seam side down, on a serving platter. Cut into slices, and serve. Yield: 6 servings.

Ham-Vegetable Filling

4 shallots, chopped
2 tablespoons butter or
  margarine, melted
¾ cup chopped fresh
  mushrooms
1 cup chopped cooked ham
1 cup chopped cooked
  spinach

1 tablespoon Dijon mustard
¼ teaspoon ground nutmeg
2 (3-ounce) packages cream
  cheese, softened
Salt and pepper to taste

Sauté shallots in butter in a large skillet until tender. Add mushrooms, and cook 3 minutes, stirring occasionally. Add ham, cooked spinach, Dijon mustard, and nutmeg; cook until mixture is thoroughly heated, stirring constantly. Add cream cheese, stirring until cheese melts. Stir in salt and pepper. Yield: 2½ cups.

Dining In
The Young Woman's League of Westport, Connecticut

Ham Loaf with Mustard Sauce

1 pound ground cooked ham	¾ cup milk
1 pound ground pork	2 eggs, beaten
1 cup tomato juice	Mustard Sauce
1 cup fine, dry breadcrumbs	

Combine ground ham, ground pork, tomato juice, breadcrumbs, milk, and beaten eggs in a large bowl; mix well. Spoon mixture into a 9- x 5- x 3-inch loafpan.

Bake at 350° for 2 hours or until done. Serve with Mustard Sauce. Yield: 6 to 8 servings.

Mustard Sauce

2 eggs, beaten	¼ teaspoon salt
¼ cup sugar	1 cup milk
2 tablespoons dry mustard	½ cup warm vinegar
1 tablespoon all-purpose flour	

Combine beaten eggs, sugar, dry mustard, flour, salt, and milk in a medium saucepan; stir well. Bring just to a boil over medium heat, stirring constantly. Slowly add vinegar; cook, stirring constantly with a wire whisk, until mixture is thickened. Yield: 2 cups.

Upper Crust: A Slice of the South
The Junior League of Johnson City, Tennessee

Pasta, Rice, & Grains

In 1904, this Italian cheese market was a thriving business that sold 27,000 to 30,000 pounds of cheese a year. The market was built in the Little Italy section of Manhattan on land once owned by Aaron Burr.

☆☆☆

Macaroni and Cheese

1 (8-ounce) package medium
 shell macaroni
1 egg, lightly beaten
2 cups small-curd cottage
 cheese
1 (8-ounce) carton
 commercial sour cream

¼ teaspoon salt
¼ teaspoon pepper
2 cups (8 ounces) shredded
 process American cheese
¼ cup soft breadcrumbs
2 teaspoons butter or
 margarine, melted

Cook macaroni according to package directions; drain. Combine macaroni, egg, and next 5 ingredients; stir well. Spoon mixture into a greased 12- x 8- x 2-inch baking dish. Combine breadcrumbs and butter, stirring well; sprinkle over macaroni. Bake at 350° for 30 minutes. Yield: 6 servings.   Arthur E. Pratt

Montgomery County Fair History Cookbook
The Montgomery County Fair Association, Inc.
Conroe, Texas

Baked Hungarian Noodles

1 (8-ounce) package medium
 egg noodles
1 (16-ounce) carton
 cream-style cottage cheese
1 (16-ounce) carton
 commercial sour cream
½ cup minced onion
2 cloves garlic, minced
2 tablespoons poppy seeds

2 tablespoons Worcestershire
 sauce
1 teaspoon salt
¼ teaspoon freshly ground
 pepper
⅛ teaspoon hot sauce
Paprika (optional)
Freshly grated Parmesan
 cheese (optional)

Cook noodles according to package directions; drain. Combine noodles, cottage cheese, and next 8 ingredients in a large bowl; stir well. Spoon mixture into a lightly greased 2-quart casserole. Bake, uncovered, at 350° for 30 minutes. If desired, sprinkle with paprika and Parmesan cheese. Serve immediately. Yield: 8 to 10 servings.

Palette to Palate
The Junior League of St. Joseph and Albrecht Art Museum
St. Joseph, Missouri

Four-Cheese Spaghetti

1 (12-ounce) package spaghetti
3 tablespoons butter or
  margarine
1½ teaspoons all-purpose
  flour
1 cup half-and-half
¾ cup (3 ounces) shredded
  Edam or Gouda cheese
¾ cup (3 ounces) shredded
  Provolone cheese

¾ cup (3 ounces) shredded
  Swiss cheese
¼ cup grated Parmesan
  cheese
½ teaspoon salt
⅛ teaspoon ground white
  pepper
1 tablespoon chopped fresh
  parsley or basil

Cook spaghetti according to package directions, omitting salt; drain. Set aside, and keep warm.

Melt butter in a heavy saucepan over low heat; add flour, stirring until smooth. Cook 1 minute, stirring constantly. Gradually add half-and-half; cook over medium heat, stirring constantly, until mixture is thickened and bubbly. Stir in cheeses, salt, and pepper. Cook, stirring constantly, until cheeses melt.

Pour cheese mixture over spaghetti; toss until spaghetti is coated. Garnish with fresh parsley. Serve immediately. Yield: 6 servings.

Palm Country Cuisine
The Junior League of Greater Lakeland, Florida

Blondie's Carbonara

1½ pounds bacon, diced
½ cup plus 3 tablespoons
  olive oil, divided
1 large onion, finely chopped
1 large green pepper, finely
  chopped
½ cup chopped fresh
  mushrooms
¾ cup Chablis or other dry
  white wine

1 (12-ounce) package
  fettuccine
½ cup butter or margarine,
  melted
2 eggs, beaten
¾ cup grated Parmesan
  cheese
¾ cup grated Romano cheese
⅓ cup chopped fresh parsley
Freshly ground pepper to taste

Cook bacon in a large skillet until crisp. Drain bacon on paper towels; discard drippings. Add 3 tablespoons olive oil to skillet. Add onion, pepper, and mushrooms, and sauté until tender. Add wine, and simmer 5 to 10 minutes.

Cook fettuccine according to package directions; drain well. Immediately toss hot fettuccine with melted butter, remaining ½ cup olive oil, eggs, Parmesan cheese, Romano cheese, and chopped parsley. Sprinkle with bacon and freshly ground pepper. Toss gently. Yield: 4 to 6 servings. Sharron Davis

Southern Elegance
The Junior League of Gaston County, North Carolina

Zucchini and Mushroom Fettuccine

1 (8-ounce) package
fettuccine
½ pound fresh mushrooms,
sliced
¼ cup butter or margarine,
melted
1½ pounds zucchini, cut into
julienne strips

1 cup whipping cream
½ cup butter or margarine
¾ cup grated Parmesan
cheese
½ cup chopped fresh parsley
Additional grated Parmesan
cheese

Cook fettuccine according to package directions; drain well, and set aside.

Sauté mushrooms in ¼ cup butter in a large skillet 2 minutes. Add zucchini, whipping cream, and ½ cup butter; simmer 3 minutes. Remove from heat. Stir in ¾ cup Parmesan cheese and chopped parsley; toss gently. Serve immediately with additional grated Parmesan cheese. Yield: 8 servings. Lee Hackney Edwards

A Dash of Down East
The Junior Guild of Rocky Mount, North Carolina

Francie's Fettuccine

2 (6-ounce) jars marinated
   artichoke hearts, undrained
½ pound bacon, cooked and
   crumbled
6 Italian-style tomatoes,
   chopped
2 (15-ounce) cans tomato
   sauce

2 cloves garlic, crushed
½ cup chopped fresh basil
3 (8-ounce) packages
   fettuccine
½ to 1 cup freshly grated
   Parmesan cheese

Drain artichoke hearts, reserving 3 tablespoons marinade; set artichoke hearts and marinade aside.

Combine bacon, tomatoes, tomato sauce, and garlic in a large saucepan. Bring to a boil; reduce heat, and simmer, uncovered, 15 minutes. Add artichoke hearts and basil; simmer 30 minutes.

Cook fettuccine according to package directions; drain well. Place fettuccine in a large serving bowl; add reserved marinade, and toss gently to coat well.

Serve tomato mixture over fettuccine; sprinkle with Parmesan cheese. Yield: 8 servings.   Francie Parker

Academic Apron
The Middlesex School
Concord, Massachusetts

Fettuccine with Asparagus

1¾ pounds fresh asparagus
   spears
½ cup butter or margarine,
   divided
½ pound fresh mushrooms,
   thinly sliced
2 sweet red peppers, cut into
   julienne strips
2 cups whipping cream

3 quarts water
12 ounces uncooked fresh
   fettuccine
4 ounces prosciutto, cut into
   julienne strips
½ teaspoon salt
¼ teaspoon pepper
1½ cups freshly grated
   Parmesan cheese, divided

Snap off tough ends of asparagus. Remove scales from stalks with a knife or vegetable peeler, if desired. Cut asparagus into 2-inch pieces. Cook asparagus, uncovered, in boiling water to cover 3 to 4 minutes or until crisp-tender. Drain and set aside.

Melt ¼ cup butter in a large skillet. Add mushrooms and sweet red pepper, and sauté until pepper is crisp-tender; set aside.

Heat whipping cream in a heavy saucepan over medium heat until simmering. Reduce heat, and continue to simmer 15 minutes or until slightly thickened. Remove from heat. Set aside, and keep whipping cream warm.

Bring water to a boil in a large Dutch oven. Add fettuccine; return to a boil. Boil 3 to 4 minutes or until fettuccine is cooked but still firm; drain well. Place fettuccine in a large bowl. Add remaining ¼ cup butter, and toss gently until butter melts. Add asparagus, sautéed vegetables, whipping cream, prosciutto, salt, pepper, and ¾ cup Parmesan cheese; toss well. Serve with remaining ¾ cup Parmesan cheese. Yield: 6 to 8 servings.

Peachtree Bouquet
The Junior League of DeKalb County, Georgia

Pasta Primavera

1 cup whipping cream
½ pound fresh snow pea
  pods, trimmed
¼ pound small fresh
  mushrooms, sliced
1 sweet red pepper, cut into
  julienne strips
1 small yellow squash, thinly
  sliced
1 cup small broccoli
  flowerets
3 tablespoons butter or
  margarine, melted
1 tablespoon vegetable oil
1 (16-ounce) package linguine
⅓ cup freshly grated
  Parmesan cheese
Freshly ground pepper to taste

Heat whipping cream in a small saucepan over low heat until warm. Set aside.

Sauté vegetables in butter and oil in a large skillet until almost crisp-tender. Add cream; cook over medium heat, stirring constantly, 5 minutes or until slightly thickened.

Cook linguine according to package directions; drain well. Place on a large serving platter. Top with vegetable mixture, and sprinkle with Parmesan cheese and pepper; toss gently. Serve immediately. Yield: 4 to 6 servings.

Hunt to Harbor
The Junior League of Baltimore, Maryland

Vegetable Lasagna

1 pound fresh spinach
2 tablespoons butter or
  margarine
Salt and pepper to taste
1 pound carrots, scraped and
  sliced
2 cups broccoli flowerets
2 cups canned diluted
  chicken broth
1 cup milk
½ cup chopped onion
¼ cup plus 2 tablespoons
  butter or margarine, melted

½ cup all-purpose flour
½ cup Chablis or other dry
  white wine
1 cup grated Parmesan
  cheese
1 cup (4 ounces) shredded
  Swiss cheese
1 cup (4 ounces) shredded
  Provolone cheese
10 lasagna noodles, cooked
  and drained
2 cups tomato sauce

Remove stems from spinach. Wash leaves thoroughly; cook spinach in a small amount of boiling water 5 to 8 minutes or until tender. Drain; place spinach on paper towels, and squeeze until barely moist. Finely chop spinach. Combine chopped spinach, 2 tablespoons butter, and salt and pepper to taste; set aside.

Cook carrots and broccoli in boiling water to cover 8 to 10 minutes or until tender; drain well. Combine spinach, carrots, and broccoli, and set aside.

Combine chicken broth and milk in a saucepan. Cook over medium heat until warm; remove from heat, and set aside.

Sauté chopped onion in ¼ cup plus 2 tablespoons butter in large skillet until tender. Add flour, and cook 3 minutes, stirring constantly. Add warm broth mixture and wine; simmer 5 minutes or until mixture is thickened, stirring constantly. Remove from heat, and set aside.

Combine Parmesan, Swiss, and Provolone cheeses. Arrange 5 lasagna noodles in a greased 13- x 9- x 2-inch baking dish. Layer one-fourth white sauce, half the vegetables, 1 cup cheese mixture, and one-fourth white sauce. Repeat layers. Spread tomato sauce over top. Sprinkle with remaining 1 cup cheese mixture. Bake, uncovered, at 350° for 35 minutes. Let lasagna stand 10 minutes before serving. Yield: 8 servings.   Diana Foster

As You Like It
St. Bernard's School
New York, New York

Lasagna Swirls

2 (10-ounce) packages frozen chopped spinach, thawed and drained
1 (16-ounce) carton ricotta cheese
2 cups (8 ounces) shredded mozzarella cheese
1½ cups grated Parmesan cheese, divided
1 (8-ounce) package cream cheese, softened
½ teaspoon dried whole basil
¼ teaspoon salt
¼ teaspoon pepper
¼ teaspoon dried whole oregano
1 (8-ounce) package lasagna noodles, cooked and drained
Light Tomato Sauce

Combine spinach, ricotta cheese, mozzarella cheese, 1 cup Parmesan cheese, softened cream cheese, basil, salt, pepper, and oregano in a large bowl; stir well.

Spread ½ cup spinach mixture on each lasagna noodle; roll up jellyroll fashion, starting at narrow end. Place lasagna rolls, coiled side down, in a 13- x 9- x 2-inch baking dish. Pour Light Tomato Sauce evenly over rolls; sprinkle with remaining ½ cup Parmesan cheese. Bake at 350° for 35 minutes. Yield: 5 servings.

Light Tomato Sauce

1 large onion, chopped
2 cloves garlic, minced
3 tablespoons butter or margarine, melted
2 (28-ounce) cans crushed tomatoes in tomato puree
1 (15½-ounce) can tomato sauce
2 tablespoons sugar
2 tablespoons olive oil
2 teaspoons dried whole basil
1 teaspoon dried Italian seasoning
¼ teaspoon salt
¼ teaspoon pepper
⅛ teaspoon sweet red pepper flakes

Sauté chopped onion and minced garlic in butter in a large skillet until tender. Add tomatoes and remaining ingredients; simmer 10 minutes. Yield: 9 cups.

A Pinch of Salt Lake
The Junior League of Salt Lake City, Utah

Spinach-Stuffed Manicotti

½ pound ground beef
2 cloves garlic, crushed
1 tablespoon olive oil
1 (10-ounce) package frozen
   chopped spinach, thawed
   and drained
1 (16-ounce) carton ricotta
   cheese
1 cup grated Romano cheese
3 eggs, beaten
½ cup Italian-seasoned
   breadcrumbs
1 teaspoon dried whole
   oregano

¼ teaspoon salt
¼ teaspoon pepper
⅛ teaspoon ground nutmeg
1 (8-ounce) package manicotti
   shells
3 cups commercial spaghetti
   sauce
¼ cup grated Parmesan
   cheese
Additional grated Parmesan
   cheese

Cook ground beef and garlic in olive oil in a large skillet until meat is browned, stirring to crumble meat; drain. Add spinach, ricotta cheese, Romano cheese, eggs, breadcrumbs, oregano, salt, pepper, and nutmeg; stir well.

Cook manicotti shells according to package directions; drain.

Stuff manicotti shells with spinach mixture, and place in a greased 13- x 9- x 2-inch baking dish. Pour spaghetti sauce over stuffed manicotti shells, and sprinkle with ¼ cup Parmesan cheese. Cover and bake at 350° for 30 minutes or until shells are thoroughly heated. Serve manicotti with additional grated Parmesan cheese. Yield: 6 to 8 servings.   Laurin Fields Stamm

Vintage Vicksburg
The Junior Auxiliary of Vicksburg, Mississippi

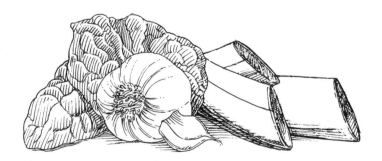

Buffet Manicotti

8 manicotti shells
3 tablespoons butter or margarine
3 tablespoons all-purpose flour
2 cups milk
1½ cups (6 ounces) shredded Muenster, Monterey Jack, or Cheddar cheese
¼ teaspoon salt
¼ teaspoon Worcestershire sauce
1½ cups chopped cooked chicken

1 cup small-curd cottage cheese
1 egg, beaten
¼ cup minced onion
2 tablespoons minced fresh parsley
½ teaspoon dried Italian seasoning
2 tablespoons butter or margarine, melted
⅛ teaspoon paprika
1 cup soft breadcrumbs

Cook manicotti shells according to package directions; drain and set aside.

Melt 3 tablespoons butter in a saucepan over low heat; add flour, stirring until smooth. Cook 1 minute, stirring constantly. Gradually add milk; cook over medium heat, stirring constantly, until mixture is thickened and bubbly. Stir in cheese, salt, and Worcestershire sauce, stirring until cheese melts. Set aside; keep warm.

Combine chicken, cottage cheese, egg, minced onion, parsley, and Italian seasoning in a medium bowl; stuff manicotti shells with chicken mixture.

Spoon ¾ cup cheese sauce into a lightly greased 13- x 9- x 2-inch baking dish. Arrange stuffed shells over sauce. Spoon remaining sauce over shells.

Combine 2 tablespoons melted butter and paprika in a small bowl; add breadcrumbs, and stir well.

Sprinkle breadcrumb mixture evenly over manicotti. Bake at 350° for 30 minutes or until manicotti is thoroughly heated and lightly browned. Yield: 4 to 6 servings.   G. Ryan

Around the World, Around Our Town
Friends of the San Pedro Library
San Pedro, California

Chicken Primavera

1 (8-ounce) package linguine
6 chicken breast halves,
  skinned, boned, and cut
  into 1-inch pieces
1 clove garlic, minced
2 tablespoons vegetable oil
3 cups broccoli flowerets
2 cups sliced fresh
  mushrooms

1 medium tomato, chopped
2 cups whipping cream
¾ cup grated Parmesan
  cheese
1 tablespoon dried whole
  basil
½ teaspoon salt
¼ teaspoon pepper

Cook linguine according to package directions; drain.

Sauté chicken and garlic in oil in a large Dutch oven. Add broccoli, mushrooms, and tomato, and sauté 3 to 5 minutes. Place chicken mixture in a large serving bowl. Add linguine, whipping cream, Parmesan cheese, basil, salt, and pepper, tossing well. Serve immediately. Yield: 4 to 6 servings.

Royle Round-Up of Recipes
The Royle School Parent-Teacher Association
Darien, Connecticut

Fusilli in Curried Cream and Salmon Sauce

1 (16-ounce) package fusilli
1½ cups commercial sour
  cream
½ cup whipping cream
2 tablespoons lemon juice
2 cloves garlic, crushed
1½ teaspoons curry powder
½ pound smoked salmon, cut
  into julienne strips

¼ cup capers, drained
2 tablespoons grated onion
¾ pound asparagus, cut into
  1-inch pieces
¼ teaspoon salt
⅛ teaspoon pepper

Cook fusilli according to package directions, omitting salt; drain and set aside.

Combine sour cream, whipping cream, lemon juice, garlic, and curry powder in container of an electric blender or food processor; cover and process until mixture is smooth. Pour sour cream mixture into a large serving bowl. Add salmon, capers, and onion to sour cream mixture, stirring well.

Arrange asparagus pieces in a steamer rack. Place rack over boiling water; cover and steam for 6 to 8 minutes or until asparagus is crisp-tender.

Add fusilli, asparagus, salt, and pepper to salmon mixture; toss gently. Serve immediately. Yield: 8 servings.

Sounds Delicious!
The Volunteer Council of the Tulsa Philharmonic Society, Inc.
Tulsa, Oklahoma

Shrimp 'n Shells

1 (8-ounce) package medium shell macaroni
1 tablespoon olive oil
1½ pounds unpeeled medium-size fresh shrimp
¼ cup butter or margarine, melted
2 tablespoons Worcestershire sauce
4 cups broccoli flowerets
2 tablespoons grated Parmesan cheese
2 tablespoons chopped onion
2 tablespoons chopped fresh parsley
1 teaspoon garlic salt
½ teaspoon salt
⅛ teaspoon pepper

Cook shell macaroni according to package directions; drain. Toss with olive oil, and set aside.

Peel and devein shrimp. Sauté shrimp in butter and Worcestershire sauce in a large skillet 3 to 5 minutes or until shrimp turn pink. Remove shrimp with a slotted spoon, and keep warm. Reserve ⅓ cup butter mixture.

Cook broccoli in a small amount of boiling water 5 minutes or until crisp-tender; drain.

Combine macaroni, shrimp, and broccoli in a large serving bowl. Add reserved butter mixture, Parmesan cheese, onion, parsley, garlic salt, salt, and pepper; toss gently to combine. Serve immediately. Yield: 4 to 6 servings.   Ann English Maybank

Charleston Receipts Repeats
The Junior League of Charleston, South Carolina

Orange Rice

⅔ cup diced celery
2 tablespoons minced
   onion
¼ cup butter or margarine,
   melted
1½ cups orange juice
1 cup water

1 cup uncooked long-grain
   rice
2 tablespoons grated orange
   rind
1 teaspoon salt
⅛ teaspoon dried whole thyme

Sauté celery and onion in butter in a large saucepan until vegetables are tender. Add orange juice, water, rice, grated orange rind, salt, and thyme, and stir well. Bring to a boil; cover, reduce heat, and simmer 25 minutes or until rice is tender and liquid is absorbed. Yield: 6 to 8 servings.   Mrs. Sam Tidwell

Kitchen Sampler
The Junior Service League of Bessemer, Alabama

Pistachio Pilaf

¾ cup shelled pistachios
1 small onion, finely chopped
2 tablespoons butter or
   margarine, melted
1 cup uncooked long-grain
   rice

2 cups canned diluted
   chicken broth
¾ cup raisins
1 tablespoon butter or
   margarine, melted
Salt and pepper to taste

Blanch pistachios by submerging in boiling water 1 minute; remove and discard skins. Set pistachios aside.

Sauté chopped onion in 2 tablespoons butter in a saucepan until tender. Add rice; cook over low heat until rice is lightly browned, stirring frequently.

Stir chicken broth and raisins into rice mixture. Bring mixture to a boil; cover, reduce heat, and simmer 20 minutes or until rice is tender and liquid is absorbed. Remove from heat; let rice mixture stand, covered, 10 minutes. Stir in blanched pistachios and 1 tablespoon melted butter. Sprinkle with salt and pepper to taste. Yield: 4 to 6 servings.

California Treasure
The Junior League of Fresno, California

Spanish Fried Rice

1½ cups uncooked long-grain
rice
1 tablespoon lard, melted
1 cup chopped tomato
¼ cup chopped onion
¼ cup chopped green pepper

3 cups canned diluted
chicken broth
1 clove garlic, minced
½ teaspoon salt
½ teaspoon cumin seeds
¼ teaspoon pepper

Sauté rice in lard in a large saucepan over medium heat until rice is lightly browned.

Add tomato, onion, and green pepper to rice mixture, and sauté until vegetables are tender.

Stir chicken broth, minced garlic, salt, cumin seeds, and pepper into vegetable mixture. Bring to a boil; cover, reduce heat, and simmer 25 minutes or until rice is tender and liquid is absorbed. Yield: 8 to 10 servings.   Bonnie Gonzalez

Parker's Blue Ribbon Recipes
The Parker Ward Relief Society
St. Anthony, Idaho

Arkansas Rice Casserole

1 (10½-ounce) can beef
consommé, undiluted
1 cup uncooked long-grain
rice
1 cup water
1 onion, diced
1 green pepper, cut into
julienne strips

¼ cup butter or margarine,
melted
1 (4-ounce) can sliced
mushrooms, drained
1 (2-ounce) jar diced
pimiento, drained
1 teaspoon salt

Combine all ingredients in a large bowl; mix well. Pour mixture into a lightly greased 12- x 8- x 2-inch baking dish. Bake at 375° for 1 hour or until rice is tender. Yield: 8 servings.

Celebration: A Taste of Arkansas
The Sevier County Cookbook Committee
Lockesburg, Arkansas

Herbed Spinach Rice

4 eggs, beaten
1 cup milk
¼ cup finely chopped onion
1 teaspoon Worcestershire sauce
½ teaspoon salt
½ teaspoon ground marjoram
½ teaspoon ground thyme
½ teaspoon dried whole rosemary

3 cups cooked long-grain rice
4 cups (16 ounces) shredded sharp Cheddar cheese
1 (10-ounce) package frozen chopped spinach, thawed and drained
¼ cup plus 2 tablespoons butter or margarine, melted
Paprika

Combine eggs and milk in a large bowl, beating well. Add onion and next 5 ingredients; stir well.

Combine rice, cheese, spinach, and butter in a large bowl, stirring well. Fold egg mixture into rice mixture. Pour rice mixture into a greased 2½-quart casserole. Sprinkle with paprika.

Set casserole in a 13- x 9- x 2-inch baking dish; pour hot water to a depth of 1 inch into dish.

Bake at 350° for 1½ hours or until a knife inserted in center comes out clean. Yield: 10 to 12 servings.

Treasured Recipes from Camargo to Indian Hill
The Indian Hill Historical Society
Cincinnati, Ohio

Herbed Lentils and Rice

1 cup (4 ounces) shredded Swiss cheese, divided
¾ cup dried lentils, washed and sorted
¾ cup chopped onion
½ cup uncooked brown rice
3½ cups canned diluted chicken broth
¼ cup Burgundy or other dry red wine

½ teaspoon dried whole basil, crushed
¼ teaspoon salt
¼ teaspoon dried whole oregano
¼ teaspoon dried whole thyme
⅛ teaspoon garlic powder
⅛ teaspoon pepper

Combine ½ cup cheese and remaining ingredients in a large bowl; stir well. Pour mixture into an ungreased 2-quart casserole. Cover and bake at 350° for 2 hours or until lentils are tender, stirring occasionally. Uncover and sprinkle with remaining cheese. Bake an additional 5 minutes or until cheese melts. Yield: 6 to 8 servings.

Tidewater on the Half Shell
The Junior League of Norfolk-Virginia Beach, Virginia

Brown Rice Pilaf with Nuts and Raisins

½ cup golden raisins
½ cup Chablis or other dry white wine
¼ cup chopped onion
¼ cup unsalted butter or margarine, melted
1 cup uncooked brown rice
1 teaspoon salt
¼ teaspoon pepper
2½ cups canned diluted chicken broth

2 tablespoons unsalted butter or margarine, melted
½ cup chopped fresh mint or cilantro
¾ cup slivered almonds, toasted
Fresh mint or cilantro sprigs (optional)

Combine raisins and wine; let stand 45 minutes. Drain.

Sauté onion in ¼ cup butter until tender. Add rice, and sauté 3 minutes. Add salt, pepper, and chicken broth. Bring to a boil; cover, reduce heat, and simmer 45 minutes or until rice is tender and liquid is absorbed. Add raisins, 2 tablespoons butter, chopped mint, and almonds, stirring well. Garnish with fresh mint sprigs, if desired. Yield: 4 servings.

South of the Fork
The Junior League of Dallas, Texas

Cauliflower and Carrots with Wild Rice

2 cloves garlic, minced
1 tablespoon butter or
  margarine, melted
1¾ cups water
½ cup uncooked wild rice
2 teaspoons chicken-flavored
  bouillon granules
½ teaspoon salt
½ teaspoon onion salt

½ cup uncooked long-grain
  rice
1 cup cauliflower flowerets
2 medium carrots, scraped
  and shredded
3 green onions, thinly sliced
2 to 3 tablespoons whipping
  cream

Sauté garlic in butter in a large saucepan. Add water and next 4 ingredients. Bring to a boil; cover, reduce heat, and simmer 25 minutes. Add rice; cover and simmer 20 minutes. Add cauliflower; cover and simmer 10 minutes or until rice is tender and liquid is absorbed. Stir in carrot, green onions, and cream. Cook until mixture is thoroughly heated. Yield: 6 to 8 servings.

Wild Rice, Star of the North
The 1006 Summit Avenue Society
St. Paul, Minnesota

Barley and Pine Nut Casserole

1 cup pearl barley
¼ cup plus 2 tablespoons
  margarine, divided
⅓ cup pine nuts
1 medium onion, chopped
½ cup minced fresh parsley

¼ cup minced fresh chives
¼ teaspoon salt
¼ teaspoon pepper
2 (14½-ounce) cans beef
  broth, undiluted
Fresh parsley sprigs (optional)

Rinse barley in cold water; drain well. Set aside.

Melt 2 tablespoons margarine in a medium skillet over medium heat; add pine nuts, and cook until lightly toasted, stirring constantly. Remove pine nuts with a slotted spoon; set aside.

Heat remaining ¼ cup margarine in skillet until melted; add reserved barley and onion. Cook, stirring constantly, until barley is lightly toasted and onion is tender. Remove from heat; stir in toasted pine nuts, parsley, chives, salt, and pepper. Spoon barley mixture into a 1½-quart casserole.

Bring beef broth to a boil in a medium saucepan; pour broth over barley mixture in casserole, and stir well. Bake, uncovered, at 375° for 1 hour and 10 minutes or until barley is tender and liquid is absorbed. Garnish casserole with fresh parsley sprigs, if desired. Yield: 6 to 8 servings.   Erika M. Daniels

Favorite Recipes
The Sponsor's Club, Robert Louis Stevenson School
Pebble Beach, California

Couscous with Almonds

¼ cup butter or margarine	½ teaspoon pepper
1 medium onion, chopped	½ cup slivered almonds,
1½ cups uncooked couscous	toasted
3 cups chicken broth	½ cup currants
½ teaspoon salt	

Melt butter in a medium saucepan over medium heat; add chopped onion, and sauté 2 minutes or until tender.

Add couscous, chicken broth, salt, and pepper to onion, stirring well. Bring mixture to a boil; reduce heat, and simmer 2 minutes. Remove from heat; cover and let stand 10 minutes or until liquid is absorbed. Stir in almonds and currants. Fluff with a fork before serving. Yield: 6 servings.

Taste of Today
BUNWC, North Shore Illinois Chapter
Northfield, Illinois

Nassau Grits

¾ pound bacon, cut into
1-inch pieces
1 medium-size green pepper,
finely chopped
1 medium onion, finely
chopped
1 cup uncooked regular grits
2 (14½-ounce) cans whole
tomatoes, undrained and
chopped

½ teaspoon salt
½ teaspoon garlic powder
½ teaspoon dried whole basil
½ teaspoon dried whole
oregano
½ teaspoon pepper
½ teaspoon hot sauce
½ teaspoon Worcestershire
sauce

Cook bacon in a Dutch oven until crisp; remove bacon, reserving drippings. Crumble bacon, and set aside.

Sauté green pepper and onion in drippings in Dutch oven until vegetables are tender. Drain vegetables, discarding drippings. Return vegetables to Dutch oven. Add grits to Dutch oven, and cook according to package directions. Add reserved bacon, tomatoes, and remaining ingredients; stir well. Cover and simmer 30 minutes. Serve immediately. Yield: 6 to 8 servings.

Unbearably Good!
The Junior Service League of Americus, Georgia

Pies & Pastries

One can almost catch the aroma of a freshly baked apple pie cooling on the window sill of this home on Lockerbie Square in Indianapolis, Indiana. With its shade trees, comfortable porches, and brick-lined streets, this midwestern neighborhood evokes a sense of a quieter, simpler time.

☆☆☆

Panache Chocolate Pie

½ cup butter or margarine
2 (1-ounce) squares
 unsweetened chocolate
2 eggs
1 cup sugar

¼ cup all-purpose flour
½ teaspoon vanilla extract
¼ cup chopped pecans
Vanilla ice cream

Place butter and chocolate in top of a double boiler; bring water to a boil. Reduce heat to low; cook until chocolate melts. Remove from heat, and let cool slightly.

Beat eggs in a large mixing bowl at medium speed of an electric mixer; gradually add sugar and flour, beating well after each addition. Stir in chocolate mixture, vanilla, and chopped pecans. Pour chocolate mixture into a well-greased 9-inch pieplate. Bake at 325° for 45 to 50 minutes or until set. Let cool. Serve with vanilla ice cream. Yield: one 9-inch pie.

Simply Sensational
TWIGS, The Auxiliary of Children's Medical Center
Dayton, Ohio

Museum Winner's Pie

1 unbaked 9-inch pastry shell
½ cup butter or margarine,
 softened
1 cup sugar
2 eggs
½ cup all-purpose flour

2 tablespoons bourbon
Pinch of salt
1 cup semisweet chocolate
 morsels
1 cup chopped pecans
Whipped cream or ice cream

Bake pastry shell at 350° for 8 minutes. Let cool.

Cream butter and sugar; add eggs, one at a time, beating well after each addition. Add flour, bourbon, and salt; beat well. Stir in chocolate morsels and pecans. Spread mixture in baked pastry shell. Bake at 350° for 35 to 40 minutes or until filling is set. Let cool completely before serving. Serve with whipped cream. Yield: one 9-inch pie.

The Kentucky Derby Museum Cookbook
The Kentucky Derby Museum
Louisville, Kentucky

Jamaican Coconut Pie

1⅓ cups flaked coconut
1 unbaked 9-inch pastry shell
3 tablespoons butter or
   margarine, softened
½ cup sugar
1 cup dark corn syrup
3 eggs
1 tablespoon rum

1 teaspoon ground nutmeg
1 teaspoon vanilla extract
⅛ teaspoon ground cinnamon
1 cup whipping cream,
   whipped
Additional toasted flaked
   coconut

Sprinkle 1⅓ cups coconut over pastry shell. Set aside.

Cream butter and sugar; add corn syrup, eggs, rum, nutmeg, vanilla, and cinnamon, beating well at medium speed of an electric mixer. Pour egg mixture over coconut in unbaked pastry shell. Bake at 350° for 45 minutes or until filling is set. Let cool completely. Top pie with whipped cream, and sprinkle with toasted coconut. Yield: one 9-inch pie.

A Taste of Almost Heaven
The Monongalia Arts Center
Morgantown, West Virginia

Pineapple Chess Pie

4 eggs, beaten
2 cups sugar
1 cup flaked coconut
1 (8-ounce) can crushed
   pineapple, undrained
½ cup butter or margarine,
   melted

1 tablespoon all-purpose flour
1 tablespoon cornmeal
1 teaspoon vanilla extract
1 unbaked 9-inch pastry shell

Combine eggs, sugar, coconut, pineapple, butter, flour, cornmeal, and vanilla in a large mixing bowl, stirring well to combine. Pour mixture into unbaked pastry shell. Bake at 350° for 45 to 50 minutes or until filling is set. Cool pie completely before serving. Yield: one 9-inch pie.   Betty Locke Taylor

Celebration: A Taste of Arkansas
The Sevier County Cookbook Committee
Lockesburg, Arkansas

Apricot-Date Prune Pie

1 (6-ounce) package dried
apricots, halved
1 cup whole pitted dates,
halved
1 cup pitted prunes, halved
1½ cups water
½ teaspoon salt

1 (6-ounce) can frozen orange
juice concentrate, thawed
and undiluted
1 teaspoon vanilla extract
Pastry for double-crust 9-inch
pie
1 tablespoon milk

Combine apricots, dates, prunes, water, and salt in a medium saucepan; bring mixture to a boil. Cover, reduce heat, and simmer 10 minutes or until fruit is softened, stirring occasionally. Remove from heat, and stir in orange juice concentrate and vanilla. Cover and chill 1 hour.

Roll out half of pastry to ⅛-inch thickness on a lightly floured surface. Place pastry in a 9-inch pieplate; trim off excess pastry along edges. Spoon fruit filling into pastry shell.

Roll remaining pastry to ⅛-inch thickness, and cut into ½-inch strips. Arrange pastry strips, lattice fashion, across top of pie filling. Trim pastry strips even with edges of pieplate; fold edges under and flute. Brush pastry with milk. (Cover edges of pastry with strips of aluminum foil to prevent excessive browning.) Bake at 425° for 30 minutes on bottom rack of oven, removing foil during last 15 minutes of baking time. Serve pie warm or let cool completely. Yield: one 9-inch pie.

Merisue Huffman

Elvis Fans Cookbook, Volume 3
The Elvis Presley Memorial Trauma Center
Memphis, Tennessee

Maple Pumpkin Pie

3 eggs, lightly beaten
2 (16-ounce) cans pumpkin
1 cup half-and-half
½ cup sugar
½ cup maple syrup
½ teaspoon salt
½ teaspoon ground cinnamon
½ teaspoon ground ginger
1 unbaked 9-inch pastry shell
2 cups whipping cream, whipped
¼ cup maple syrup

Combine first 8 ingredients in a large mixing bowl; stir well. Pour two-thirds of pumpkin mixture into pastry shell. Place on lowest rack of oven. Pour remaining pumpkin mixture into pastry shell. Bake at 400° for 10 minutes. Reduce heat to 350°, and bake 1 hour or until filling is set. Let cool. Just before serving, pipe whipped cream in rosettes on top of pie, and drizzle with maple syrup. Yield: one 9-inch pie.   Jerretta Mulvey

State Hospital Cooks
Patient/Staff Advocacy Committee, Vermont State Hospital
Waterbury, Vermont

Sour Cream-Pear Pie

½ cup sugar
2 tablespoons all-purpose flour
¼ teaspoon salt
1 egg
½ teaspoon vanilla extract
1 cup commercial sour cream
4 cups peeled, sliced pears (about 5 large pears)
Nut Crust
Crumble Topping

Combine sugar, flour, and salt in a large bowl; stir well. Stir in egg, vanilla, and sour cream. Fold in pear slices. Pour mixture into Nut Crust. Bake at 400° for 30 minutes. (Cover edges of pastry with strips of aluminum foil to prevent excessive browning, if necessary.) Remove foil, and sprinkle Crumble Topping over pie. Bake an additional 25 to 30 minutes or until topping is golden brown. Let cool 20 minutes before serving. Yield: one 9-inch pie.

Nut Crust

¼ cup hazelnuts
1¼ cups all-purpose flour
¼ cup sifted powdered sugar
½ cup butter or margarine

Toast hazelnuts at 400° for 6 minutes. Rub briskly with a towel to remove skins. Finely chop nuts.

Combine chopped hazelnuts, flour, and powdered sugar in a large bowl. Cut in butter with a pastry blender until mixture holds together. Press mixture on bottom and up sides of a 9-inch pieplate. Yield: one 9-inch crust.

Crumble Topping

¼ cup all-purpose flour

2 tablespoons sugar

½ teaspoon ground cinnamon

¼ cup butter or margarine

Combine first 3 ingredients. Cut in butter with a pastry blender until mixture is crumbly. Yield: ½ cup.   Denise Moran

La Salette's Favorite Recipes
The La Salette Shrine
Attleboro, Massachusetts

Sour Cream-Apple Pie

1 cup commercial sour cream

¾ cup sugar

2 tablespoons all-purpose flour

¼ teaspoon salt

1 teaspoon vanilla extract

1 egg, lightly beaten

4 cups peeled, sliced cooking apples

1 unbaked 9-inch pastry shell

½ cup firmly packed brown sugar

⅓ cup all-purpose flour

¼ cup butter or margarine

Combine first 6 ingredients in a large mixing bowl; beat at medium speed of an electric mixer 3 minutes. Gently fold in apple slices. Spoon mixture into pastry shell. Bake at 400° for 25 minutes. (Cover edges of pastry with strips of aluminum foil to prevent excessive browning, if necessary.)

Combine brown sugar and ⅓ cup flour; cut in butter with a pastry blender until mixture resembles coarse meal. Sprinkle brown sugar mixture over pie. Bake an additional 20 minutes. Serve warm or let cool. Yield: one 9-inch pie.   Betty Fulgham

Southern Secrets
SouthTrust Corporation
Birmingham, Alabama

Sour Cream-Raisin Pie

1 cup raisins
1 cup boiling water
1 cup sugar
¼ cup plus 2 tablespoons
  all-purpose flour
⅛ teaspoon salt
2¼ cups milk
3 eggs, separated
½ cup commercial sour
  cream
¼ cup butter
1 baked 9-inch pastry shell
½ teaspoon cream of tartar
¼ cup plus 2 tablespoons
  sugar

Cover raisins with boiling water; let stand 5 minutes. Drain; set aside. Combine 1 cup sugar, flour, and salt in a saucepan; stir well. Gradually stir in milk. Cook over medium heat, stirring constantly, until mixture thickens and comes to a boil. Reduce heat; cook 2 minutes, stirring constantly. Remove from heat. Beat egg yolks until thick and lemon colored. Gradually stir about 1 cup of hot milk mixture into yolks; add to remaining hot mixture, stirring constantly. Bring to a boil, and cook 2 minutes, stirring constantly. Remove from heat. Add raisins, sour cream, and butter; stir well. Spoon into pastry shell. Beat egg whites (at room temperature) and cream of tartar at high speed of an electric mixer 1 minute. Add ¼ cup plus 2 tablespoons sugar, 1 tablespoon at a time, beating until stiff peaks form. Spread meringue over hot filling, sealing to edge of pastry. Bake at 350° for 12 to 15 minutes or until golden. Yield: one 9-inch pie.   LaVon Rasmussen

Thou Preparest a Table Before Me
East Avenue United Methodist Church Women
York, Nebraska

Sour Cream-Lemon Pie

1¼ cups sugar
¼ cup plus 2 tablespoons
  cornstarch
½ teaspoon salt
2 cups hot water
3 egg yolks
2 tablespoons grated
  lemon rind
⅓ cup fresh lemon juice
1 tablespoon butter
1 cup commercial sour cream
1 baked 9-inch pastry shell
1 cup whipping cream
¼ cup sifted powdered sugar

Combine 1¼ cups sugar, cornstarch, and salt in a heavy saucepan; stir well. Gradually stir in water; cook over medium heat, stirring constantly, until mixture thickens and comes to a boil. Boil 1 minute, stirring constantly. Remove from heat.

Beat egg yolks until thick and lemon colored. Gradually stir about one-fourth of hot mixture into yolks; add to remaining hot mixture, stirring constantly. Cook over medium heat 2 to 3 minutes, stirring constantly. Remove from heat. Add lemon rind, lemon juice, and butter, stirring until butter melts. Let cool. Stir in sour cream. Spoon sour cream mixture into baked pastry shell.

Beat whipping cream at high speed of an electric mixer until foamy; gradually add powdered sugar, beating until soft peaks form. Spread sweetened whipped cream over pie filling. Chill thoroughly. Yield: one 9-inch pie.

Very Innovative Parties
The Loma Linda University School of Dentistry Auxiliary
Loma Linda, California

Glazed Peach Pie

5 cups peeled, sliced fresh peaches, divided
½ cup water
1 cup sugar
3 tablespoons cornstarch
2 tablespoons butter
¼ teaspoon almond extract
1 baked 9-inch pastry shell
Whipped cream or vanilla ice cream

Place 2 cups peach slices and water in container of an electric blender or food processor; cover and process until smooth. Pour pureed mixture into a medium saucepan.

Combine sugar and cornstarch, stirring well; add sugar mixture to pureed mixture in saucepan, and stir well. Cook over medium-high heat 5 minutes or until mixture is thickened and clear, stirring constantly. Remove from heat. Add butter and almond extract, stirring until butter melts; let cool.

Arrange remaining 3 cups peach slices in baked pastry shell. Pour glaze mixture over peach slices. Chill thoroughly. Serve with whipped cream. Yield: one 9-inch pie.

Hunt to Harbor
The Junior League of Baltimore, Maryland

Sinful Chocolate-Berry Pie

30 chocolate wafer cookies, crushed (1½ cups)

⅓ cup butter or margarine, melted

½ cup plus 2 tablespoons semisweet chocolate morsels, divided

1 (8-ounce) package cream cheese, softened

¼ cup firmly packed brown sugar

½ teaspoon vanilla extract

1 cup whipping cream, whipped

1 pint fresh strawberries, hulled

1 teaspoon shortening

Combine cookie crumbs and butter in a medium bowl, stirring well. Firmly press over bottom and sides of a lightly greased 9-inch pieplate. Bake at 325° for 10 minutes. Let cool completely.

Place ½ cup chocolate morsels in top of a double boiler; bring water to a boil. Reduce heat to low; cook until chocolate melts, stirring occasionally. Remove from heat; cool to lukewarm.

Beat cream cheese at medium speed of an electric mixer until smooth. Add brown sugar and vanilla, beating well. Add cooled chocolate; beat well. Fold whipped cream into chocolate mixture. Spoon filling into cooled crust. Cover and chill at least 8 hours.

Reserve 1 whole strawberry for garnish; slice remaining strawberries. Arrange strawberry slices over chilled pie. Place reserved whole strawberry in center.

Combine remaining 2 tablespoons morsels and shortening in a saucepan. Cook over low heat until chocolate and shortening melt, stirring frequently. Remove from heat; cool slightly. Drizzle melted chocolate mixture over strawberries. Yield: one 9-inch pie.

The Mystic Seaport All Seasons Cookbook
Mystic Seaport Museum Stores
Mystic, Connecticut

Winning Peanut Butter Pie

25 vanilla wafers, crushed
½ cup finely chopped
  unsalted, blanched peanuts
¼ cup butter or margarine,
  melted
1 (8-ounce) package cream
  cheese, softened

1 cup creamy peanut butter
1 cup sugar
1 cup whipping cream
1 teaspoon vanilla extract
Hot Fudge Sauce, divided

Combine vanilla wafers, peanuts, and melted butter in a small bowl, stirring well. Firmly press crumb mixture evenly over bottom and sides of an ungreased 10-inch pieplate. Bake at 350° for 15 minutes; let cool.

Combine cream cheese and peanut butter in a large mixing bowl; beat at medium speed of an electric mixer until light and fluffy. Gradually add sugar, and beat until smooth.

Beat whipping cream until soft peaks form; beat in vanilla. Gently fold whipped cream into peanut butter mixture, blending until smooth. Spoon peanut butter filling into prepared crust. Cover and chill at least 2 hours.

Spread ½ cup lukewarm Hot Fudge Sauce over peanut butter filling. If desired, make a flower design by swirling sauce into the filling with a small spatula. Chill at least 6 hours or until firm. Store remaining Hot Fudge Sauce in refrigerator. To serve, heat Hot Fudge Sauce in a small saucepan over low heat, stirring until smooth; remove from heat, and let cool to lukewarm. Serve pie with remaining Hot Fudge Sauce. Yield: one 10-inch pie.

Hot Fudge Sauce

1 (14-ounce) can sweetened
  condensed milk
2 (1-ounce) squares semisweet
  chocolate

1 tablespoon vanilla extract
2 tablespoons butter or
  margarine

Combine sweetened condensed milk and chocolate in top of a double boiler; bring water to a boil. Reduce heat to low; cook until chocolate melts and mixture thickens, stirring occasionally. Add vanilla and butter, stirring until butter melts. Remove from heat. Let cool to lukewarm. Yield: 1⅔ cups.

A Pinch of Salt Lake
The Junior League of Salt Lake City, Utah

Chocolate Sabayon Pie

1 (8½-ounce) package
  chocolate wafers, crushed
½ cup sifted powdered sugar
½ cup butter or margarine,
  melted
10 (1-ounce) squares
  semisweet chocolate
2 egg yolks, lightly beaten
¼ cup water

1 tablespoon sugar
2 tablespoons white crème de
  menthe
2 tablespoons white crème de
  cacao
1 cup whipping cream,
  whipped
Additional whipped cream
  (optional)

Combine chocolate wafer crumbs, ½ cup powdered sugar, and butter; stir well. Firmly press crumb mixture evenly over bottom and 1¼ inches up sides of a 9-inch springform pan. Chill until firm.

Place chocolate squares, egg yolks, and water in top of a double boiler; bring water to a boil. Reduce heat to low; cook until chocolate melts, stirring constantly. Remove from heat, and let cool. Combine 1 tablespoon sugar and liqueurs, stirring until sugar dissolves. Gradually stir liqueur mixture into chocolate mixture. Gently fold whipped cream into chocolate mixture; spoon into prepared pan. Chill 8 hours or until firm. Garnish with additional whipped cream, if desired. Yield: one 9-inch pie. Sarah Voorhis

Academic Apron
The Middlesex School
Concord, Massachusetts

Pumpkin-Almond Pie

24 vanilla wafers, divided
1 pint vanilla ice cream,
  softened
1 (16-ounce) can pumpkin
1½ cups sugar
1 teaspoon ground cinnamon
½ teaspoon salt
½ teaspoon ground ginger

¼ teaspoon ground cloves
1 teaspoon vanilla extract
1 cup whipping cream,
  whipped
¼ cup sugar
1 cup sliced, blanched
  almonds

Arrange 14 vanilla wafers in the bottom of a 9-inch pieplate. Spread ice cream evenly over wafers. Arrange remaining wafers around edge of pieplate. Cover and freeze until firm.

Combine pumpkin and next 6 ingredients in a large bowl, stirring well. Gently fold whipped cream into pumpkin mixture. Spread pumpkin mixture over ice cream layer. Cover and freeze until firm.

Place ¼ cup sugar in a small heavy saucepan. Cook over medium heat until sugar melts and turns a light golden brown, stirring constantly. Remove from heat, and stir in almonds. Spoon almond mixture onto wax paper. Let cool completely. Break almond mixture into small pieces.

Remove pie from freezer 10 minutes before slicing. Sprinkle almond pieces over pie. Cut pie into wedges, and serve immediately. Yield: one 9-inch pie.

Bound to Please
The Junior League of Boise, Idaho

Caramel-Coffee Ice Cream Pie

1 egg white
¼ teaspoon salt
¼ cup sugar
1½ cups chopped walnuts
1 quart vanilla ice cream, softened
1 quart coffee ice cream, softened

2 tablespoons butter or margarine
½ cup firmly packed brown sugar
¼ cup half-and-half
2 tablespoons chopped walnuts
½ teaspoon vanilla extract

Beat egg white (at room temperature) and salt in a small bowl at high speed of an electric mixer 1 minute. Add ¼ cup sugar, 1 tablespoon at a time, beating until stiff peaks form and sugar dissolves (2 to 4 minutes). Fold in 1½ cups chopped walnuts. Spread meringue mixture over bottom and sides of a greased 9-inch pie-plate. Bake at 400° for 10 minutes. Let cool completely.

Combine softened ice creams in a large bowl; spoon into cooled crust. Freeze until firm.

Melt butter in a saucepan over medium heat; stir in brown sugar. Remove from heat. Gradually stir in half-and-half. Cook over medium heat 1 minute, stirring constantly. Stir in 2 tablespoons walnuts and vanilla. Serve sauce over pie. Yield: one 9-inch pie.

Necessities and Temptations
The Junior League of Austin, Texas

Peppermint-Fudge Ribbon Pie

1 quart peppermint ice
  cream, softened
1 baked 9-inch pastry shell
Fudge Sauce
3 egg whites
¼ teaspoon cream of tartar

¼ cup plus 2 tablespoons
  sugar
½ teaspoon vanilla extract
Crushed hard peppermint
  candy

Spoon half of ice cream into pastry shell, spreading evenly; freeze until firm. Spread half of Fudge Sauce over ice cream layer; freeze until firm. Repeat layers, freezing until firm. Beat egg whites (at room temperature) and cream of tartar at high speed of an electric mixer 1 minute. Add sugar, 1 tablespoon at a time, beating until stiff peaks form and sugar dissolves. Beat in vanilla. Spread meringue over pie. Top with candy. Broil 6 inches from heat 1 minute or until browned. Serve immediately. Yield: one 9-inch pie.

Fudge Sauce

1 cup sugar
1 (5.3-ounce) can evaporated
  milk
2 (1-ounce) squares
  unsweetened chocolate

2 tablespoons butter or
  margarine
1 teaspoon vanilla extract

Combine all ingredients in a small saucepan. Cook over medium heat until thickened and bubbly, stirring constantly. Let cool to room temperature. Yield: 1¼ cups.

Palm Country Cuisine
The Junior League of Greater Lakeland, Florida

Walnut Tassies

2 (3-ounce) packages cream
  cheese, softened
¾ cup butter, softened
1½ cups all-purpose flour
2 eggs
1½ cups firmly packed brown
  sugar

1½ cups finely chopped
  walnuts
1½ teaspoons vanilla extract
2 tablespoons butter, melted

Combine cream cheese and butter in a medium bowl; beat at medium speed of an electric mixer until well blended. Add flour; mix well. Shape dough into 48 balls; chill. Place in miniature (1¾-inch) muffin pans, shaping each ball into a tart shell. Set aside.

Combine eggs, sugar, walnuts, and vanilla; stir well. Add melted butter, stirring well. Spoon walnut mixture into tart shells, filling three-fourths full. Bake at 375° for 20 minutes or until lightly browned. Yield: 4 dozen.   Angela Costigliola

From Start to Finish
The Rhode Island Special Olympics
Warwick, Rhode Island

Brownie Tarts

1 cup all-purpose flour	2 eggs
½ cup cold butter	⅔ cup sugar
1 (3-ounce) package cream cheese	Pinch of salt
	½ teaspoon vanilla extract
4 (1-ounce) squares semisweet chocolate	½ cup chopped walnuts
2 tablespoons butter or margarine	

Position knife blade in food processor bowl; add flour, ½ cup cold butter, and cream cheese. Cover and process until mixture forms a ball. Press mixture firmly into 6 (4-inch) shallow tart or quiche pans.

Combine chocolate and 2 tablespoons butter in top of a double boiler; bring water to a boil. Reduce heat to low, and cook until chocolate and butter melt, stirring occasionally. Remove from heat. Set mixture aside.

Beat eggs at medium speed of an electric mixer until thick and lemon colored; gradually add sugar, beating well. Add chocolate mixture, salt, and vanilla; beat at low speed 1 minute.

Sprinkle chopped walnuts evenly in tart shells. Spoon chocolate mixture over walnuts in tart shells. Bake at 350° for 30 minutes. Yield: 6 (4-inch) tarts.   Margaret Gustin

Compliments to the Cook
YWCA of Salt Lake City, Utah

Czechoslovakian Tart

1 cup butter or margarine, softened	2 cups all-purpose flour
1 cup sugar	1 cup finely chopped pecans
2 egg yolks	1 teaspoon vanilla extract
	2¼ cups apricot preserves

Cream butter; gradually add sugar, beating at medium speed of an electric mixer. Add egg yolks, beating well. Fold in flour, pecans, and vanilla until mixture forms a dough.

Press half of dough into a greased and floured 13- x 9- x 2-inch baking pan. Top with apricot preserves, spreading to within ¼ inch of edges. Press remaining half of dough over preserves. Bake at 350° for 50 minutes or until lightly browned. Cool and cut into squares. Yield: 12 servings.   Mildred Goldberger

I Must Have That Recipe
Albert Einstein College of Medicine, Yeshiva University
Bronx, New York

Almond-Toffee Tart

2 cups all-purpose flour	1½ cups sugar
3 tablespoons sugar	¼ teaspoon salt
¾ cup butter	2 cups sliced, blanched
2 egg yolks, lightly beaten	almonds
1½ cups whipping cream	¼ teaspoon almond extract

Combine flour and 3 tablespoons sugar in a medium bowl; cut in butter with a pastry blender until mixture resembles coarse meal.

Add egg yolks, stirring until dry ingredients are slightly moistened; shape into a ball. Gently press pastry over bottom and sides of an 11-inch tart pan. Bake at 325° for 10 minutes (pastry will be pale).

Combine whipping cream, 1½ cups sugar, and salt in a heavy saucepan; bring to a boil. Reduce heat to medium, and cook 5 minutes, stirring constantly. Remove from heat; stir in almonds and almond extract. Pour almond mixture into pastry shell. Bake at 375° for 35 to 40 minutes or until lightly browned. Let cool to room temperature. Carefully remove sides of tart pan before serving. Yield: 10 to 12 servings.

Crème de LA Coast
Small World Guild-Childrens Hospital of Orange County, California

Bavarian Apple Tart

½ cup butter, softened
⅓ cup sugar
¼ teaspoon vanilla extract
1 cup all-purpose flour
1 (8-ounce) package cream cheese, softened
¼ cup sugar

1 egg
½ teaspoon vanilla extract
⅓ cup sugar
½ teaspoon ground cinnamon
4 cups peeled, sliced cooking apples

Cream butter and ⅓ cup sugar; add ¼ teaspoon vanilla, beating well. Add flour, beating well. Spread pastry in bottom and 2 inches up sides of a well-greased 9-inch springform pan. Set aside.

Combine cream cheese and ¼ cup sugar in a medium bowl; beat until light and fluffy. Add egg and ½ teaspoon vanilla; beat well. Spread cream cheese mixture evenly over pastry.

Combine ⅓ cup sugar and cinnamon in a large bowl; stir well. Add apple slices, and toss gently to coat well. Arrange apple slices evenly over cream cheese mixture.

Bake at 450° for 10 minutes. Reduce heat to 400°, and bake 25 minutes. Let cool completely. Carefully remove sides of springform pan before serving. Yield: one 9-inch tart.

Even More Special
The Junior League of Durham and Orange Counties, North Carolina

Caramel-Apple Tart

3 cups all-purpose flour
¼ cup sugar
1½ teaspoons salt
½ cup butter or margarine
1 egg
¼ cup cold water
¼ cup vegetable oil
½ pound caramels (about 28)
½ cup evaporated milk
6 cups peeled, sliced cooking
  apples

1 cup sugar
⅓ cup all-purpose flour
2 teaspoons grated lemon
  rind
3 tablespoons fresh lemon
  juice
⅓ cup sugar
1 (8-ounce) package cream
  cheese, softened
1 egg
½ cup chopped walnuts

Combine 3 cups flour, ¼ cup sugar, and salt in a medium mixing bowl, and stir well; cut in butter with a pastry blender until mixture resembles coarse meal.

Combine 1 egg, water, and oil; sprinkle evenly over surface of flour mixture, and stir with a fork until dry ingredients are moistened. Shape into a ball.

Place dough on an 18- x 14-inch sheet of heavy-duty aluminum foil. Roll dough to a 17- x 12-inch rectangle. Fold edge of aluminum foil to form standing rim; flute edges of pastry. Place foil and pastry on a large baking sheet.

Combine caramels and evaporated milk in top of a double boiler. Bring water to a boil; reduce heat to low. Cook until caramels melt and mixture is smooth, stirring constantly. Set caramel mixture aside, and keep warm.

Combine apple slices, 1 cup sugar, ⅓ cup flour, lemon rind, and lemon juice in a large mixing bowl, tossing gently to coat well. Arrange apple slices evenly over pastry.

Pour caramel sauce in 5 lengthwise strips over apples.

Combine ⅓ cup sugar, cream cheese, and 1 egg, beating at medium speed of an electric mixer until smooth. Spoon cream cheese mixture between strips of caramel sauce. Sprinkle with chopped walnuts. Bake at 375° for 30 to 35 minutes or until apples are tender. Yield: 8 servings.   Mary Lou Wheeldon

Lorimor Centennial Cookbook, Volume II
The Centennial Committee
Lorimor, Iowa

Apple Crisp

6 large cooking apples,
  peeled, cored, and chopped
  (about 2½ pounds)
½ cup sugar
2 teaspoons lemon juice
½ teaspoon ground cinnamon
¼ teaspoon ground cloves
¾ cup all-purpose flour
½ cup sugar
⅛ teaspoon salt
¼ cup plus 2 tablespoons
  butter or margarine
½ cup chopped walnuts or
  pecans

Combine first 5 ingredients in a large bowl; stir well. Place apple mixture in a 2-quart casserole.

Combine flour, ½ cup sugar, and salt in a medium mixing bowl; cut in butter with a pastry blender until mixture resembles coarse meal. Stir in chopped walnuts, and sprinkle mixture evenly over apples. Bake at 350° for 45 minutes to 1 hour or until lightly browned. Yield: 8 servings.   Carolyn Clarke

Montgomery County Fair History Cookbook
The Montgomery County Fair Association, Inc.
Conroe, Texas

Cranberry-Apple Crisp

3 cups peeled, coarsely
  chopped cooking apples
2 cups fresh cranberries
1 cup sugar
1 tablespoon fresh lemon
  juice
1 teaspoon ground cinnamon
1½ cups regular oats,
  uncooked
1 cup firmly packed brown
  sugar
½ teaspoon salt
½ cup butter or margarine,
  softened

Combine first 5 ingredients in a large mixing bowl; toss gently. Place apple mixture in a greased 8-inch square baking dish. Combine oats, brown sugar, and salt; stir well. Cut in butter with a pastry blender until mixture resembles coarse meal. Sprinkle oat mixture over fruit mixture. Bake at 350° for 1 hour. Serve warm. Yield: 6 to 8 servings.   Jill Walpert

Another Taste of Palm Springs
Tiempo de Los Niños, an Auxiliary of Desert Hospital
Palm Springs, California

Crisped Almond Apples

5 large Granny Smith or
  other cooking apples
¾ cup plus 2 tablespoons
  sugar, divided
1 tablespoon plus 1½
  teaspoons lemon juice
1 cup all-purpose flour
¼ teaspoon salt
¼ teaspoon ground cinnamon
⅔ cup finely chopped
  blanched almonds
½ cup unsalted butter or
  margarine, melted
¾ teaspoon vanilla extract
1½ cups whipping cream
2 tablespoons sugar

Peel and core apples; cut into 1-inch-thick slices. Combine apple slices, 2 tablespoons sugar, and lemon juice in a large bowl; toss gently. Arrange apple slices in a greased 13- x 9- x 2-inch baking dish in 3 lengthwise rows. Set aside.

Combine flour, ¾ cup sugar, salt, and cinnamon in a medium mixing bowl, stirring well. Stir in almonds. Add melted butter and vanilla; stir until mixture resembles coarse meal. Sprinkle almond mixture evenly over apples. Bake at 400° for 30 to 35 minutes or until golden brown. Cool 10 to 15 minutes on a wire rack.

Beat whipping cream until foamy. Gradually add 2 tablespoons sugar, beating until soft peaks form. Serve warm apples with sweetened whipped cream. Yield: 6 to 8 servings.

California Treasure
The Junior League of Fresno, California

Poultry

A winding, tree-lined country roadway leading to a small farm in the Litchfield hills of Connecticut expresses the rural charm of this southernmost of the New England states.

☆☆☆

Garlic Chicken

1 whole garlic bulb,
   minced
1½ teaspoons salt
1½ teaspoons paprika

½ teaspoon pepper
1 (3½-pound) broiler-fryer
½ cup water

Combine garlic, salt, paprika, and pepper in a small bowl; mash with the back of a spoon to form a paste. Rub garlic mixture inside chicken cavity and over outside of chicken. Cover chicken, and chill at least 8 hours.

Place chicken, breast side up, in a large shallow roasting pan; add ½ cup water to pan. Loosely cover chicken with aluminum foil. Bake at 425° for 30 minutes. Reduce heat to 375°, and bake 1 hour or until done, basting occasionally and adding water to pan, if necessary. Yield 4 servings.   Irene Saiger

Pesach Potpourri
The Sinai Akiba Academy
Los Angeles, California

Baked Chicken Curry

½ cup honey
¼ cup prepared mustard
3 tablespoons butter or
   margarine, melted
3 tablespoons milk
2 teaspoons curry powder
1 teaspoon salt

⅛ teaspoon ground white
   pepper
1 (2½- to 3-pound)
   broiler-fryer, cut up
½ cup raisins
¼ cup chopped pecans
¼ cup shredded coconut

Combine honey, mustard, butter, milk, curry powder, salt, and pepper in a small bowl; stir well. Dip chicken in curry mixture. Place chicken in a greased 12- x 8- x 2-inch baking dish. Reserve remaining curry mixture, and set aside.

Bake chicken at 350° for 1 hour, basting occasionally with reserved curry mixture. Remove chicken from oven; sprinkle with raisins, pecans, and coconut. Bake an additional 15 minutes or until chicken is done. Yield: 4 servings.

Winning at the Table
The Junior League of Las Vegas, Nevada

Breast of Chicken Jubilee

4 chicken breast halves
¼ teaspoon salt
¼ teaspoon garlic salt
¼ teaspoon pepper
¼ cup butter or margarine
2 medium onions, sliced
1 (12-ounce) bottle chili sauce
½ cup firmly packed brown
  sugar
½ cup raisins
1 tablespoon Worcestershire
  sauce
1 cup dry sherry
1 (16-ounce) can pitted dark
  sweet cherries, drained
Hot cooked rice

Sprinkle chicken breast halves evenly with salt, garlic salt, and pepper. Melt butter in a large skillet over medium heat; add chicken breast halves, and cook until golden brown. Place chicken in a 2½-quart casserole.

Combine onion, chili sauce, sugar, raisins, and Worcestershire sauce in a medium bowl; spoon onion mixture over chicken. Cover and bake at 325° for 1 hour. Add sherry and sweet cherries to chicken mixture; cover and bake an additional 15 minutes or until chicken is done.

Remove chicken mixture to a serving platter, using a slotted spoon. Serve chicken with hot cooked rice. Yield: 4 servings.

Steeped in Tradition
The Junior Service League of DeLand, Florida

Herbed Chicken Breasts

3 tablespoons plus 1½
  teaspoons butter or
  margarine, melted
1 tablespoon grated onion
1 large clove garlic,
  crushed
1 teaspoon dried whole
  thyme
½ teaspoon salt
½ teaspoon pepper
½ teaspoon dried whole
  rosemary
¼ teaspoon rubbed sage
⅛ teaspoon dried whole
  marjoram
⅛ teaspoon hot sauce
4 large chicken breast halves,
  boned
1 tablespoon plus 1½
  teaspoons chopped fresh
  parsley (optional)

Combine melted butter, onion, garlic, thyme, salt, pepper, rosemary, sage, marjoram, and hot sauce in a small bowl, stirring well. Dip each chicken breast half in sauce, coating well. Tuck edges of chicken breasts under; place chicken, skin side up, in a greased 8-inch square baking dish. Bake at 425° for 20 minutes or until chicken is done, basting occasionally with sauce. Garnish with fresh parsley, if desired. Yield: 4 servings.   Hilary Rodham Clinton

Celebration: A Taste of Arkansas
The Sevier County Cookbook Committee
Lockesburg, Arkansas

Rice-Stuffed Chicken Breasts

½ pound sliced fresh mushrooms
1 small onion, chopped
½ cup chopped green pepper
1 tablespoon butter or margarine, melted
1 cup cooked long-grain rice
1 cup cooked wild rice
½ teaspoon salt
½ teaspoon Worcestershire sauce
¼ teaspoon pepper
⅛ teaspoon rubbed sage
8 chicken breast halves
1 cup butter or margarine, melted
Juice of 1 lime
1 tablespoon paprika

Sauté mushrooms, onion, and green pepper in 1 tablespoon butter in a large skillet. Remove from heat, and stir in rices, salt, Worcestershire sauce, pepper, and sage.

Gently separate chicken skin from flesh, forming pockets. Stuff pockets with rice mixture, and secure with wooden picks. Place stuffed chicken breast halves, skin side up, in an ungreased 13- x 9- x 2-inch baking dish.

Combine 1 cup butter, lime juice, and paprika; brush butter mixture over stuffed chicken breast halves. Bake at 350° for 1 hour, or until chicken is done, basting frequently with remaining butter mixture. Yield: 8 servings.   Kathleen Waguespack

The Bishop's Bounty
St. Mary's Training School for Retarded Children
Alexandria, Louisiana

Stuffed Chicken Breasts

2 cups ricotta cheese
½ pound fresh spinach, washed and chopped
½ cup grated Parmesan cheese
½ cup (2 ounces) shredded Gruyère or Swiss cheese
2 cloves garlic, minced
¼ teaspoon salt
¼ teaspoon pepper
1 egg
4 chicken breasts, boned
2 tablespoons butter or margarine

Combine ricotta cheese, spinach, Parmesan cheese, Gruyère cheese, garlic, salt, pepper, and egg in a large bowl, stirring well. Gently separate chicken skin from flesh, forming pockets. Stuff each pocket with 1 cup spinach mixture, and secure with a wooden pick. Place chicken breasts, skin side up, in a greased 13- x 9- x 2-inch baking dish; dot with butter. Bake at 350° for 50 to 60 minutes or until done, basting every 10 minutes with pan juices. Cut chicken breasts in half before serving. Yield: 8 servings.

Palette to Palate
The Junior League of St. Joseph and Albrecht Art Museum
St. Joseph, Missouri

Pesto-Stuffed Chicken Breasts

8 chicken breast halves, skinned and boned
1 pound fresh spinach
3 shallots, finely chopped
2 tablespoons unsalted butter or margarine, melted
Pesto Sauce, divided
½ cup ricotta cheese
1 egg yolk
¼ cup pine nuts, toasted
½ teaspoon seasoned salt
⅛ teaspoon pepper
4 (⅛-inch-thick) slices prosciutto
3 tablespoons lemon juice
3 tablespoons unsalted butter or margarine, melted
¼ cup mayonnaise

Place each chicken breast half between 2 sheets of wax paper, and flatten to ¼-inch thickness, using a meat mallet or rolling pin; set chicken aside.

Remove stems from spinach; wash leaves thoroughly, and tear into large pieces. Steam spinach in a 10-inch skillet over medium heat 2 minutes. Drain. Place spinach between layers of paper towels, and squeeze until barely moist; coarsely chop spinach.

Sauté shallots in 2 tablespoons butter in a small skillet until tender; drain. Combine shallots, ¼ cup Pesto Sauce, ricotta cheese, egg yolk, pine nuts, seasoned salt, and pepper in a large bowl; stir well. Add spinach, stirring well.

Cut prosciutto slices in half. Place one-half slice prosciutto on each chicken breast half. Spread about two tablespoons spinach mixture over prosciutto; roll up jellyroll fashion, starting with short side. Place chicken, seam side down, in an ungreased 13- x 9- x 2-inch baking dish. Combine lemon juice and 3 tablespoons butter; pour over chicken. Bake, uncovered, at 375° for 40 minutes or until done, basting occasionally with pan juices. Chill. Combine remaining ¾ cup Pesto Sauce and mayonnaise, stirring well. Slice chicken rolls crosswise, and serve with mayonnaise mixture. Yield: 8 servings.

Pesto Sauce

¼ cup pine nuts
3 cloves garlic, sliced
2 cups fresh basil leaves
½ teaspoon salt

½ cup olive oil
½ cup grated Parmesan
    cheese

Position knife blade in food processor bowl; add pine nuts and garlic. Cover and process until mixture forms a paste. Add basil and salt. With processor running, pour olive oil through food chute in a slow, steady stream until thoroughly combined. Cover and chill. Add Parmesan cheese, stirring well. Store Pesto Sauce in an airtight container in the refrigerator. Pesto Sauce may be refrigerated up to 1 week. Yield: 1 cup.

South of the Fork
The Junior League of Dallas, Texas

Champagne Chicken for Two

2 chicken breast halves, skinned and boned	1 tablespoon plus 1 teaspoon butter or margarine
Dash of salt	¼ pound fresh mushrooms, quartered
¼ teaspoon pepper	
2 teaspoons all-purpose flour	¾ cup whipping cream
1 tablespoon vegetable oil	¼ cup champagne

Sprinkle chicken breast halves with salt and pepper; dredge in flour. Heat oil in a large skillet over medium heat; add chicken, and cook until golden brown, turning to brown both sides. Remove chicken from skillet, reserving pan drippings. Drain chicken on paper towels, and set aside.

Add butter to pan drippings in skillet. Add mushrooms, and sauté until tender. Stir in cream and champagne. Return chicken to skillet. Bring to a boil; cover, reduce heat, and simmer 8 to 10 minutes or until chicken is done. Transfer chicken to a serving platter; set aside, and keep warm.

Cook sauce over medium heat 5 minutes or until liquid is reduced and sauce is thickened, stirring constantly. Pour sauce over chicken. Yield: 2 servings.   Steve Jones

Southern Secrets
SouthTrust Corporation
Birmingham, Alabama

Sherried Chicken with Artichokes

8 chicken breast halves, skinned and boned	¼ teaspoon garlic salt
½ cup all-purpose flour	¼ teaspoon onion salt
½ cup butter or margarine	¼ teaspoon dried whole rosemary
¾ pound fresh mushrooms, quartered	¼ teaspoon dried whole thyme
1 (9-ounce) package frozen artichoke hearts, thawed and drained	¼ teaspoon freshly ground pepper
⅓ cup chopped green onions	1 cup dry sherry
⅓ cup chopped fresh parsley	¾ cup canned diluted chicken broth
2 tablespoons lemon juice	2 bay leaves
	½ cup whipping cream

Dredge chicken in flour. Melt butter in a skillet over medium heat; add chicken, and cook until brown. Place in a 13- x 9- x 2-inch baking dish; add mushrooms and next 9 ingredients. Pour sherry and broth over chicken; top with bay leaves. Cover and bake at 350° for 40 to 50 minutes or until chicken is done.

Remove chicken and vegetables to a serving platter, using a slotted spoon; keep warm. Remove and discard bay leaves. Place remaining liquid in a saucepan, and cook over medium heat until mixture is reduced by half. Stir in cream, and continue cooking until mixture is slightly thickened. Pour sauce over chicken and vegetables. Yield: 8 servings.

Sounds Delicious!
The Volunteer Council of the Tulsa Philharmonic Society, Inc.
Tulsa, Oklahoma

Herbed Chicken

8 chicken breast halves, skinned and boned
4 green onions, chopped
¾ teaspoon dried whole tarragon
2 tablespoons butter or margarine
½ teaspoon salt
⅛ teaspoon pepper
½ cup Chablis or other dry white wine
1 egg white
⅔ cup mayonnaise
½ cup grated Parmesan cheese
Chopped fresh parsley (optional)

Place chicken in a 13- x 9- x 2-inch baking dish. Sprinkle with green onions and tarragon; dot with butter. Sprinkle with salt and pepper; add wine. Bake, uncovered, at 350° for 30 minutes. Remove chicken from oven; keep warm.

Beat egg white (at room temperature) at high speed of an electric mixer until soft peaks form; fold in mayonnaise. Top chicken with dollops of mayonnaise mixture, and sprinkle with Parmesan cheese. Bake an additional 10 to 15 minutes or until lightly browned. Garnish with parsley, if desired. Yield: 8 servings.

A Slice of Nantucket
St. Mary's Guild, St. Mary-Our Lady of the Isle Church
Nantucket, Massachusetts

Bourbon-Mustard Chicken

4 chicken breast halves,
  skinned and boned
¼ cup firmly packed dark
  brown sugar
¼ cup Dijon mustard
¼ cup bourbon
2 green onions, thinly sliced

1 teaspoon salt
1 teaspoon Worcestershire
  sauce
1 tablespoon butter or
  margarine
1 tablespoon vegetable oil

Place chicken between 2 sheets of wax paper; pound to ¼-inch thickness, using a meat mallet or rolling pin. Place chicken in a shallow baking dish.

Combine brown sugar and next 5 ingredients, stirring well. Brush mustard mixture evenly over both sides of chicken breast halves. Cover and marinate in refrigerator 1 hour.

Remove chicken from marinade, reserving marinade. Combine butter and oil in a large skillet, and place over medium-high heat. Sauté chicken 3 to 4 minutes on each side or until done. Remove chicken to a serving platter, and keep warm. Drain and discard pan drippings. Add reserved marinade to skillet; bring to a boil, stirring constantly. Pour sauce over chicken. Yield: 4 servings.

Gatherings
The Junior League of Milwaukee, Wisconsin

Pecan-Breaded Chicken Breasts with Mustard Sauce

4 chicken breast halves,
  skinned and boned
½ teaspoon salt
¼ teaspoon freshly ground
  pepper
¼ cup plus 2 tablespoons
  butter or margarine, melted
3 tablespoons Dijon mustard

1½ cups ground pecans
¼ cup butter or margarine
2 tablespoons vegetable oil
¾ cup canned diluted
  chicken broth
⅔ cup commercial sour
  cream

Place chicken between 2 sheets of wax paper; flatten to ¼-inch thickness, using a meat mallet or rolling pin. Sprinkle chicken with salt and pepper.

Combine ¼ cup plus 2 tablespoons butter and mustard in a small bowl, stirring with a wire whisk until smooth. Dip chicken in mustard mixture; dredge in ground pecans.

Melt ¼ cup butter in a large skillet over medium heat; stir in oil. Add chicken, and cook 3 to 4 minutes on each side or until golden brown. Remove chicken from skillet, and drain on paper towels; keep warm.

Drain and discard pan drippings. Add chicken broth to skillet, and cook over medium heat, scraping sides and bottom of pan to loosen any remaining cooked on pieces of chicken and pecans. Add sour cream, and cook over medium heat until thoroughly heated, stirring constantly (do not boil). Serve sauce with chicken. Yield: 2 to 4 servings.   Mr. and Mrs. Charles S. Robb

VIP Cookbook, Volume VI
The American Cancer Society, Virginia Division
Vienna, Virginia

Chicken Saltimbocca

6 chicken breast halves,
   skinned and boned
3 (1-ounce) slices cooked
   ham, cut in half
3 (1-ounce) slices mozzarella
   cheese, cut in half
¾ teaspoon rubbed sage

⅓ cup fine, dry breadcrumbs
2 tablespoons grated
   Parmesan cheese
2 tablespoons chopped fresh
   parsley
¼ cup butter or margarine,
   melted

Place chicken breast halves between 2 sheets of wax paper; flatten to ¼-inch thickness, using a meat mallet or rolling pin. Top each piece of chicken with a ham slice and mozzarella cheese slice. Sprinkle ⅛ teaspoon sage over each cheese slice. Roll up jellyroll fashion, and secure with wooden picks.

Combine breadcrumbs, Parmesan cheese, and parsley. Dip chicken in butter; dredge in breadcrumb mixture. Place chicken in a greased 8-inch square baking dish. Bake at 350° for 45 minutes or until chicken is done. Yield: 6 servings.   Karen Duell

Remembering Our Heritage
Herndon Covenant Church Women
Herndon, Kansas

Chicken-Mushroom Kabobs

¼ cup cider vinegar
¼ cup soy sauce
2 tablespoons vegetable oil
2 tablespoons honey
2 small green onions, minced
4 chicken breast halves,
 skinned, boned, and cut
 into 1½-inch pieces

10 large fresh mushrooms,
 halved
10 slices bacon
1 (8-ounce) can sliced
 pineapple, drained
Vegetable cooking spray

Combine first 5 ingredients; stir well. Add chicken and mushrooms. Cover and marinate in refrigerator 2 hours.

Remove chicken and mushrooms from marinade, reserving marinade. Slice bacon in half crosswise. Place a piece of chicken and a mushroom half together, and wrap with a piece of bacon. Cut each pineapple slice into three pieces. Alternate chicken, mushrooms, and pineapple on 6 (12-inch) skewers, placing a mushroom half on each end of skewer. Place kabobs on a broiler rack coated with cooking spray; place in broiler pan. Broil 6 inches from heat 15 minutes or until chicken is done, turning and basting often with marinade. Yield: 4 servings.

Rave Revues
Lakewood Center Associates, Lakewood Center for the Arts
Lake Oswego, Oregon

Twin Pepper Chicken

8 chicken breast halves,
 skinned and boned
1 tablespoon cornstarch
2 tablespoons dry sherry
2 tablespoons soy sauce
2 tablespoons vegetable oil
2 cloves garlic, minced
¼ cup plus 1 tablespoon
 vegetable oil, divided
6 dried red pepper pods
1 sweet red pepper, cut into
 ¼-inch strips

½ pound fresh mushrooms,
 thinly sliced
3 green onions, sliced
 diagonally into 1-inch
 pieces
1 tablespoon cornstarch
¾ cup canned diluted
 chicken broth
2 tablespoons sesame oil

Slice chicken crosswise into ¼-inch strips. Combine 1 tablespoon cornstarch and next 4 ingredients in a large bowl, stirring well. Add chicken pieces; cover and marinate in refrigerator at least 1 hour.

Pour 3 tablespoons vegetable oil around top of preheated wok, coating sides; heat at medium high (325°) for 2 minutes. Add dried red pepper pods, and stir-fry 20 seconds or until peppers turn dark.

Add chicken pieces, and stir-fry 5 to 8 minutes. Remove chicken and peppers from wok; set aside. Add remaining 2 tablespoons vegetable oil to wok; heat 1 minute. Add sweet red pepper, and stir-fry 30 seconds. Add mushrooms and onions; stir-fry 1 minute. Return chicken and peppers to wok; stir gently to combine.

Combine 1 tablespoon cornstarch and chicken broth, stirring well. Add cornstarch mixture to chicken mixture, and stir-fry 1 minute or until mixture is thickened. Stir in sesame oil. Serve immediately. Yield: 6 to 8 servings.

Even More Special
The Junior League of Durham and Orange Counties,
North Carolina

Chicken Upside Down

⅔ cup butter or margarine	2½ cups cooked chicken, cut
⅔ cup all-purpose flour	into ½-inch cubes
3 cups chicken broth	1 egg
2 cups milk	⅔ cup milk
1 teaspoon salt	3 tablespoons vegetable oil
½ teaspoon pepper	1 cup self-rising cornmeal
2 tablespoons lemon juice	1 teaspoon sugar

Melt butter in a saucepan over medium heat. Add flour, stirring constantly. Gradually add chicken broth and milk; cook over medium heat, stirring constantly, until thickened and bubbly. Stir in salt, pepper, lemon juice, and chicken. Pour mixture into a greased 13- x 9- x 2-inch baking dish. Combine egg and remaining ingredients, stirring well; pour over chicken. Bake at 350° for 50 to 60 minutes or until golden brown. Yield: 6 to 8 servings.

Uptown Down South
The Junior League of Greenville, South Carolina

Chicken with Fruit and Almonds

2 cups milk
1 cup grated coconut
3 medium onions, sliced
2 cloves garlic, crushed
2 tablespoons grated lemon
  rind
3 tablespoons lemon juice
2 tablespoons Damson plum
  jam or preserves
1 tablespoon ground
  coriander
1 teaspoon sugar
1 teaspoon salt

1 teaspoon anise seeds,
  crushed
1 teaspoon ground ginger
½ teaspoon ground saffron
¼ teaspoon chili powder
1 tablespoon vegetable oil
3 tablespoons butter
12 (4-ounce) chicken breast
  halves, skinned, boned, and
  cut into 1-inch pieces
1 cup whole blanched
  almonds
Hot cooked rice

Combine milk and coconut in a saucepan. Bring just to a boil over medium heat; remove from heat, and let stand 30 minutes. Drain well, reserving milk. Press coconut between paper towels to remove excess moisture; set aside.

Combine onion and next 11 ingredients; stir well. Set aside.

Combine oil and butter in a large skillet; cook over medium heat until butter melts. Add reserved coconut, and cook until lightly browned, stirring constantly. Remove coconut with a slotted spoon; set aside. Add chicken to oil in skillet; cook until lightly browned, stirring occasionally. Add reserved onion mixture; stir gently. Stir in reserved milk, coconut, and almonds. Bring to a boil; cover, reduce heat, and simmer 10 minutes or until chicken is tender. Serve over hot cooked rice. Yield: 12 servings.   Jane Mold

Elizabeth H. Brown Humane Society Cookbook
The Elizabeth H. Brown Humane Society, Inc.
Orleans, Vermont

Janet and Gana's Enchilada Suisse

½ cup chopped onion
1 clove garlic, minced
¼ cup vegetable oil, divided
2 cups diced cooked chicken
½ cup green chile salsa
¼ cup chopped green chiles
2 tablespoons chopped fresh parsley
2 teaspoons all-purpose flour
2 chicken-flavored bouillon cubes

Dash of paprika
1 cup milk
½ cup whipping cream
1½ cups (6 ounces) shredded Monterey Jack cheese, divided
6 (6-inch) corn tortillas
Salsa (recipe follows)

Sauté onion and garlic in 1 tablespoon oil until tender. Remove from heat, and set aside.

Combine chicken and next 3 ingredients; add sautéed onion mixture to chicken mixture, tossing gently. Set aside.

Combine flour, bouillon cubes, and paprika in a heavy saucepan. Gradually add milk and whipping cream; cook over medium heat until bouillon cubes dissolve and mixture is thickened and bubbly, stirring constantly. Add ½ cup cheese, stirring until cheese melts. Pour sauce into a large shallow dish; set aside.

Fry tortillas, one at a time, in remaining 3 tablespoons oil in a medium skillet, 5 seconds on each side or just until tortillas are softened. Drain on paper towels. Dip each tortilla, one at a time, in cheese sauce.

Place 2 tablespoons chicken mixture on each tortilla; roll up tortillas, and place seam side down in a 2-quart casserole. Pour remaining cheese sauce over tortillas. Sprinkle remaining 1 cup cheese over tortillas. Cover and bake at 350° for 15 minutes. Uncover and bake an additional 15 minutes. Spoon salsa down center of casserole. Yield: 6 servings.

Salsa

⅔ cup chopped tomato
½ cup chopped green onions

⅓ cup diced green chiles

Combine all ingredients in a small mixing bowl, and stir well. Yield: 1½ cups.

Cathy Carson

Diamonds in the Desert
The Woman's League of Ozona, Texas

Chicken Livers Supreme

12 slices bacon
1 medium onion, thinly
  sliced
1 green pepper, cut into
  ¼-inch strips
1 pound chicken livers
3 tablespoons butter or
  margarine, melted

⅓ cup sliced pimiento-stuffed
  olives
⅓ cup sliced ripe olives
3 tablespoons dry sherry
Toasted and buttered English
  muffins

Cook bacon in a large skillet until crisp; remove bacon, reserving drippings in skillet. Crumble bacon, and set aside. Sauté onion and green pepper in drippings until tender. Drain and set aside.

Sauté livers in butter in a large skillet 5 to 8 minutes or until livers are browned. Stir in bacon, sautéed vegetables, olives, and sherry. Cook over medium heat until thoroughly heated. Serve over English muffins. Yield: 6 servings.   Helen L. Cashman

The Great Entertainer Cookbook
The Buffalo Bill Historical Center
Cody, Wyoming

Fruited Rock Cornish Game Hens

2 (1-pound) Cornish hens
½ teaspoon onion salt
¼ teaspoon pepper
½ cup butter, melted
1 (11-ounce) can mandarin
  oranges, undrained

1 (10-ounce) jar maraschino
  cherries, undrained
1 tablespoon cornstarch
⅛ teaspoon salt
2 tablespoons lemon juice
2 tablespoons rum or brandy

Remove giblets from hens; reserve for other uses. Rinse hens with cold water, and pat dry. Sprinkle cavities with onion salt and pepper. Close cavities, securing with wooden picks; truss.

Place hens, breast side up, in a shallow roasting pan; brush hens with melted butter. Bake at 400° for 45 to 60 minutes or until juices run clear when thigh is pierced with a fork, basting occasionally with pan drippings. Remove from oven, and keep warm.

Drain oranges and cherries, reserving syrups; set fruit aside. Combine syrups, adding water to measure 1 cup, if necessary.

Combine cornstarch, ⅛ teaspoon salt, and lemon juice in a saucepan; stir well. Add syrup mixture. Bring to a boil over medium heat, and cook 1 minute, stirring constantly. Stir in fruit; cook until thoroughly heated. Transfer to a chafing dish; keep warm.

Place rum in a small long-handled saucepan; heat until warm (do not boil). Remove from heat. Ignite with a long match, and pour over fruit sauce. Stir until flames die down. Serve fruit sauce with hens. Yield: 2 servings.

Crème de LA Coast
Small World Guild-Childrens Hospital of Orange County,
California

Quail in Orange Sauce

½ cup all-purpose flour
1 teaspoon seasoned salt
¼ teaspoon pepper
8 quail, cleaned
½ cup vegetable oil
½ cup chopped onion
½ green pepper, chopped
2 cloves garlic, minced
1 carrot, scraped and sliced
1 cup canned diluted chicken broth
1 cup Chablis or other dry white wine
1 tablespoon grated orange rind
1 teaspoon Worcesteshire sauce
Commercial sour cream (optional)

Combine flour, salt, and pepper. Dredge quail in flour mixture; brown in hot oil in a large skillet. Remove quail to a 13- x 9- x 2-inch baking dish, reserving drippings in skillet.

Sauté onion, green pepper, and garlic in drippings in skillet until tender. Add carrot, chicken broth, and wine, stirring well. Cover and simmer 15 minutes. Strain sauce, discarding vegetables. Pour sauce over quail. Sprinkle orange rind and Worcestershire sauce over quail. Cover and bake at 350° for 45 minutes. Turn off oven; leave quail in oven 30 minutes. Serve quail with a dollop of sour cream, if desired. Yield: 4 servings.   Vicki Rado

Lone Star Legacy II
The Junior Forum of Austin, Texas

Norma's Turkey alla Lombarda

1 (10- to 12-pound) turkey
3 cups water
8 cups soft breadcrumbs or
  unseasoned croutons
¼ cup grated Parmesan
  cheese
2 tablespoons poultry
  seasoning
1 teaspoon dried whole
  oregano
1 teaspoon freshly ground
  pepper

⅓ pound Italian sausage
4 cups chopped onion
2 cups peeled, chopped
  cooking apples
⅔ cup canned chestnuts,
  chopped
⅓ cup pine nuts
2 eggs, beaten
1 teaspoon dried whole
  rosemary, crushed
1½ cups Chablis or other dry
  white wine

Remove giblets and neck from turkey; rinse and place in a small saucepan with 3 cups water. Bring to a boil; cover, reduce heat, and simmer 30 minutes. Remove giblets and neck from broth, reserving broth. Set aside, and let cool.

Combine breadcrumbs and next 4 ingredients in a large bowl, stirring well. Set aside.

Remove sausage from casing. Cook sausage in a large skillet over high heat until sausage browns, stirring to crumble meat. Remove meat with a slotted spoon, reserving pan drippings in skillet. Add sausage to breadcrumb mixture; stir well. Add onion to pan drippings in skillet; cook over medium heat until golden. Remove with a slotted spoon, and stir into breadcrumb mixture. Combine apple, chestnuts, and pine nuts. Add to breadcrumb mixture, stirring well. Remove meat from reserved turkey neck; coarsely chop meat and giblets. Stir meat and giblets into breadcrumb mixture. Combine eggs and 1 cup reserved broth; stir well. Pour over breadcrumb mixture, and stir well.

Rinse turkey with cold water; pat dry. Stuff dressing into body cavities of turkey. If excess skin around tail has been cut away, tuck legs under flap of skin around tail. If skin is intact, close cavity with skewers, and truss. Tie ends of legs to tail with cord. Lift wingtips up and over back, and tuck under bird. Spoon remaining dressing into a greased 11- x 7- x 2-inch baking dish. Cover and chill.

Place turkey in a shallow roasting pan, breast side up; rub bird with crushed rosemary. Pour wine in roasting pan around bird. Insert meat thermometer in meaty part of turkey thigh, making sure thermometer does not touch bone. Bake at 325° until meat thermometer reaches 185°. If turkey starts to brown too much, cover loosely with aluminum foil.

When turkey is two-thirds done, cut the cord or band of skin holding drumstick ends to tail; this will ensure that the thighs are cooked internally. Turkey is done when drumsticks are easily moved up and down. Let stand 15 minutes before carving.

Bake remaining dressing at 350° for 30 to 40 minutes. Yield: 18 to 20 servings.   Paola Stearns

The Spence Collection
The Spence School
New York, New York

Spicy Grilled Turkey Breast

1½ teaspoons salt
1½ teaspoons dry mustard
1½ teaspoons chili powder
2½ teaspoons tarragon vinegar
1 (5½- to 6-pound) turkey breast, skinned and boned
3 tablespoons chopped onion
3 tablespoons vegetable oil
½ cup water
¼ cup tarragon vinegar
3 tablespoons butter
2 tablespoons Worcestershire sauce
1 tablespoon plus 1 teaspoon sugar
2 teaspoons salt
2 teaspoons dry mustard
2 teaspoons chili powder
2 teaspoons pepper
2 cloves garlic, minced
½ teaspoon hot sauce
⅛ teaspoon sweet red pepper flakes

Combine first 4 ingredients; stir well. Brush mixture evenly over both sides of turkey breast; place in a large shallow dish. Cover and chill at least 1 hour.

Sauté onion in oil in a saucepan until tender. Stir in water and remaining ingredients; simmer 20 minutes. Set aside.

Insert meat thermometer in meaty portion of breast, making sure it does not touch bone. Grill over medium coals 45 minutes to 1½ hours or until meat thermometer registers 185°, turning and basting frequently with sauce. Cover and let stand 10 minutes before slicing. Yield: 10 to 12 servings.

California Heritage Continues
The Junior League of Pasadena, California

Turkey-Wild Rice Supreme

1 cup uncooked wild rice
½ cup chopped onion
½ cup butter or margarine,
  melted
¼ cup all-purpose flour
2 (3-ounce) cans mushroom
  slices, broiled in butter and
  undrained
1½ cups half-and-half

3 cups diced cooked turkey
1 (4-ounce) jar diced
  pimiento, drained
2 tablespoons chopped fresh
  parsley
1½ teaspoons salt
¼ teaspoon pepper
½ cup slivered blanched
  almonds

Wash wild rice in 3 changes of hot water; drain. Cook wild rice according to package directions, omitting salt.

Sauté onion in butter in a large Dutch oven. Add flour, stirring until smooth. Cook 1 minute, stirring constantly. Drain mushrooms, reserving liquid. Set mushrooms aside. Add water to reserved liquid to measure 1½ cups. Gradually add liquid and half-and-half to onion mixture, and cook until slightly thickened and bubbly, stirring constantly. Remove from heat. Stir in wild rice, mushrooms, turkey, pimiento, parsley, salt, and pepper. Spoon into a greased 2½-quart casserole. Sprinkle with almonds. Bake at 350° for 40 minutes. Yield: 6 to 8 servings.

Wild Rice, Star of the North
The 1006 Summit Avenue Society
St. Paul, Minnesota

Salads &
Salad Dressings

Sandy beaches, sunbathers, and palm trees swaying in warm breezes are as standard as abundant sunshine and citrus fruit in Florida. This state is the leading producer of our country's oranges, grapefruit, and tangerines.

☆☆☆

Carrot Salad

1½ cups shredded carrot
1½ cups unpeeled red apple, chopped
1 tablespoon finely chopped onion
2 tablespoons vegetable oil

2 tablespoons pineapple juice
1½ teaspoons cider vinegar
⅛ teaspoon salt
⅛ teaspoon ground ginger
2 tablespoons chopped pecans or walnuts

Combine carrot, apple, and onion in a bowl; toss gently. Set aside. Combine oil and next 4 ingredients, stirring well. Pour dressing over carrot mixture; toss gently. Cover and chill. Add pecans, and toss gently just before serving. Yield: 4 servings.   Donna Huffman

M.A.E.H. Cook Book
The Michigan Association of Extension Homemakers
Hastings, Michigan

Broccoli and Cauliflower Salad

1 lemon
2 cloves garlic
3 tablespoons salt
3 quarts water
1 medium cauliflower, broken into flowerets

4 cups broccoli flowerets
1 pint cherry tomatoes
1 cup mayonnaise
2 tablespoons fresh lemon juice
½ teaspoon dry mustard

Remove rind from lemon; set lemon aside. Combine lemon rind, garlic, salt, and water in a large Dutch oven. Bring to a boil over high heat; boil 5 minutes. Add cauliflower and broccoli flowerets; boil 5 minutes or until vegetables are crisp-tender. Drain vegetables, discarding lemon rind and garlic cloves. Rinse vegetables under cold running water.

Arrange broccoli and cauliflower in rings around edge of a serving platter. Place tomatoes in center of ring. Cover and chill.

Combine mayonnaise, lemon juice, and mustard in a small bowl, stirring well. Cover and chill thoroughly; serve dressing with salad. Yield: 6 to 8 servings.   Viola Petty

. . . More Than Cookies!
The Northwest Georgia Girl Scout Council, Inc.
Atlanta, Georgia

Fresh Mushroom Salad

¼ cup vegetable oil
¼ cup olive oil
1 green onion, minced
1 tablespoon lemon juice
1 tablespoon white wine vinegar
1 tablespoon whipping cream
1 teaspoon chopped fresh basil leaves
½ teaspoon dry mustard
¼ teaspoon salt
¼ teaspoon freshly ground pepper
1 pound fresh mushrooms, sliced
Bibb or Boston lettuce leaves
6 cherry tomatoes, halved

Combine oils, green onion, lemon juice, vinegar, whipping cream, basil, mustard, salt, and pepper in a jar; cover tightly, and shake vigorously. Place mushrooms in a large serving bowl. Pour dressing over mushrooms, and toss gently. Serve mushroom mixture on lettuce leaves. Top with cherry tomato halves. Yield: 6 servings.

Even More Special
The Junior League of Durham and Orange Counties,
North Carolina

Tomatoes Vinaigrette

12 (½-inch-thick) slices tomato
1 cup olive oil
⅓ cup red wine vinegar
2 cloves garlic, crushed
2 teaspoons dried whole oregano
1 teaspoon salt
½ teaspoon dry mustard
½ teaspoon pepper
Lettuce leaves
2 green onions, minced
2 teaspoons chopped fresh parsley

Place tomato slices in a large shallow dish. Combine oil and next 6 ingredients in a small bowl; beat with a wire whisk until blended. Pour vinaigrette over tomatoes. Cover and chill at least 2 hours, basting tomatoes with vinaigrette occasionally.

To serve, remove tomatoes from vinaigrette, and arrange on lettuce leaves. Sprinkle tomatoes with a small amount of vinaigrette. Garnish with green onions and parsley. Yield: 4 to 6 servings.

Winning at the Table
The Junior League of Las Vegas, Nevada

Dick Reynolds' Favorite New Potato Salad

2½ pounds new potatoes
Mustard Vinaigrette
¼ cup finely chopped fresh dillweed
2 green onions, finely chopped

¼ teaspoon salt
⅛ teaspoon freshly ground pepper
1 cup commercial sour cream

Wash potatoes; cook in boiling water to cover 15 to 20 minutes or until tender. Drain and cool slightly. Cut potatoes in half, and place in a large bowl.

Pour Mustard Vinaigrette over potatoes; add dillweed and green onions, and toss gently. Sprinkle with salt and pepper. Gently fold in sour cream. Serve immediately. Yield: 8 servings.

Mustard Vinaigrette

¼ cup white wine vinegar
1 tablespoon Dijon mustard
1 teaspoon salt

⅛ teaspoon freshly ground pepper
1 cup olive oil

Combine all ingredients except oil in container of an electric blender; with blender running, gradually add oil in a slow, steady stream, processing until mixture is smooth and slightly thickened. Yield: 1¼ cups.

Dick Reynolds

Sooner Sampler
The Junior League of Norman, Oklahoma

German Potato Salad

2 pounds red potatoes
6 thick slices bacon
½ cup finely chopped onion
⅓ cup vinegar
⅓ cup water
1 teaspoon sugar
½ teaspoon pepper

Cook potatoes in boiling water to cover 15 minutes or until tender. Drain; cool slightly. Peel and slice potatoes. Place in a bowl; set aside. Cook bacon in a skillet until crisp; remove bacon, reserving ½ cup drippings in skillet. Crumble bacon; set aside. Sauté onion in drippings until tender. Stir in vinegar, water, sugar, and pepper. Cook 1 minute; add bacon, and cook until heated. Pour over potatoes; toss gently. Serve immediately. Yield: 6 servings.

The Minnesota Ethnic Food Book
The Minnesota Historical Society
St. Paul, Minnesota

Spicy Thai Slaw

1 medium cucumber
2 serrano chiles
1 small Savoy cabbage, shredded (about 1 pound)
4 green onions, minced
½ cup unsalted dry-roasted peanuts, chopped
2 cloves garlic, minced
⅓ cup vegetable oil
¼ cup rice wine vinegar
3 tablespoons chopped fresh cilantro
2 tablespoons sugar
2 tablespoons light sesame oil
½ teaspoon curry powder
⅛ teaspoon soy sauce

Peel cucumber, and cut in half lengthwise; scoop out and discard seeds. Coarsely chop cucumber; set aside.

Rinse chiles; remove and discard stem ends. Cut chiles in half lengthwise; remove and discard seeds. Chop chiles. (Wear rubber gloves when working with chiles.) Combine cucumber, chiles, cabbage, green onions, peanuts, and garlic in a bowl; toss well. Combine oil and remaining ingredients; stir with a wire whisk until well blended. Pour dressing over cabbage mixture; toss gently. Cover and chill at least 3 hours before serving. Yield: 6 to 8 servings.

Delicious Decisions
The Junior League of San Diego, California

Hawaiian Coleslaw

4 cups finely shredded
   cabbage
1 (11-ounce) can mandarin
   oranges, drained
1 (8-ounce) can crushed
   pineapple, drained
½ cup mayonnaise

2 tablespoons frozen orange
   juice concentrate, thawed
½ teaspoon salt
¼ teaspoon ground white
   pepper
¼ teaspoon ground ginger
¼ teaspoon ground nutmeg

Combine cabbage, oranges, and pineapple; toss gently, and set aside. Combine mayonnaise and remaining ingredients; stir well. Pour dressing over cabbage mixture; toss gently. Cover and chill at least 6 hours. Yield: 6 servings.   Janina Larson

A Slice of Nantucket
St. Mary's Guild, St. Mary-Our Lady of the Isle Church
Nantucket, Massachusetts

Spinach Salad with Sweet-Sour Dressing

1 pound fresh spinach
1 (16-ounce) can bean
   sprouts, drained
1 (8-ounce) can sliced water
   chestnuts, drained
8 slices bacon, cooked and
   crumbled
4 hard-cooked eggs, sliced
½ cup sugar

1 medium onion, grated
½ cup vegetable oil
⅓ cup catsup
¼ cup red wine vinegar
2 tablespoons Worcestershire
   sauce
1 tablespoon sesame oil
½ teaspoon salt

Remove stems from spinach; wash leaves thoroughly, and pat dry. Tear into bite-size pieces. Combine spinach, bean sprouts, and next 3 ingredients; toss salad gently. Chill. Combine sugar and remaining ingredients in a jar. Cover tightly, and shake vigorously. Chill. Shake dressing well before pouring over salad; toss salad gently. Yield: 6 to 8 servings.   Dixie Harlan

The Bishop's Bounty
St. Mary's Training School for Retarded Children
Alexandria, Louisiana

Tri-Color Salad

1 large head Belgian endive
1 large head radicchio, torn
  into bite-size pieces
1 bunch watercress, trimmed
  and torn into bite-size
  pieces

½ pound bacon, cooked and
  crumbled
2 tablespoons pine nuts,
  toasted
Dressing (recipe follows)

Peel leaves from core of endive. Wash leaves, and pat dry with
paper towels. Arrange endive, radicchio, and watercress on individual salad plates. Chill thoroughly. Sprinkle crumbled bacon and
toasted pine nuts evenly over salads. Drizzle dressing evenly over
salads. Yield: 4 to 6 servings.

Dressing

3 tablespoons olive oil
3 tablespoons walnut oil
2 tablespoons raspberry
  vinegar

½ teaspoon sugar
½ teaspoon salt
⅛ teaspoon pepper

Combine all ingredients in a jar. Cover tightly, and shake
vigorously. Yield: ½ cup.

Make It Miami
The Guild of the Museum of Science, Inc.
Miami, Florida

Bishie's Rice Salad

1½ cups uncooked long-grain
  rice
1 cup frozen English peas
½ cup water
½ teaspoon sugar
½ teaspoon dried whole
  rosemary
¾ cup thinly sliced
  celery
¾ cup slivered almonds,
  toasted

½ cup raisins
½ cup commercial sour
  cream
½ cup mayonnaise
¼ cup plus 1 tablespoon
  chutney, chopped
1 teaspoon curry powder
¼ teaspoon salt
⅛ teaspoon pepper

Cook rice according to package directions; chill.

Combine peas, water, rosemary, and sugar in a saucepan. Bring to a boil; cover, reduce heat, and simmer 10 minutes. Drain; let cool.

Combine rice, peas, celery, almonds, and raisins in a large bowl; toss gently. Combine sour cream and remaining ingredients, stirring well. Add sour cream mixture to rice mixture, stirring well. Cover and chill at least 8 hours. Yield: 6 servings.   Bishie Beatty

A Visual Feast
The Founders Society, Detroit Institute of Arts
Detroit, Michigan

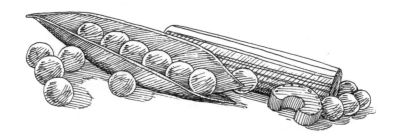

Wild Rice and Artichoke Heart Salad

1 cup uncooked wild rice
2 (6-ounce) jars quartered and marinated artichoke hearts, undrained
3 medium tomatoes, chopped
1 (8-ounce) can sliced water chestnuts, drained
1 (4-ounce) can sliced mushrooms, drained
1 cup commercial Italian salad dressing

Wash rice in 3 changes of hot water; drain. Cook according to package directions, omitting salt. Let cool.

Drain 1 jar artichoke hearts; discard marinade. Combine rice, drained artichoke hearts, undrained artichoke hearts, chopped tomato, water chestnuts, and mushrooms in a large bowl. Pour dressing over vegetable mixture; toss gently. Cover and chill at least 8 hours. Drain before serving. Yield: 8 to 10 servings.

Wild Rice, Star of the North
The 1006 Summit Avenue Society
St. Paul, Minnesota

North Shore Chicken Salad

¼ cup rice wine vinegar
2 cloves garlic, minced
1 tablespoon Dijon mustard
½ teaspoon salt
¼ teaspoon sugar
¼ teaspoon freshly ground
  pepper
⅓ cup vegetable oil
4 cups cooked wild rice
  (cooked in chicken broth)
1½ cups chopped cooked
  chicken

½ cup diced sweet red
  pepper
½ cup fresh snow pea pods,
  trimmed and cut into
  1-inch pieces
3 green onions, chopped
2 tablespoons lemon juice
1 or 2 avocados, cut into
  1-inch pieces
1 cup pecan halves, toasted
Lettuce leaves

Combine first 6 ingredients in container of an electric blender; cover and process at high speed 10 seconds or until thoroughly blended. With blender running, gradually add oil in a slow, steady stream; process 30 seconds or until thickened. Set aside.

Combine wild rice, chicken, sweet red pepper, snow peas, green onions, and lemon juice in a large bowl, tossing gently. Pour dressing over chicken mixture, tossing gently. Cover and chill 2 to 4 hours. Stir in avocado and pecans. Serve salad over lettuce leaves. Yield: 6 servings.

Celebrated Seasons
The Junior League of Minneapolis, Minnesota

Wild Rice-Seafood Salad

3 cups cooked wild rice
½ pound fresh lump
  crabmeat, drained and flaked
1 large tomato, peeled,
  seeded, and chopped
1 cup thinly sliced celery
½ cup chopped green onions
¼ teaspoon salt

⅛ teaspoon pepper
⅓ cup mayonnaise
⅓ cup commercial sour cream
¼ cup chili sauce
1 tablespoon lemon juice
1 teaspoon Dijon mustard
Lettuce leaves
Fresh parsley sprigs

Combine first 7 ingredients in a large bowl; toss well. Combine mayonnaise, sour cream, chili sauce, lemon juice, and mustard; stir well. Add mayonnaise mixture to wild rice mixture, stirring well.

Cover and chill. To serve, spoon salad onto lettuce leaves. Garnish with parsley sprigs. Yield: 6 servings.

Concertos for Cooks
The North Group, Symphony Women's Committee
Indianapolis, Indiana

Green Pasta Salad

¾ cup fresh spinach leaves, chopped
½ cup fresh parsley sprigs, chopped
4 green onions, cut into 1-inch pieces
1 clove garlic, crushed
¾ cup mayonnaise
¾ cup plain yogurt
3 tablespoons pesto sauce
2 tablespoons minced fresh chives
½ teaspoon salt
¼ teaspoon pepper

3 cups water
1 pound unpeeled medium-size fresh shrimp
6 quarts water
2 tablespoons olive oil
1 tablespoon salt
1 clove garlic, crushed
1 (12-ounce) package rotini
1 tablespoon olive oil
1 (10-ounce) package frozen English peas, thawed
¼ pound salami, chopped
1 (2-ounce) jar sliced pimiento, drained

Combine first 4 ingredients in container of an electric blender; cover and process until minced. Add mayonnaise, yogurt, pesto sauce, chives, ½ teaspoon salt, and pepper; process until well blended, scraping sides of container occasionally. Chill.

Bring 3 cups water to a boil; add shrimp, and cook 3 to 5 minutes. Drain; rinse with cold water. Chill. Peel and devein shrimp. Set aside.

Combine 6 quarts water, 2 tablespoons olive oil, 1 tablespoon salt, and 1 clove garlic in a large Dutch oven; bring to a boil. Add rotini; cook 8 minutes or until tender. Drain. Rinse with cold water; drain.

Combine rotini and 1 tablespoon olive oil in a large bowl; toss lightly to coat. Add mayonnaise mixture, shrimp, peas, salami, and pimiento; toss well. Cover and chill thoroughly. Yield: 10 servings.

Rave Revues
Lakewood Center Associates, Lakewood Center for the Arts
Lake Oswego, Oregon

Lemon-Cream Dressing

½ cup mayonnaise
½ teaspoon prepared mustard
1 tablespoon grated lemon
rind

3 tablespoons fresh lemon
juice
½ cup whipping cream,
whipped

Combine mayonnaise and mustard in a small bowl; stir in lemon rind and lemon juice. Fold in whipped cream. Serve dressing over fruit. Yield: 1⅔ cups.   Narice Sutton

Calling All Cooks Two
The Telephone Pioneers of America
Birmingham, Alabama

Poppy Seed Dressing

2 cups vegetable oil
1½ cups sugar
⅔ cup vinegar
3 tablespoons onion juice

2 teaspoons salt
2 teaspoons prepared mustard
2 teaspoons poppy seeds

Combine first 6 ingredients, stirring until smooth. Stir in poppy seeds. Cover and chill. Stir dressing well before serving over salad greens. Yield: 3½ cups.   Alice Watson

Thou Preparest a Table Before Me
East Avenue United Methodist Church Women
York, Nebraska

Five-Herb Vinaigrette

½ cup vegetable oil
1 tablespoon sugar
2 tablespoons lemon juice
2 tablespoons vinegar
½ teaspoon salt
½ teaspoon dry mustard
½ teaspoon paprika
¼ teaspoon dried whole
tarragon

¼ teaspoon dried whole basil
¼ teaspoon dried whole
marjoram
¼ teaspoon dried whole
oregano
¼ teaspoon dried parsley
flakes
⅛ teaspoon garlic powder
⅛ teaspoon curry powder

Combine all ingredients in a jar; cover tightly, and shake vigorously. Chill thoroughly. Shake again before serving over salad greens. Yield: ¾ cup.

Taste of Today
BUNWC, North Shore Illinois Chapter
Northfield, Illinois

French Vinaigrette Dressing

½ cup fresh parsley sprigs
1 clove garlic
½ cup olive oil
½ cup vegetable oil
¼ cup red wine vinegar

2 tablespoons lemon juice
2 tablespoons Dijon mustard
1 teaspoon sugar
¼ teaspoon salt
⅛ teaspoon pepper

Position knife blade in food processor bowl; add parsley. Cover and process until finely chopped. Add garlic through food chute; pulse 3 or 4 times until finely minced. Add oils and remaining ingredients; process 3 to 5 seconds or until well blended. Cover and chill. Serve dressing over salad greens. Yield: 1½ cups.

Peachtree Bouquet
The Junior League of DeKalb County, Georgia

Favorite Green Salad Dressing

1 cup vegetable oil
¼ cup white wine vinegar
¼ cup commercial sour cream
2 tablespoons sugar
2 teaspoons chopped fresh parsley

1½ teaspoons salt
2 cloves garlic, crushed
½ teaspoon dry mustard
¼ teaspoon pepper

Combine all ingredients, stirring until well blended. Cover and chill. Serve dressing over salad greens. Yield: about 1½ cups.

Palm Country Cuisine
The Junior League of Greater Lakeland, Florida

True Blue Cheese Dressing

1 cup mayonnaise
1 (4-ounce) package blue
  cheese, crumbled
3 tablespoons milk
2 tablespoons lemon juice
1 tablespoon chopped onion

2 teaspoons sugar
¼ teaspoon salt
¼ teaspoon dry mustard
¼ teaspoon Worcestershire
  sauce

Combine all ingredients; stir well. Cover and chill. Serve dressing over salad greens. Yield: about 1¾ cups.   Betty Anderson

One Hundred Years of Sharing
Calvary Covenant Church Women
Evansville, Minnesota

Ranch Dressing

2 cups mayonnaise
2 cups buttermilk
1½ teaspoons chopped fresh
  parsley

1 teaspoon onion powder
1 teaspoon garlic powder
1 teaspoon garlic salt
⅛ teaspoon pepper

Combine all ingredients in a small bowl, stirring well. Cover tightly, and chill at least 8 hours. Serve dressing over salad greens. Yield: 4 cups.   Peg Oehrtman

Calvary Collections
Calvary Lutheran Church
Kalispell, Montana

Sauces &
Condiments

Sugar time in Vermont is an age-old spring rite. "Sap's a-runnin' " means the long winter is coming to an end, and it's time for the concentrated sap from the sugar maples to be harvested. Maple syrup was first prepared by Indians by dropping hot rocks into the sap to evaporate the water.

☆☆☆

Chocolate Sauce

½ cup butter or margarine
1 cup sugar
⅓ cup cocoa
1 cup whipping cream
2 tablespoons Kahlúa or other
coffee-flavored liqueur

1 teaspoon instant coffee
granules
1 teaspoon vanilla extract

Melt butter in a medium saucepan over low heat. Add sugar, cocoa, whipping cream, and Kahlúa, stirring well. Bring mixture to a boil over medium heat, stirring constantly. Add coffee granules, stirring until granules dissolve; reduce heat, and simmer 5 minutes or until sauce is smooth and slightly thickened. Remove from heat; stir in vanilla. Serve Chocolate Sauce warm or cold over ice cream or cake. Yield: 2¼ cups.   Mary Jones

Keeping the Feast
Episcopal Church Women of St. Thomas Church
Abingdon, Virginia

Fudge Sauce

½ cup butter or margarine
1 (6-ounce) package
semisweet chocolate
morsels
1 (13-ounce) can evaporated
milk

1½ cups sifted powdered
sugar
1 teaspoon vanilla extract

Combine butter and chocolate morsels in top of a double boiler; bring water to a boil. Reduce heat to low; cook until chocolate morsels melt, stirring occasionally.

Add evaporated milk and powdered sugar to chocolate mixture, stirring well. Cook, stirring constantly, until sauce is smooth and thickened. Remove from heat, and stir in vanilla. Serve Fudge Sauce warm or cold over ice cream. Yield: 2¾ cups.   Marian Worum

A Rainbow of Recipes
The Education Department/Regional Treatment Center
Fergus Falls, Minnesota

Valley Raisin Dessert Sauce

½ cup raisins
½ cup dark rum
½ cup sugar
¼ cup water
1 (2½-inch) stick cinnamon,
  broken in half

½ cup chopped pecans
1 tablespoon grated lemon
  rind
1 tablespoon grated orange
  rind
½ teaspoon vanilla extract

Combine raisins and rum in a small bowl; set aside.

Combine sugar and water in a heavy saucepan, stirring well; add cinnamon. Bring to a boil over medium heat; boil 2 minutes. Stir in raisin mixture; reduce heat, and cook 5 minutes. Remove from heat; stir in pecans, lemon and orange rind, and vanilla. Serve sauce warm or cold over ice cream or pound cake. Yield: 1½ cups.

California Treasure
The Junior League of Fresno, California

Praline Sauce

1½ cups firmly packed light
  brown sugar
¾ cup light corn syrup
¼ cup butter

1 (5-ounce) can evaporated
  milk
¾ cup chopped pecans

Combine brown sugar, corn syrup, and butter in a medium saucepan, stirring well. Bring to a boil; reduce heat, and simmer 3 to 4 minutes, stirring constantly. Remove from heat, and let cool to lukewarm. Gradually stir in evaporated milk and pecans. Serve warm over ice cream. Yield: 2 cups.

Noteworthy
The Ravinia Festival
Highland Park, Illinois

Parsley-Garlic Sauce

2 egg yolks
1 tablespoon chopped fresh
 chives
1 tablespoon chopped fresh
 parsley
2 cloves garlic, crushed
1 tablespoon plus 1½
 teaspoons lemon juice

¼ teaspoon dry mustard
⅛ teaspoon ground red
 pepper
Dash of salt
½ cup butter or margarine,
 softened

Combine egg yolks, chives, parsley, garlic, lemon juice, mustard, red pepper, and salt in top of a double boiler. Place over hot (not boiling) water. Stir with a wire whisk until well blended. Add butter, 1 tablespoon at a time, stirring constantly with wire whisk until butter melts. Continue whisking until sauce is thickened. Serve over seafood, beef, or vegetables. Yield: ¾ cup.

Steeped in Tradition
The Junior Service League of DeLand, Florida

Lemon Barbecue Sauce

1 clove garlic, minced
1 cup butter or margarine,
 melted
1 tablespoon plus 1 teaspoon
 all-purpose flour
⅔ cup water
¼ cup plus 2 tablespoons
 lemon juice

1 tablespoon plus 1 teaspoon
 salt
1 tablespoon sugar
½ teaspoon dried whole
 thyme
¼ teaspoon pepper
¼ teaspoon hot sauce

Sauté garlic in butter in a medium saucepan 3 to 4 minutes or until tender. Add flour, stirring until smooth. Add water, lemon juice, salt, sugar, thyme, pepper, and hot sauce; stir well. Cook over medium heat, stirring constantly, 3 minutes or until sauce is slightly thickened. Let cool. Use Lemon Barbecue Sauce to baste beef, pork, or chicken during cooking. Yield: 1¾ cups.

Southern Elegance
The Junior League of Gaston County, North Carolina

Teriyaki Sauce

¼ cup vegetable oil
¼ cup soy sauce
2 tablespoons catsup
1 tablespoon red wine
   vinegar

2 cloves garlic, crushed
¼ teaspoon pepper

Combine all ingredients in a small bowl; stir well. Use Teriyaki Sauce to marinate chicken, beef, or shrimp before cooking; use sauce to baste during cooking. Yield: ¾ cup.   P. Wallor

Firehouse Favorites
The Women's Auxiliary-Haddam Volunteer Fire Department
Higganum, Connecticut

Green Tomato Mincemeat

18 medium-size green
   tomatoes, chopped (about
   6 pounds)
8 tart apples, peeled, cored,
   and chopped (about 3
   pounds)
1 (15-ounce) package raisins
2 cups sugar
1½ cups firmly packed brown
   sugar

¼ cup minced lemon or
   orange peel
2 teaspoons salt
1 tablespoon ground
   cinnamon
¼ teaspoon ground allspice
¼ teaspoon ground cloves
1 cup water
¾ cup vinegar
¼ cup lemon juice

Combine all ingredients in a Dutch oven. Cook over high heat, stirring constantly, until mixture comes to a boil. Reduce heat, and simmer 1½ hours or until mixture is thickened, stirring occasionally. Spoon hot mixture into hot sterilized jars, leaving ¼-inch headspace. Remove air bubbles; wipe jar rims. Cover at once with metal lids, and screw on bands. Process in boiling-water bath 25 minutes. Use Green Tomato Mincemeat to make pies. Yield: 5 quarts.

The Mystic Seaport All Seasons Cookbook
Mystic Seaport Museum Stores
Mystic, Connecticut

Cranberries au Grand Marnier

1 (16-ounce) package fresh
cranberries
2 cups sugar

½ cup Grand Marnier or
other orange-flavored
liqueur

Wash cranberries, and drain well. Place cranberries in an ungreased 13- x 9- x 2-inch baking dish; sprinkle with sugar. Cover and bake at 350° for 1 hour. Remove from oven, and let cool. Stir in Grand Marnier. Chill until ready to serve. Serve as a condiment with beef, pork, or poultry. Yield: 3 cups.

The Gathering
The Blue Bird Circle
Houston, Texas

Cranberry Fruit Conserve

1 (16-ounce) package fresh
cranberries
1½ cups water
2½ cups sugar
1 cup golden raisins,
chopped
1 medium-size cooking apple,
peeled, cored, and chopped

1 tablespoon plus ½ teaspoon
grated orange rind
1 teaspoon grated lemon rind
¼ cup orange juice
2 tablespoons fresh lemon
juice
1 cup chopped walnuts

Wash cranberries, and drain. Combine cranberries and water in a large Dutch oven; bring to a boil. Cover, reduce heat, and simmer 6 to 8 minutes or until cranberry skins pop. Add sugar and next 6 ingredients; bring to a boil over medium heat, stirring frequently. Cover, reduce heat, and simmer 15 minutes. Remove from heat, and stir in walnuts.

Quickly spoon hot conserve into hot sterilized jars, leaving ¼-inch headspace. Remove air bubbles; wipe jar rims. Cover at once with metal lids, and screw on bands. Process in boiling-water bath 10 minutes. Yield: 3 pints.   Loris Birnkrant

A Visual Feast
The Founders Society, Detroit Institute of Arts
Detroit, Michigan

Plum Nutty Jam

2½ pounds fresh plums
1½ teaspoons grated orange
   rind
½ cup orange juice
1 (1¾-ounce) package
   powdered fruit pectin

5½ cups sugar
½ cup finely chopped
   walnuts

Remove and discard pits from plums (do not peel). Chop plums into ½-inch pieces. Combine chopped plums, orange rind, and orange juice in a large Dutch oven. Stir in powdered fruit pectin. Bring mixture to a rolling boil, stirring constantly. Stir in sugar. Return to a rolling boil; boil 1 minute, stirring constantly. Remove from heat; skim off foam. Stir 5 minutes. Stir in walnuts.

Quickly spoon hot mixture into hot sterilized jars, leaving ¼-inch headspace. Remove air bubbles; wipe jar rims. Cover at once with metal lids, and screw on bands. Process in boiling-water bath 15 minutes. Yield: 9 half pints.   Deb Williams

Pot Luck
Village Green
Temple, New Hampshire

Spiced Pear Butter

¾ cup unsalted butter,
   softened
1 large ripe pear, peeled,
   cored, and cut into 1-inch
   pieces
½ teaspoon ground cinnamon

¼ teaspoon grated lemon
   rind
⅛ teaspoon ground nutmeg
2 tablespoons honey
1 teaspoon fresh lemon
   juice

Position knife blade in food processor bowl; add butter. Cover and process until smooth. Gradually add pear through food chute; process until smooth. Add cinnamon and remaining ingredients; process until well blended. Use as a spread for muffins, scones, or toast. Yield: 1½ cups.

Boston Tea Parties
The Museum of Fine Arts
Boston, Massachusetts

Lemon Curd

4 eggs, beaten
1½ cups sugar
½ cup lemon juice

½ cup butter or margarine
1 tablespoon grated lemon
  rind

Combine all ingredients in top of a double boiler, and stir well. Bring water to a boil; reduce heat, and cook 15 minutes or until mixture thickens, stirring constantly. Remove from heat, and let cool. Store in refrigerator. Use Lemon Curd as a spread for toast. Yield: 2¼ cups.   Frances Williams

The Share-Cropper
The Central Delta Academy Parent-Teacher Organization
Inverness, Mississippi

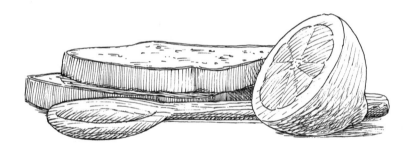

Jane's Family Refrigerator Pickles

6 cups thinly sliced
  cucumbers
2 cups thinly sliced onions,
  separated into rings
1½ cups sugar

1½ cups vinegar
½ teaspoon salt
½ teaspoon mustard seeds
½ teaspoon celery seeds
½ teaspoon ground turmeric

Layer cucumber and onion alternately in a large glass bowl or crock; set aside.

Combine sugar and remaining ingredients in a saucepan; bring to a boil. Cook until sugar dissolves, stirring frequently. Pour boiling mixture over cucumber and onion. Let cool slightly. Cover and chill at least 24 hours before serving. Yield: 6 cups.   Jane M. Kelley

VIP Cookbook, Volume VI
The American Cancer Society, Virginia Division
Vienna, Virginia

Harvest Corn Relish

2 tablespoons cornstarch
⅓ cup vinegar (5% acidity)
4 cups frozen whole kernel
  corn, thawed
1 cup chopped celery
⅓ cup chopped onion
¼ cup chopped dill pickles

3 tablespoons chopped
  pimiento
⅓ cup sugar
1 teaspoon salt
1 teaspoon caraway seeds
¼ teaspoon dry mustard
Pepper to taste

Combine cornstarch and vinegar in a small bowl, stirring well. Set mixture aside.

Combine corn and remaining ingredients in a medium saucepan; add cornstarch mixture. Cook over medium heat until thickened, stirring constantly.

Quickly spoon corn mixture into hot sterilized jars, leaving ¼-inch headspace. Remove air bubbles, and wipe jar rims. Cover at once with metal lids, and screw on bands. Process in boiling-water bath 15 minutes. Yield: 2 pints.

Gatherings
The Junior League of Milwaukee, Wisconsin

Sauerkraut Relish

2 (16-ounce) jars sauerkraut,
  drained
1 cup shredded carrot
1 cup diced celery
1 cup diced green pepper

½ cup sliced pimiento
1 small onion, finely chopped
1 cup sugar
½ cup vinegar
½ cup vegetable oil

Combine sauerkraut, carrot, celery, green pepper, pimiento, and onion in a large glass bowl; toss gently, and set aside.

Combine sugar, vinegar, and oil in a small heavy saucepan. Cook vinegar mixture over medium heat until sugar dissolves, stirring constantly. Remove from heat, and let cool. Pour vinegar mixture over vegetable mixture. Cover and marinate in refrigerator at least 8 hours. Yield: 7 cups.   Priscilla A. Parker

Elvis Fans Cookbook, Volume 3
The Elvis Presley Memorial Trauma Center
Memphis, Tennessee

Zucchini Relish

12 cups coarsely chopped
zucchini
1½ cups chopped onion
1 cup chopped green pepper
4 cloves garlic, crushed
1 tablespoon plus ½ teaspoon
salt

Ice water
1 cup water
5 cups sugar
3 cups vinegar
2 teaspoons mustard seeds
2 teaspoons ground turmeric
2 teaspoons prepared mustard

Combine zucchini, onion, green pepper, garlic, and salt in a large bowl; add ice water to cover. Let stand 3 hours; drain well.

Combine 1 cup water, sugar, vinegar, mustard seeds, turmeric, and mustard in a large Dutch oven; bring to a boil. Add zucchini mixture, and boil 10 minutes.

Quickly ladle hot mixture into hot sterilized jars, leaving ¼-inch headspace. Remove air bubbles, and wipe jar rims. Cover at once with metal lids, and screw on bands. Process in boiling-water bath 10 minutes. Yield: 4 quarts.   Alice Shuffleburg

What's Cooking in the District?
The Wildwood Fire Company Auxiliary, Inc.
Kennebunkport, Maine

Broccoli Pesto

2 cups broccoli flowerets
½ cup coarsely chopped
fresh basil leaves
2 large cloves garlic
¼ cup pine nuts

½ teaspoon Kosher salt
½ teaspoon pepper
1 cup olive oil
½ cup grated Parmesan
cheese

Position knife blade in food processor bowl; add first 6 ingredients. Cover and process until smooth. With processor running, pour oil through food chute in a slow, steady stream, processing until mixture is blended. Transfer broccoli mixture to a small bowl, and stir in cheese. Serve immediately with warm buttered pasta. Yield: 2 cups.   Carole Hicks

Another Taste of Palm Springs
Tiempo de Los Niños, an Auxiliary of Desert Hospital
Palm Springs, California

Hot Sweet Mustard

1 (4-ounce) can dry mustard	2 eggs
¾ cup Chablis or other dry white wine	½ cup honey
½ cup vinegar	2 cups mayonnaise

Combine mustard, wine, and vinegar in a medium bowl; stir well. Cover and let stand at room temperature at least 8 hours.

Combine eggs and honey in top of a double boiler. Bring water to a boil; reduce heat to medium, and cook over simmering water until mixture is thickened, stirring constantly. Remove from heat; let cool. Stir in mustard mixture and mayonnaise. Store in refrigerator. Yield: 4¼ cups.   Wilma V. Corbin

The Glory of Cooking
The National Grange
Washington, DC

Laura's Mustard Mousse

1 envelope unflavored gelatin	3 tablespoons Dijon mustard
¼ cup lemon juice	½ teaspoon salt
4 eggs	1 cup whipping cream
¾ cup sugar	2 tablespoons chopped fresh parsley
½ cup cider vinegar	
½ cup water	

Sprinkle gelatin over lemon juice; let stand 5 minutes.

Combine eggs and next 5 ingredients in a medium saucepan; stir in gelatin mixture. Cook over medium heat 1 minute or until gelatin dissolves, stirring constantly. Remove from heat; chill until mixture is consistency of unbeaten egg whites.

Beat whipping cream at high speed of an electric mixer until stiff peaks form. Fold whipped cream and parsley into mustard mixture. Pour mixture into a lightly oiled 4-cup mold. Cover and chill 8 hours. Yield: 8 servings.

Treasured Recipes from Camargo to Indian Hill
The Indian Hill Historical Society
Cincinnati, Ohio

Soups & Stews

An old covered bridge like this one crossing a stream in Groveton, New Hampshire, is a typical New England sight. The continental ice sheet once covered the entire state and in receding, rerouted water courses into the numerous streams and lakes to be found throughout the state.

☆☆☆

Apple-Butternut Squash Soup

2 medium leeks
1 medium onion,
 chopped
½ cup chopped celery
3 tablespoons butter or
 margarine, melted
1 (1-pound) butternut squash,
 peeled, seeded, and
 chopped
2 large Granny Smith apples,
 peeled, cored, and chopped
1 small turnip, peeled and
 chopped
½ cup chopped carrot
4 cups canned diluted
 chicken broth

¼ cup plus 2 tablespoons
 butter or margarine
¼ cup all-purpose flour
1 cup apple cider
½ teaspoon salt
¼ teaspoon ground nutmeg
¼ teaspoon dried whole
 rosemary, crushed
¼ teaspoon dried whole sage,
 crushed
¼ teaspoon pepper
½ cup (2 ounces) shredded
 Gruyère cheese
½ cup whipping cream
Croutons (optional)

Remove root, tough outer leaves, and tops from leeks, leaving 2 inches of dark leaves; wash leeks, and chop.

Sauté leeks, onion, and celery in 3 tablespoons butter in a large Dutch oven until vegetables are tender. Add squash, apple, turnip, carrot, and chicken broth, stirring to combine. Bring mixture to a boil; cover, reduce heat, and simmer 45 minutes or until vegetables are tender. Remove 1 cup liquid from vegetable mixture, and set liquid aside.

Melt ¼ cup plus 2 tablespoons butter in a heavy saucepan over low heat; add flour, stirring until smooth. Cook over medium heat 3 minutes, stirring constantly. Remove from heat. Gradually add 1 cup reserved liquid, stirring constantly with a wire whisk until mixture is thickened and smooth. Add flour mixture to soup, stirring well. Add apple cider, salt, nutmeg, rosemary, sage, and pepper; stir well. Simmer soup, uncovered, 10 minutes or until thoroughly heated. Add shredded cheese and whipping cream, stirring until cheese melts. Ladle soup into individual serving bowls. Garnish with croutons, if desired. Yield: 12 cups.

Dining In
The Young Woman's League of Westport, Connecticut

Celeriac Soup

2 medium leeks
3 tablespoons unsalted butter
  or margarine, melted
2 medium potatoes, peeled
  and diced
2 stalks celery, diced

1 (¾-pound) celeriac root,
  peeled and diced
2 (14.5-ounce) cans chicken
  broth, undiluted
½ cup milk
½ cup whipping cream

Remove root, tough outer leaves, and tops from leeks, leaving white part only. Wash leeks, and chop. Sauté leeks in butter in a large Dutch oven 2 minutes. Add potato, celery, and celeriac; sauté until vegetables are tender. Stir in chicken broth. Bring mixture to a boil; cover, reduce heat, and simmer 30 minutes.

Pour vegetable mixture into container of an electric blender or food processor; cover and process until smooth. Return pureed vegetable mixture to Dutch oven; stir in milk and whipping cream. Cook over low heat until soup is thoroughly heated, stirring constantly. Yield: 7 cups.   Nancy Hoffmann

The Spence Collection
The Spence School
New York, New York

Mexican Maize Olé

4 cups frozen whole kernel
  corn, thawed
2 cups water
¼ cup thinly sliced onion
1 clove garlic, halved
2 tablespoons butter or
  margarine
2 tablespoons all-purpose
  flour

2 cups milk
1¼ teaspoons salt
¼ teaspoon pepper
1 teaspoon chili powder
¼ teaspoon ground cumin
½ cup (2 ounces) shredded
  Cheddar cheese
¼ cup chopped ripe olives
16 tortilla chips, crushed

Combine first 4 ingredients in a medium saucepan. Bring to a boil; cover, reduce heat, and simmer 5 minutes or until tender. Remove and discard garlic; set mixture aside.

Melt butter in a heavy saucepan over low heat; add flour, stirring until smooth. Cook 1 minute, stirring constantly. Gradually add milk; cook over medium heat, stirring constantly, until mixture is thickened and bubbly. Add corn mixture, salt, and pepper; stir well, and set aside.

Position knife blade in food processor bowl. Add corn mixture to bowl; cover and process until smooth. Return mixture to saucepan; stir in chili powder and cumin. Cook over medium heat until thoroughly heated (do not boil). Ladle into individual bowls, and top with cheese, olives, and tortilla chips. Yield: 6 cups.

Sounds Delicious!
The Volunteer Council of the Tulsa Philharmonic Society, Inc.
Tulsa, Oklahoma

Cheddar Cheese Soup

½ cup diced bacon
1 cup finely chopped carrot
1 cup finely chopped celery
1 cup finely chopped onion
¾ cup finely chopped green pepper
3 cups canned diluted chicken broth
1½ cups beer

3½ cups milk
⅔ cup all-purpose flour
4 cups (16 ounces) shredded Cheddar cheese
½ cup whipping cream
½ teaspoon salt
¼ teaspoon pepper
Chopped fresh parsley

Cook bacon in a large Dutch oven until crisp; remove bacon, reserving drippings in skillet. Set bacon aside.

Sauté carrot, celery, onion, and green pepper in bacon drippings until onion is tender. Stir in chicken broth and beer. Bring mixture to a boil; reduce heat, and simmer until vegetables are tender. Remove from heat, and set aside.

Combine milk and flour in a saucepan, stirring well. Cook over medium heat until thickened, stirring constantly. Add cheese, and stir until cheese melts. Add cheese mixture to broth mixture, stirring well. Add whipping cream, salt, and pepper, stirring well. Ladle soup into individual soup bowls, and top with reserved bacon and parsley. Yield: 10 cups.   Mary-Frances Below

Let's Table It
The Vermont Center for Independent Living
Montpelier, Vermont

Potato-Cheese Soup

2 cups finely chopped onion
2 cups finely chopped carrot
¼ cup unsalted butter or
  margarine, melted
5 cups vegetable broth
3 cups peeled, chopped
  potatoes

6 sprigs fresh parsley
2 to 3 tablespoons chopped
  fresh dillweed
3 cups (12 ounces) shredded
  Cheddar cheese
½ teaspoon salt
¼ teaspoon pepper

Sauté onion and carrot in butter in a Dutch oven until tender. Stir in broth, potato, and parsley. Bring mixture to a boil; reduce heat, and simmer, uncovered, until potatoes are tender. Remove from heat. Add dillweed, stirring well; let stand 5 minutes. Transfer mixture in batches to container of an electric blender; cover and process until smooth. Return pureed mixture to Dutch oven. Add cheese, salt, and pepper; stir well. Cook over low heat until cheese melts, stirring constantly. Yield: 8 cups.   Marie Weitzman

Pesach Potpourri
The Sinai Akiba Academy
Los Angeles, California

Pumpkin Soup

6 thick slices bacon, cut into
  small pieces
½ pound fresh spinach
3 medium leeks
¼ cup unsalted butter or
  margarine, melted
4 cups canned diluted
  chicken broth
1⅓ cups cooked, mashed
  pumpkin
3 medium potatoes, peeled
  and thinly sliced

1 tablespoon chopped fresh
  parsley
1 bay leaf
½ teaspoon dried whole
  thyme
⅛ teaspoon ground nutmeg
1½ cups whipping cream
½ cup freshly grated
  Parmesan cheese
Salt and pepper to taste

Cook bacon in large skillet until almost crisp; remove bacon, and drain on paper towels. Set aside. Discard bacon drippings.

Remove and discard stems from spinach; wash leaves thoroughly, and chop. Set chopped spinach aside.

Remove roots, tough leaves, and tops from leeks, leaving white part only; wash leeks, and finely chop. Sauté in butter in a Dutch oven until tender. Add bacon, broth, and next 6 ingredients; stir well. Bring to a boil; reduce heat, and simmer 30 minutes, stirring occasionally. Remove and discard bay leaf.

Transfer vegetable mixture in batches to container of an electric blender or food processor; cover and process until smooth. Return pureed mixture to Dutch oven. Stir in whipping cream. Cook over low heat 20 minutes or until thoroughly heated (do not boil). Stir in chopped spinach, Parmesan cheese, and salt and pepper to taste just before serving. Yield: 9 cups.   Russell Carlson

Elizabeth H. Brown Humane Society Cookbook
The Elizabeth H. Brown Humane Society, Inc.
Orleans, Vermont

Ham and Wild Rice Soup

¾ cup uncooked wild rice
1 tablespoon vegetable oil
4 cups water
1 medium onion, diced
1 stalk celery, diced
1 carrot, scraped and diced
½ cup butter or margarine, melted
½ cup all-purpose flour

3 cups canned diluted chicken broth
2 cups half-and-half
1 cup diced cooked ham
½ teaspoon dried whole rosemary
¼ teaspoon salt
¼ teaspoon pepper
Chopped fresh parsley

Wash rice in 3 changes of hot water; drain. Sauté rice in hot oil in a skillet until lightly browned. Add water, and simmer, uncovered, 30 minutes. Drain, reserving 1½ cups liquid. Set aside.

Sauté onion, celery, and carrot in butter in a Dutch oven until vegetables are tender. Stir in flour; bring to a boil over low heat. Cook 5 minutes. Add reserved liquid and broth, stirring well. Bring to a boil, stirring constantly. Cook 1 minute. Add rice, half-and-half, and next 4 ingredients; stir well. Simmer, uncovered, 20 minutes. Garnish with fresh parsley. Yield: 8 cups.

Wild Rice, Star of the North
The 1006 Summit Avenue Society
St. Paul, Minnesota

Minestrone with Pesto

1 cup dried Great Northern
  beans
9½ cups water
2 (10¾-ounce) cans chicken
  broth, undiluted
5 ounces salt pork
2 teaspoons salt
1 medium cabbage, shredded
4 carrots, scraped and cut
  into ¼-inch diagonal slices
2 medium potatoes, peeled
  and cut into ½-inch cubes
1 (16-ounce) can Italian-style
  tomatoes, undrained
2 medium onions, thinly
  sliced

¼ cup olive oil
1 stalk celery, cut into ⅛-inch
  diagonal slices
2 zucchini, cut into ¼-inch
  slices
1 large tomato, peeled and
  cut into ½-inch pieces
1 clove garlic, crushed
½ teaspoon salt
¼ teaspoon pepper
¼ cup chopped fresh parsley
4 ounces uncooked spaghetti,
  broken in half
Pesto Sauce

Sort and wash beans; place in a large Dutch oven. Cover with water 2 inches above beans; let soak 8 hours. Drain.

Combine beans, 9½ cups water, chicken broth, salt pork, and 2 teaspoons salt in a large stockpot. Bring mixture to a boil; reduce heat, cover, and simmer 1 hour. Add shredded cabbage, sliced carrot, cubed potato, and Italian-style tomatoes; cover and simmer mixture 30 minutes.

Sauté sliced onion in hot vegetable oil in a large skillet 5 minutes or until onion is tender. Add celery, zucchini, tomato pieces, garlic, ½ teaspoon salt, and pepper to onion; cook vegetable mixture over low heat 20 minutes. Add vegetable mixture to bean mixture; stir in parsley and spaghetti. Cover and cook over low heat 30 minutes, stirring occasionally. Remove and discard salt pork. To serve, ladle Minestrone into individual soup bowls. Top each serving with a dollop of Pesto Sauce. Yield: 24 cups.

Pesto Sauce

¼ cup butter or margarine,
  softened
½ cup finely chopped fresh
  parsley
¼ cup grated Parmesan
  cheese

1 clove garlic, crushed
1 teaspoon dried whole basil
½ teaspoon dried whole
  marjoram
¼ cup olive oil
¼ cup chopped pine nuts

Cream butter; add parsley, Parmesan cheese, garlic, basil, and marjoram, stirring well. Gradually add oil, stirring well. Add pine nuts, stirring until mixture is blended. Yield: 1 cup.

Palette to Palate
The Junior League of St. Joseph and Albrecht Art Museum
St. Joseph, Missouri

Beef-Lentil Soup

3 tablespoons all-purpose
  flour
2 teaspoons salt
¼ teaspoon pepper
2 pounds beef for stewing,
  cut into ½-inch cubes
3 tablespoons vegetable oil
5 to 6 cups water
5 medium carrots, scraped
  and thinly sliced

2 cups sliced celery
2 large onions, chopped
1 cup dried lentils, washed
  and sorted
1 tablespoon lemon juice
1½ teaspoons salt
1 teaspoon dried whole
  thyme

Combine flour, 2 teaspoons salt, and pepper in a medium bowl; dredge beef in flour mixture.

Heat oil in a large Dutch oven. Add beef, and cook until browned on all sides. Add water; cover and simmer 45 minutes. Skim off fat, if necessary. Stir in carrot, celery, onion, lentils, lemon juice, 1½ teaspoons salt, and thyme. Cover and simmer 1 hour or until meat and vegetables are tender, stirring occasionally. Yield: 12 cups.

First There Must Be Food
Northwestern Memorial Hospital
Chicago, Illinois

Oxtail Soup

3 quarts water
2 pounds oxtails or short ribs
2 medium onions, chopped
1 bay leaf
1 tablespoon salt
½ teaspoon pepper
1 (1-pound) can tomatoes, undrained and chopped
1 medium potato, peeled and chopped
1 cup diced carrot
1 cup chopped celery
1 cup frozen cut green beans
½ cup pearl barley
¼ cup tomato paste
2 tablespoons chopped fresh parsley

Combine water, oxtails, onion, bay leaf, salt, and pepper in a large Dutch oven. Bring mixture to a boil; cover, reduce heat, and simmer 3 hours or until meat is tender. Skim fat from soup. Add tomatoes, potato, carrot, celery, green beans, barley, and tomato paste, stirring well. Bring mixture to a boil; cover, reduce heat, and simmer 30 minutes or until vegetables are tender.

Remove and discard bay leaf. Remove oxtails from soup. Remove and discard fat and bones from oxtails. Chop meat, and return meat to soup; stir in fresh parsley. Ladle soup into individual soup bowls. Yield: 12 cups.   Celia Dlugoleski

Our Favorite Recipes
E. J. Noble Hospital Staff and Friends
Gouverneur, New York

Vegetable Clam Soup

1 (16-ounce) can whole tomatoes, undrained and chopped
1 medium carrot, scraped and diced
1 medium-size green pepper, diced
1 small onion, chopped
1 stalk celery, diced
2 (6½-ounce) cans minced clams, undrained
1 tablespoon chopped fresh parsley
1 teaspoon salt
¼ teaspoon garlic powder
¼ teaspoon pepper
Pinch of dried whole tarragon
2 tablespoons dry sherry
1 tablespoon butter or margarine
1 teaspoon Worcestershire sauce

Combine tomatoes, carrot, green pepper, onion, and celery in a large Dutch oven. Bring mixture to a boil; cover, reduce heat, and simmer 10 minutes or until vegetables are tender. Add clams and remaining ingredients; stir well. Cook until mixture is thoroughly heated. Yield: 5 cups.

Parishables
St. Paul's Episcopal Church
Cleveland Heights, Ohio

Bouillabaisse, American Style

1 medium onion, chopped
1 stalk celery, chopped
1 leek, finely chopped
1 clove garlic, minced
¼ cup olive oil
2 (28-ounce) cans Italian-style tomatoes, drained and chopped
2 cups clam juice
2 cups Chablis or other dry white wine
2 tablespoons chopped fresh parsley
1 small bay leaf
1 teaspoon fennel seeds, crushed
½ teaspoon salt
½ teaspoon dried whole thyme
¼ teaspoon pepper
⅛ teaspoon ground saffron
1 pound unpeeled medium-size fresh shrimp
1 (½-pound) fresh lobster tail, split, cleaned, and coarsely chopped
½ pound fresh sea scallops
Grated Parmesan cheese

Sauté onion, celery, leek, and garlic in olive oil in a large Dutch oven 5 minutes or until vegetables are tender. Add tomatoes and next 9 ingredients; stir well. Bring mixture to a boil; reduce heat, and simmer, uncovered, 15 minutes.

Peel and devein shrimp. Add shrimp, lobster, and sea scallops to tomato mixture, stirring well; cook 5 minutes or until shrimp turn pink and lobster and scallops are done. Remove and discard bay leaf. Ladle into individual soup bowls, and sprinkle each serving with grated Parmesan cheese. Yield: 11 cups.

The True Essentials of a Feast
The Library of Congress/LC Cooking Club
Washington, DC

Catfish Gumbo

1 cup chopped celery
1 cup chopped onion
1 cup chopped green pepper
2 cloves garlic, minced
⅓ cup vegetable oil
4 beef-flavored bouillon cubes
4 cups boiling water
2 (16-ounce) cans whole tomatoes, undrained and chopped
2 (10-ounce) packages frozen okra, thawed
1 (6-ounce) can vegetable juice cocktail
1 tablespoon plus 1 teaspoon salt
½ teaspoon dried whole thyme
½ teaspoon pepper
¼ teaspoon ground bay leaves
2 pounds farm-raised catfish fillets, skinned and cut into 1-inch pieces
Hot cooked rice

Sauté celery, onion, green pepper, and garlic in oil in a Dutch oven until vegetables are tender. Dissolve bouillon cubes in water; add to vegetable mixture. Stir in tomatoes and next 6 ingredients. Cover, reduce heat, and simmer 30 minutes, stirring frequently. Add fish; stir well. Cover and simmer 20 minutes. Serve gumbo over rice. Yield: 18 cups.   Doris Boyer

The Share-Cropper
The Central Delta Academy Parent-Teacher Organization
Inverness, Mississippi

Red Beans and Rice

1 pound dried red beans
1 meaty ham bone
2 quarts water
3 cups chopped onion
1 cup chopped green onions
¼ cup tomato sauce
2 cloves garlic, minced
1 tablespoon salt
1 tablespoon Worcestershire sauce
1 teaspoon pepper
½ teaspoon sugar
¼ teaspoon dried whole oregano
¼ teaspoon dried whole thyme
⅛ teaspoon ground red pepper
⅛ teaspoon hot sauce
Hot cooked rice
Additional chopped green onions

Sort and wash beans; place in a Dutch oven. Add ham bone and water; bring to a boil, and boil 3 minutes. Remove from heat, and let stand 1 hour. Return mixture to a boil; cover, reduce heat, and simmer 3 hours. Remove ham bone; remove and discard fat and bone. Shred meat, and return to bean mixture. Stir in onion and next 11 ingredients. Bring to a boil; reduce heat, and simmer 1 hour. Remove ½ cup beans; mash beans, and return to Dutch oven, stirring well. Serve beans over rice. Top each serving with green onions. Yield: 10 cups.

The Market Place
The Junior Woman's Club of Augusta, Georgia

Corn Chowder

2 cups milk
½ cup diced salt pork
2 slices onion
2 cups water
1 cup chopped potatoes
5 sprigs fresh parsley
1 small bay leaf
½ teaspoon salt
¼ teaspoon pepper
⅛ teaspoon dried whole sage
3 tablespoons all-purpose flour
3 tablespoons water
2½ cups whole kernel corn
2 egg yolks, lightly beaten
1 tablespoon butter or margarine
Paprika

Heat milk in a small saucepan to 120° to 130°. Set aside.

Brown salt pork in a Dutch oven. Add onion, and cook until tender. Add 2 cups water and next 6 ingredients; stir well. Bring to a boil; reduce heat, and simmer 10 minutes or until potatoes are tender. Remove and discard bay leaf.

Combine flour and 3 tablespoons water, stirring until smooth. Add to potato mixture, stirring well. Cook over medium heat until mixture thickens. Stir in corn and warm milk; cook until thoroughly heated. Stir about ½ cup hot mixture into egg yolks; add to remaining hot mixture, stirring constantly. Add butter, stirring until butter melts. Ladle into individual soup bowls; sprinkle each serving with paprika. Yield: 5 cups.

Shirley Frey

Home at the Range
Chapter EX-P.E.O.
Oakley, Kansas

Connecticut Coastline Seafood Chowder

¼ pound diced salt pork
2 large onions, chopped
2 leeks, thinly sliced
3 cups peeled, chopped
   potatoes
2 cups clam juice
1 cup water
1 stalk celery, sliced
1 bay leaf
1 tablespoon chopped fresh
   parsley
½ teaspoon dried whole
   oregano

½ teaspoon dried whole
   thyme
¼ teaspoon freshly ground
   pepper
3 dozen Quahog clams,
   coarsely chopped
½ pound fresh bay scallops
½ pound fish fillets, cubed
4 cups half-and-half
2 tablespoons unsalted butter
   or margarine
¼ teaspoon hot sauce

Cook salt pork in a large Dutch oven until crisp. Add onion and leeks, and sauté until vegetables are tender. Add potato and next 8 ingredients, stirring well. Bring mixture to a boil; reduce heat, cover, and simmer 15 minutes or until potatoes are tender. Cool slightly; remove and discard bay leaf. Cover and chill 8 hours.

Bring chilled mixture to a boil. Add clams, scallops, and fish; reduce heat, and simmer 3 minutes or until fish flakes easily when tested with a fork. Stir in half-and-half, butter, and hot sauce; cook until thoroughly heated. Serve immediately. Yield: 12 cups.

Off the Hook
The Junior League of Stamford-Norwalk
Darien, Connecticut

Block Island Scallop Stew

2 pounds fresh sea scallops
⅓ cup dry white vermouth
1 clove garlic, minced
2 onions, thinly sliced
¼ cup plus 1 tablespoon
   olive oil
2 cups peeled, chopped
   Italian-style tomatoes

3 tablespoons butter or
   margarine
2 tablespoons minced fresh
   parsley
½ teaspoon salt
¼ teaspoon freshly ground
   pepper
Toasted French bread slices

Combine first 3 ingredients; stir well. Let stand 30 minutes.

Sauté onion in olive oil in a Dutch oven until onion is tender. Add chopped tomatoes; cover and cook until tomatoes soften. Add scallop mixture, butter, minced parsley, salt, and pepper; cook, uncovered, until scallops are done. Serve stew over toasted French bread slices. Yield: 7 cups.   Peter J. B. Vercelli

A Taste of Salt Air and Island Kitchens
Ladies Auxiliary of the Block Island Volunteer Fire Department
Block Island, Rhode Island

Stew with Onions

1 tablespoon mixed pickling spices
3 pounds boneless beef chuck, cut into 1½-inch cubes
¼ cup olive oil
2 pounds boiling onions, peeled
1 (14.5-ounce) can tomato wedges, undrained
1 (8-ounce) can tomato sauce
1 (6-ounce) can tomato paste
¼ cup vinegar
3 cloves garlic, minced
2 bay leaves
1 tablespoon brown sugar
½ teaspoon salt
¼ teaspoon pepper
1 (10-ounce) package frozen Italian green beans

Place pickling spices on a piece of cheesecloth; tie ends securely.

Brown beef in hot oil in a Dutch oven; drain, discarding oil. Return meat to Dutch oven. Add spice bag, onions, and next 9 ingredients, stirring well. Bring to a boil; cover, reduce heat, and simmer 2 hours or until meat is tender. Add beans, and cook 30 minutes. Remove and discard bay leaves. Yield: 12 cups.

The Minnesota Ethnic Food Book
The Minnesota Historical Society
St. Paul, Minnesota

Beer Stew

¼ cup all-purpose flour
1 to 2 teaspoons salt
½ teaspoon pepper
2 pounds beef for stewing,
  cut into 1-inch pieces
¼ cup vegetable oil
4 medium onions, sliced
1 (12-ounce) can beer
2 bay leaves
1 clove garlic, crushed

1 tablespoon soy sauce
1 tablespoon steak sauce
1 tablespoon Worcestershire
  sauce
½ teaspoon dried whole
  thyme
4 cups peeled, cubed potatoes
1 (10-ounce) package frozen
  English peas

Combine flour, salt, and pepper; lightly dredge meat in flour mixture. Brown meat in hot oil in a Dutch oven. Add onion and next 7 ingredients, stirring well. Bring mixture to a boil; cover, reduce heat, and simmer 1½ hours. Add potato, and cook 20 minutes. Stir in peas, and cook 10 minutes or until vegetables are tender. Remove and discard bay leaves before serving. Yield: 10 cups.

Rockport Collection
The Rockport Art Association
Rockport, Texas

Beef Stew

3 tablespoons vegetable oil
2 pounds beef for stewing,
  cut into 1-inch pieces
1 clove garlic, minced
1 medium onion, chopped
2 tablespoons all-purpose
  flour
4 beef-flavored bouillon cubes
¾ teaspoon salt

½ teaspoon pepper
½ teaspoon Worcestershire
  sauce
4 cups water
4 cups peeled, cubed potatoes
2 cups cubed carrots
1 cup chopped celery
1 cup frozen English peas

Heat oil in a Dutch oven; add beef, and cook until browned on all sides. Set beef aside, and keep warm; reserve drippings.
Sauté garlic in pan drippings in Dutch oven until browned. Add onion, and sauté until tender. Add flour; cook 1 minute, stirring constantly. Return beef to Dutch oven. Add bouillon cubes, salt,

pepper, Worcestershire sauce, and ½ cup water; stir well. Stir in remaining 3½ cups water. Bring mixture to a boil. Cook, stirring frequently, until mixture is thickened. Cover, reduce heat, and simmer 1½ hours. Add potato and carrot; simmer 10 minutes. Add celery and peas; simmer 8 minutes or until vegetables are tender. Yield: 8 cups.   Joyce Ridley

Good Cooking Cookbook
United Lutheran Church
Langdon, North Dakota

Kerry's "Get the Red Out" Chili

4½ pounds ground chuck
2 (28-ounce) cans whole
   tomatoes, undrained
3 to 4 tablespoons finely
   ground mild red chile
   peppers
2 to 4 tablespoons finely
   ground hot red chile
   peppers
2 cloves garlic, minced
3 to 5 teaspoons chili powder
2 teaspoons ground cumin
1¼ teaspoons salt
1¼ teaspoons dried whole
   oregano, crushed

¼ teaspoon ground red
   pepper
1 or 2 jalapeño peppers,
   seeded and chopped
1 or 2 (12-ounce) cans beer
2 (15-ounce) cans pinto
   beans, undrained
1 (8-ounce) can tomato sauce
¼ to ½ cup masa harina
Chopped onion
Chopped green chiles
Shredded Monterey Jack
   cheese
Commercial sour cream

Brown ground chuck in a large Dutch oven, stirring to crumble meat; drain. Add tomatoes and next 8 ingredients, stirring well. Bring mixture to a boil; boil 15 minutes. Reduce heat to low; cook, uncovered, 30 minutes. Add jalapeño pepper, stirring well. Simmer 1 hour, uncovered, adding beer to mixture as mixture is reduced. Add pinto beans, tomato sauce, and masa harina, stirring well. Simmer 1 to 2 hours, uncovered, stirring occasionally.

Ladle chili into individual serving bowls. Top each serving with onion, green chiles, cheese, and sour cream. Yield: 12 cups.

A Pinch of Salt Lake
The Junior League of Salt Lake City, Utah

Male Chauvinist Chili

6 slices bacon
⅔ pound hot Italian sausage, cut into 1-inch pieces
⅔ pound ground beef
1 large onion, coarsely chopped
1 green pepper, coarsely chopped
1 clove garlic, minced
1 small jalapeño pepper, seeded and minced
1 cup Burgundy or other dry red wine
½ cup Worcestershire sauce

1½ teaspoons chili powder
1½ teaspoons freshly ground pepper
1 teaspoon celery seeds
1 teaspoon dry mustard
½ teaspoon salt
6 cups chopped Italian-style tomatoes (about 4 pounds)
1 (15-ounce) can garbanzo beans, undrained
1 (15-ounce) can kidney beans, undrained
1 (15-ounce) can pinto beans, undrained

Cook bacon in a 4½-quart Dutch oven until crisp; remove bacon, and crumble. Set bacon aside. Discard drippings.

Brown sausage in Dutch oven, stirring occasionally. Drain well, reserving drippings. Set sausage aside. Brown ground beef in Dutch oven, stirring to crumble meat. Drain, reserving drippings. Set ground beef aside.

Sauté onion, green pepper, garlic, and jalapeño pepper in pan drippings in Dutch oven 2 minutes. Add wine and Worcestershire sauce; simmer, uncovered, 10 minutes. Add chili powder, pepper, celery seeds, mustard, and salt, stirring well; simmer, uncovered, 10 minutes. Mash tomatoes; add tomatoes and liquid to mixture in Dutch oven, stirring well. Add reserved bacon, sausage, and ground beef to mixture in Dutch oven, stirring well. Bring mixture to a boil; cover, reduce heat, and simmer 30 minutes, stirring occasionally. Add beans; stir well. Cover and simmer 1 hour. Ladle into individual bowls. Yield: 10 cups.   Dwayne Tallman

. . . More Than Cookies!
The Northwest Georgia Girl Scout Council, Inc.
Atlanta, Georgia

Vegetables

Mitchell's Handi-Market in Fort Payne, Alabama, is one of hundreds of roadside markets in the South that sell fresh-from-the-garden produce nearly year-round. These open-air markets are especially prevalent in Alabama where more than half of the land is devoted to agriculture.

☆☆☆

Green Beans in Sour Cream

2 pounds fresh green beans	1 to 2 teaspoons grated lemon
1 medium onion, chopped	rind
2 tablespoons minced fresh	1 teaspoon salt
parsley	¼ teaspoon freshly ground
2 tablespoons butter or	pepper
margarine, melted	1 cup buttered soft
1 (8-ounce) carton	breadcrumbs
commercial sour cream	

Wash beans and remove strings. Cut green beans into 1-inch pieces. Cook in a small amount of boiling water 6 minutes or until tender. Drain; transfer beans to a 2-quart casserole. Set aside.

Sauté onion and parsley in butter 2 minutes or until onion is tender. Stir in sour cream, lemon rind, salt, and pepper. Spoon sour cream mixture over beans. Sprinkle breadcrumbs over sour cream mixture. Bake, uncovered, at 350° for 20 minutes or until thoroughly heated. Yield: 8 servings.

The Stenciled Strawberry Cookbook
The Junior League of Albany, New York

Baked Beans

1 pound dried navy beans	¼ cup plus 2 tablespoons
½ cup chopped salt pork or	firmly packed brown sugar
bacon	¼ cup chopped onion
3½ cups water	2 teaspoons salt
1 cup vegetable juice cocktail	2 teaspoons dry mustard
½ cup molasses	¼ teaspoon pepper

Sort and wash beans; place in a large Dutch oven. Cover with water 2 inches above beans; let soak 8 hours. Drain.

Sauté salt pork in a skillet until lightly browned; drain. Add salt pork, 3½ cups water, and remaining ingredients to beans; stir well. Cover and bake at 350° for 5 to 6 hours, adding additional water, if necessary. Yield: 6 to 8 servings.   Shirley Wildes

Pot Luck
Village Green
Temple, New Hampshire

Julienne Beets with Horseradish

1 (16-ounce) can sliced beets,
  undrained
¼ cup sugar
2 tablespoons vinegar
1 tablespoon cornstarch
1 tablespoon lemon juice
½ teaspoon salt
2½ tablespoons prepared
  horseradish
1 tablespoon butter or
  margarine
Commercial sour cream
  (optional)

Drain beets, reserving liquid. Set liquid aside. Slice beets into julienne strips; set aside.

Combine beet liquid, sugar, vinegar, cornstarch, lemon juice, and salt in a medium saucepan, stirring well. Cook over medium heat until thickened, stirring constantly. Add horseradish and butter, stirring until butter melts. Gently stir in beets, and bring mixture to a boil. Reduce heat, and simmer 5 to 10 minutes or until mixture is thoroughly heated. Top each serving with a dollop of sour cream, if desired. Yield: 4 servings.

First There Must Be Food
Northwestern Memorial Hospital
Chicago, Illinois

Brussels Sprouts with Walnut-Cream Sauce

3 tablespoons butter or
  margarine
3 tablespoons all-purpose
  flour
2 cups whipping cream
2 cloves garlic, minced
¼ teaspoon ground bay
  leaves
Salt and ground white pepper
  to taste
⅔ cup half-and-half
3 tablespoons grated
  Parmesan cheese
1 cup walnuts, ground
2½ pounds fresh brussels
  sprouts
1¾ cups water

Melt butter in a heavy saucepan over low heat; add flour, stirring until smooth. Cook 1 minute, stirring constantly. Gradually add whipping cream; cook over medium heat until mixture is thickened and bubbly, stirring constantly. Add garlic, bay leaves, salt, and pepper; cook 3 minutes, stirring constantly. Beat half-and-half and Parmesan cheese into whipping cream mixture with a wire whisk. Stir in ground walnuts. Remove from heat; cover and let stand 5 minutes. Keep sauce warm.

Wash brussels sprouts thoroughly, and remove discolored leaves. Cut off stem ends, and slash bottom of each sprout with a shallow X. Combine brussels sprouts and water in a large saucepan; bring to a boil. Cover, reduce heat, and simmer 10 to 12 minutes or until brussels sprouts are tender; drain well. Transfer brussels sprouts to a serving bowl. Pour warm sauce over brussels sprouts, and toss gently. Serve immediately. Yield: 10 servings.   Bill Harris

Favorite Recipes from Friends
The Town Hill School
Lakeville, Connecticut

Nutty Carrots

1½ pounds carrots, scraped
  and cut into julienne strips
1½ cups water
½ teaspoon salt
¼ cup butter, melted
1 teaspoon salt
¼ teaspoon coarsely ground
  pepper

¼ teaspoon grated lemon
  rind
2 tablespoons lemon juice
2 teaspoons honey
½ cup coarsely chopped
  walnuts

Combine carrots, water, and ½ teaspoon salt in a heavy saucepan. Bring to a boil; cover, reduce heat, and simmer 15 minutes or until carrots are tender. Drain well. Set aside, and keep warm.

Combine butter, 1 teaspoon salt, pepper, lemon rind, lemon juice, and honey in a small saucepan, and stir well. Cook over medium heat until mixture is thoroughly heated, stirring constantly. Pour sauce over carrots. Add chopped walnuts, and toss gently. Yield: 6 to 8 servings.   Pam Hamer

Deep in the Heart
The Junior Forum of Dallas, Texas

Red Cabbage and Cranberries

2 tablespoons butter or
  margarine
1½ pounds red cabbage,
  shredded
¼ cup red wine vinegar
1¼ cups sugar

⅓ cup orange juice
1 (3-inch) stick cinnamon
1 pound fresh cranberries
1 tablespoon plus 1 teaspoon
  grated orange rind

Melt butter in a large Dutch oven over medium-high heat. Add cabbage, and cook 5 to 6 minutes or just until cabbage is tender. Stir in vinegar, and bring mixture to a boil; cook 2 minutes. Add sugar, orange juice, and cinnamon stick, stirring well. Cover, reduce heat, and simmer 8 minutes. Add cranberries, stirring well; cook over medium-high heat, uncovered, 5 to 6 minutes or until cranberry skins pop. Remove from heat; remove and discard cinnamon. Stir in orange rind. Serve warm. Yield: 8 servings.

Taste of Today
BUNWC, North Shore Illinois Chapter
Northfield, Illinois

Herbed Grilled Corn

8 ears fresh corn
½ cup butter or margarine,
  softened
2 tablespoons chopped fresh
  parsley

2 tablespoons chopped fresh
  chives
½ teaspoon salt
Dash of pepper

Remove husks and silks from corn just before cooking. Combine remaining ingredients; stir well. Spread butter mixture on corn, and place each ear on a piece of aluminum foil; wrap tightly.

Grill over medium coals 20 minutes or until corn is tender, turning several times. Yield: 8 servings.   Evelyn Staley

We, The Women of Hawaii Cookbook
We, The Women of Hawaii
Waialua, Oahu

Bart Conner's Eggplant Parmigiana

1 egg, lightly beaten
1 cup milk
1 tablespoon vegetable oil
1 cup all-purpose flour
2 medium eggplants, peeled and cut into ½-inch slices
Vegetable oil
1 (29-ounce) can tomato sauce
1 (12-ounce) can tomato paste
1 (16-ounce) can tomatoes, drained
¼ cup Burgundy or other dry red wine

1 teaspoon dried whole oregano
½ teaspoon dried whole basil
¼ teaspoon garlic salt
¼ teaspoon dried whole thyme
2 (6-ounce) packages mozzarella cheese slices
¼ cup grated Parmesan cheese

Combine egg, milk, and 1 tablespoon vegetable oil in a large bowl; gradually add flour, stirring until smooth. Dredge eggplant in flour mixture, and fry in hot oil (375°) until golden brown. Drain on paper towels; set aside.

Combine tomato sauce, tomato paste, tomatoes, wine, oregano, basil, garlic salt, and thyme in a medium saucepan, stirring well. Bring mixture to a boil; reduce heat, and simmer 10 minutes.

Arrange half of eggplant slices in a lightly greased 13- x 9- x 2-inch baking dish. Layer with half each of mozzarella slices and tomato sauce mixture; repeat layers with eggplant slices, mozzarella cheese, and tomato sauce mixture. Sprinkle top with Parmesan cheese. Bake at 350° for 30 minutes or until mixture is thoroughly heated. Yield: 8 servings.   Bart Conner

Sooner Sampler
The Junior League of Norman, Oklahoma

Mushroom Casserole

2 pounds medium-size fresh
  mushrooms
¼ cup plus 2 tablespoons
  butter or margarine,
  softened
3 tablespoons all-purpose
  flour
2 teaspoons salt

2 teaspoons prepared mustard
¼ teaspoon ground nutmeg
¼ teaspoon pepper
1 (8-ounce) carton
  commercial sour cream
¼ cup minced fresh parsley
¼ cup minced onion

Clean mushrooms with damp paper towels. Remove stems, and reserve for other uses. Slice mushroom caps, and set aside.

Cream butter, flour, salt, mustard, nutmeg, and pepper at medium speed of an electric mixer. Add sour cream, parsley, and onion, stirring well.

Place half of mushroom slices in a greased 2-quart baking dish. Top mushroom slices with half of sour cream mixture, spreading evenly. Repeat layers. Bake at 325° for 1 hour or until casserole is thoroughly heated. Yield: 6 to 8 servings.   Jane Langford

Compliments to the Cook
The YWCA of Salt Lake City, Utah

Okra and Tomatoes

1 large green pepper,
  chopped
1 medium onion, chopped
2 tablespoons bacon
  drippings
4 cups sliced fresh okra

3 large tomatoes, peeled and
  chopped
1 teaspoon sugar
¾ teaspoon salt
¼ teaspoon pepper

Sauté chopped green pepper and onion in bacon drippings in a medium skillet until vegetables are tender. Add okra, tomatoes, sugar, salt, and pepper, and stir gently. Cover and simmer 10 minutes or until okra is tender, stirring occasionally. Serve immediately. Yield: 6 servings.   Frankie Elkins

Celebration: A Taste of Arkansas
The Sevier County Cookbook Committee
Lockesburg, Arkansas

Walla Walla Onion Casserole

5 cups chopped Walla Walla
  onions or other sweet
  yellow onions
¼ cup butter or margarine,
  melted

1 cup cooked long-grain rice
1 (8-ounce) carton
  commercial sour cream
1 cup (4 ounces) shredded
  Swiss or Cheddar cheese

Sauté onion in butter in a large skillet until tender. Remove from heat. Stir in rice and sour cream.

Spread half the onion mixture in a greased 12- x 8- x 2-inch baking dish. Sprinkle with ½ cup cheese. Repeat layers. Cover and bake at 350° for 30 minutes. Uncover and bake an additional 15 minutes or until lightly browned. Yield: 6 to 8 servings.

Rave Revues
Lakewood Center Associates, Lakewood Center for the Arts
Lake Oswego, Oregon

Idaho Curried Onions

5 medium onions, thinly
  sliced
1 cup water
3 tablespoons butter or
  margarine
2 tablespoons all-purpose
  flour

2 teaspoons beef-flavored
  bouillon granules
1 teaspoon curry powder
1 cup milk
½ cup (2 ounces) shredded
  Cheddar cheese, divided

Combine onion and water in a large skillet. Bring to a boil. Cover, reduce heat, and simmer until onions are tender; drain. Transfer onions to a greased 2-quart casserole.

Melt butter in a heavy saucepan over low heat; add flour, bouillon granules, and curry powder, stirring until smooth. Cook 1 minute, stirring constantly. Gradually add milk; cook over medium heat, stirring constantly, until mixture is thickened and bubbly. Add ⅓ cup cheese, stirring until cheese melts. Pour sauce over onions in casserole. Top with remaining cheese. Bake at 325° for 30 minutes. Serve immediately. Yield: 8 servings.

Bound to Please
The Junior League of Boise, Idaho

Snow Peas with Cashews

1 pound fresh snow pea pods
1 (10-ounce) package frozen
English peas
¼ cup unsalted butter or
margarine
1 cup unsalted cashews
2 tablespoons chopped green
onions

1 clove garlic, minced
¼ cup finely chopped fresh
parsley
½ teaspoon salt
¼ teaspoon freshly ground
pepper

Wash snow pea pods; trim ends, and remove any tough strings. Cook snow peas in a small amount of boiling water 5 minutes or until crisp-tender; drain.

Cook English peas in a small amount of boiling water 3 minutes or just until tender. Drain. Combine snow peas and English peas in a large bowl; set aside.

Melt butter in a medium saucepan over medium heat. Add cashews, green onions, and garlic; cook 1 minute. Stir in parsley, salt, and pepper. Pour butter mixture over peas, and toss gently. Yield: 6 to 8 servings.

California Heritage Continues
The Junior League of Pasadena, California

Scalloped Potatoes and Carrots

¾ cup water
2 cups thinly sliced carrots
2 tablespoons chopped onion
1½ teaspoons butter or
margarine
¼ teaspoon salt
1 tablespoon butter or
margarine, melted
2 pounds red potatoes, peeled
and sliced ⅛-inch thick

3 tablespoons butter or
margarine
1 teaspoon salt
1 teaspoon dried whole
rosemary
⅛ teaspoon pepper
1 cup (4 ounces) shredded
Swiss cheese
1¼ cups whipping cream
Fresh mint sprigs (optional)

Bring water to a boil in a medium saucepan; add carrot, onion, 1½ teaspoons butter, and ¼ teaspoon salt. Cover, reduce heat, and simmer 20 minutes or until carrots are tender. Drain.

Brush 1 tablespoon melted butter in the bottom of a shallow 2½-quart casserole. Layer potato slices in casserole. Arrange carrots over potatoes; dot with 3 tablespoons butter. Sprinkle with 1 teaspoon salt, rosemary, pepper, and cheese.

Place whipping cream in a small saucepan. Cook over low heat until warm; pour over vegetable mixture. Bake at 300° for 1 hour and 45 minutes or until lightly browned. Garnish with fresh mint sprigs, if desired. Yield: 6 to 8 servings.

Cooking with the Santa Fe Opera
The Santa Fe Opera Guild
Santa Fe, New Mexico

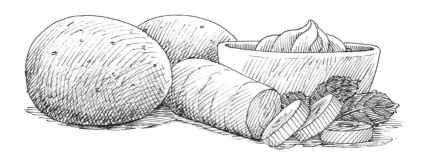

Louisiana Praline Yams

3 cups cooked, mashed yams
½ cup sugar
2 eggs, beaten
¼ cup milk
½ teaspoon salt
¼ teaspoon vanilla extract

1 cup firmly packed brown sugar
1 cup chopped pecans
½ cup all-purpose flour
¼ cup butter or margarine

Combine first 6 ingredients in container of an electric blender or food processor; cover and process until smooth. Spoon mixture into a greased shallow 2-quart casserole.

Combine brown sugar, pecans, flour, and butter; sprinkle over yam mixture. Bake at 350° for 25 to 30 minutes or until thoroughly heated. Yield: 8 to 10 servings.

Artist's Palate Cookbook
New Orleans Museum of Art-Women's Volunteer Committee
New Orleans, Louisiana

Spinach Pudding

1 (10-ounce) package frozen
chopped spinach
¾ cup milk
1 tablespoon butter or
margarine
2 eggs, beaten
¾ cup (3 ounces) shredded
Swiss cheese

1 (2-ounce) can mushroom
stems and pieces, drained
1 tablespoon finely chopped
onion
½ teaspoon salt
Dash of pepper
⅛ teaspoon ground nutmeg

Cook spinach according to package directions; drain well, and set spinach aside.

Combine milk and butter in a medium saucepan; cook over medium heat until butter melts, stirring occasionally. Remove from heat. Add spinach, eggs, Swiss cheese, mushrooms, onion, salt, and pepper; stir well. Pour spinach mixture into a greased 1-quart casserole. Sprinkle with nutmeg.

Set casserole in a 9-inch square baking pan; pour hot water to a depth of 1 inch into pan. Bake at 325° for 50 to 55 minutes or until a knife inserted in center comes out clean. Remove casserole from water. Yield: 4 to 6 servings.   Eloise Knoll

Around the World, Around Our Town
Friends of the San Pedro Library
San Pedro, California

Souffléed Acorn Squash

2 small acorn squash (about
¾-pound each)
¼ cup butter or margarine
1 egg, separated
1 tablespoon plus 1 teaspoon
brown sugar

¼ teaspoon salt
¼ teaspoon ground cinnamon
⅛ teaspoon freshly ground
pepper
Dash of ground nutmeg
⅛ teaspoon salt

Cut squash in half crosswise; remove and discard seeds and membranes. Place squash, cut side down, in a shallow baking dish. Pour boiling water to a depth of ½ inch into dish. Bake, uncovered, at 400° for 30 minutes. Turn squash cut side up. Place 1 tablespoon butter in each squash cavity. Bake an additional 30 minutes or until squash is tender. Remove squash from baking dish; drain and reserve melted butter. Let squash cool slightly. Remove pulp, leaving a ¼-inch-thick shell.

Position knife blade in food processor bowl; add reserved melted butter, squash pulp, egg yolk, brown sugar, and next 4 ingredients. Cover and process until smooth. Transfer squash mixture to a medium bowl; set aside.

Beat egg white (at room temperature) in a small bowl at high speed of an electric mixer until foamy; add ⅛ teaspoon salt, and beat until stiff but not dry. Gently fold beaten egg white into squash mixture. Spoon squash mixture into squash shells; place shells on a baking sheet. Bake at 400° for 25 minutes or until puffed and golden brown. Yield: 4 servings.   Susan Webb

The Spence Collection
The Spence School
New York, New York

Cranberry-Orange Acorn Squash

2 acorn squash
¼ teaspoon salt
3 tablespoons unsalted butter
   or margarine
3 tablespoons dark brown
   sugar

3 tablespoons orange
   marmalade
¾ cup fresh cranberries,
   coarsely chopped

Cut squash in half lengthwise; remove and discard seeds and membranes. Sprinkle cut sides of squash with salt. Place squash, cut side down, in a buttered shallow baking dish. Bake, uncovered, at 350° for 35 minutes.

Melt butter in a small saucepan over medium heat. Add sugar, stirring until sugar dissolves. Add marmalade and cranberries, stirring well. Remove from heat.

Turn squash over; fill squash cavities with cranberry mixture. Bake stuffed squash at 350° for 30 to 40 minutes or until squash is tender. Yield: 4 servings.

Even More Special
The Junior League of Durham and Orange Counties,
North Carolina

Glazed Acorn Squash

1 large acorn squash
1/3 cup orange juice
1/2 cup firmly packed brown
   sugar
1/4 cup light corn syrup

1/4 cup butter or margarine
2 teaspoons grated lemon
   rind
1/8 teaspoon salt

Cut squash into 3/4-inch-thick slices; remove and discard seeds and membrane. Arrange squash slices in a single layer in a lightly greased shallow baking dish. Pour orange juice over squash. Cover and bake at 350° for 30 minutes.

Combine brown sugar, corn syrup, butter, lemon rind, and salt in a small saucepan. Bring mixture to a boil; reduce heat, and simmer 5 minutes or until mixture is slightly thickened. Pour sugar mixture over squash slices. Bake, uncovered, an additional 15 to 20 minutes or until squash is tender, basting occasionally with pan liquids. Yield: 2 to 4 servings.   Terry Routman

Temptations
Presbyterian Day School
Cleveland, Mississippi

Summer Squash with Sun-Dried Tomatoes

1/2 (6-ounce) jar sun-dried
   tomatoes, undrained
4 medium-size yellow squash
1 tablespoon chopped fresh
   rosemary

1/4 teaspoon salt
1/8 teaspoon freshly ground
   pepper

Drain sun-dried tomatoes, reserving 2 tablespoons oil. Cut tomatoes into julienne strips; set aside.

Cut squash crosswise into 1/4-inch slices. Sauté squash slices in reserved oil in a large skillet over medium-high heat 5 minutes or until squash is lightly browned. Add reserved tomato strips, rosemary, salt, and pepper, and toss gently to mix well. Serve immediately. Yield: 4 servings.

Celebrated Seasons
The Junior League of Minneapolis, Minnesota

Cheese-Stuffed Zucchini

2 medium zucchini
¼ cup minced onion
1 tablespoon butter or
   margarine, melted
2 tablespoons grated
   Parmesan cheese
2 tablespoons Italian-seasoned
   breadcrumbs

¼ teaspoon pepper
⅛ teaspoon salt
3 slices bacon, cooked and
   crumbled
¼ cup (1 ounce) shredded
   Cheddar cheese

Cook whole zucchini in boiling water in a medium saucepan 8 to 10 minutes or until tender. Drain and let cool slightly. Slice zucchini in half lengthwise. Carefully scoop out zucchini pulp, leaving ¼-inch-thick shells. Finely chop zucchini pulp. Set zucchini pulp and shells aside.

Sauté minced onion in butter in a skillet over medium heat until onion is tender. Add chopped zucchini pulp, grated Parmesan cheese, Italian-seasoned breadcrumbs, pepper, and salt. Cook until vegetable mixture is thoroughly heated. Stir in crumbled bacon. Spoon vegetable mixture evenly into reserved zucchini shells. Top vegetable mixture with shredded Cheddar cheese.

Place stuffed zucchini shells on an ungreased baking sheet. Bake at 450° for 8 to 10 minutes or until stuffed zucchini shells are thoroughly heated and cheese melts. Serve immediately. Yield: 4 servings.

The Gathering
The Blue Bird Circle
Houston, Texas

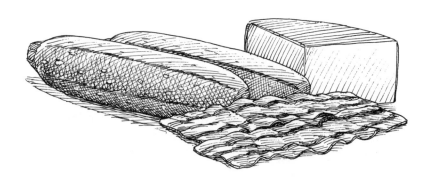

Zucchini-Cottage Cheese Puff

2 eggs, separated
1 cup low-fat cottage cheese
1 small onion, chopped
¾ cup soft whole wheat
    breadcrumbs

1 cup diced cooked zucchini
¾ cup (3 ounces) shredded
    Monterey Jack cheese

Combine egg yolks, cottage cheese, and onion in container of an electric blender; cover and process until smooth. Transfer mixture to a medium bowl. Stir in breadcrumbs, zucchini, and cheese. Set mixture aside.

Beat egg whites (at room temperature) at high speed of an electric mixer until stiff peaks form. Gently fold egg whites into zucchini mixture. Pour mixture into a greased 1-quart casserole. Bake at 350° for 40 minutes or until set. Serve hot. Yield: 4 to 6 servings.

West Central Vegetarian Cookbook
West Central Seventh Day Adventist Church
Oak Park, Illinois

Tomatoes Stuffed with Mushrooms

4 medium tomatoes
¼ teaspoon salt
¼ teaspoon sugar
6 green onions, thinly sliced
2 tablespoons butter or
    margarine, melted
¾ pound fresh mushrooms,
    thinly sliced
1 tablespoon plus 1½
    teaspoons lemon juice

1 tablespoon tarragon vinegar
1 teaspoon paprika
½ teaspoon salt
¾ cup half-and-half
3 tablespoons freshly grated
    Parmesan cheese
3 tablespoons (¾ ounce)
    shredded Gruyère cheese

Cut top quarter off each tomato; reserve top quarter for other uses. Scoop out tomato pulp; chop pulp, and set aside. Sprinkle inside of tomato shells with ¼ teaspoon salt and sugar, and invert on paper towels to drain 30 minutes.

Sauté green onions in butter in a large skillet over medium heat until onions are tender. Add sliced mushrooms, and sauté until mushrooms are tender. Stir in reserved tomato pulp, lemon juice, tarragon vinegar, paprika, and ½ teaspoon salt. Cook 2 minutes, stirring constantly. Stir in half-and-half; cook 10 to 12 minutes or until liquid is reduced and mixture is thickened and bubbly. Spoon mixture into tomato shells; place shells in a lightly greased 9-inch square baking dish. Combine Parmesan and Gruyère cheeses, and sprinkle evenly over tomatoes.

Bake at 400° for 10 minutes. Broil 6 inches from heat 3 to 4 minutes or until cheese is lightly browned. Serve immediately. Yield: 4 servings.

Very Innovative Parties
The Loma Linda University School of Dentistry Auxiliary
Loma Linda, California

Turnip Puree with Cheese and Pears

1 pound turnips, peeled and cut in half	¼ cup (1 ounce) shredded Gorgonzola cheese
1 pound pears, peeled and cored	Salt and pepper to taste
⅓ cup minced shallots	Dash of nutmeg
2 tablespoons butter or margarine, melted	

Place turnips in a vegetable steamer over boiling water. Cover and steam 15 to 20 minutes or until turnips are tender. Set turnips aside. Place pears in steamer over boiling water. Cover and steam 5 to 10 minutes or until pears are tender.

Sauté shallots in butter in a small skillet until tender. Transfer shallot mixture to container of an electric blender or food processor. Add half the turnips, half the pears, and 2 tablespoons cheese; cover and process until smooth. Transfer mixture to a serving bowl. Repeat procedure with turnips, pears, and cheese. Sprinkle turnip mixture with salt, pepper, and nutmeg; stir well. Serve hot or chilled. Yield: 6 to 8 servings.   Parker Dexter

Academic Apron
The Middlesex School
Concord, Massachusetts

Barbecued Confetti Vegetables

8 to 10 cherry tomatoes, halved

1½ cups corn, cut from cob

1 sweet red pepper, cut into julienne strips

½ medium-size green pepper, cut into julienne strips

1 small onion, sliced

1 tablespoon chopped fresh basil leaves

¼ teaspoon grated lemon rind

Salt and freshly ground pepper to taste

1 tablespoon plus 1 teaspoon unsalted butter or margarine, cut into pieces

Combine all ingredients except butter in a large bowl; toss gently to mix well. Divide vegetable mixture in half. Place each half in center of a 12- x 12-inch piece of heavy-duty aluminum foil. Dot vegetables with butter. Bring corners of foil together to form a pyramid; twist to seal. Grill foil packets over medium hot coals 15 to 20 minutes or until vegetables are tender. Serve immediately. Yield: 4 servings.

Delicious Decisions
The Junior League of San Diego, California

Ghivetch

1 small cauliflower, broken into flowerets

2 medium carrots, scraped and thinly sliced

2 medium-size baking potatoes, peeled and diced

2 medium tomatoes, peeled and quartered

¼ pound fresh green beans, sliced diagonally into ½-inch pieces

1 stalk celery, sliced diagonally into ¼-inch pieces

1 yellow squash, thinly sliced

1 medium zucchini, thinly sliced

1 onion, thinly sliced

1 small sweet red pepper, cut into strips

1 small green pepper, cut into strips

1 cup chicken broth

½ cup olive oil

3 cloves garlic, minced

2 teaspoons salt

½ teaspoon ground savory

¼ teaspoon dried whole tarragon

1 bay leaf

Combine first 11 ingredients in a large bowl; toss well. Spoon vegetable mixture into a deep 5-quart casserole; set aside.

Combine broth and remaining ingredients in a saucepan; bring mixture to a boil. Pour over vegetables. Cover and bake at 350° for 1 hour or until vegetables are tender, stirring occasionally. Remove and discard bay leaf before serving. Yield: 8 to 10 servings.

Noteworthy
The Ravinia Festival
Highland Park, Illinois

Spicy Mexican Pickled Vegetables

12 cloves garlic
1 medium onion, cut into wedges
¾ cup olive oil
4 medium carrots, scraped and thinly sliced
1 teaspoon black peppercorns
1½ cups vinegar
2 cups water
½ (7-ounce) can whole pickled jalapeño peppers, drained
1 medium cauliflower, broken into flowerets

3 tablespoons salt
3 medium zucchini, thinly sliced
12 small bay leaves
¾ teaspoon dried whole marjoram
¾ teaspoon dried whole oregano
¾ teaspoon dried whole thyme
1 (7-ounce) jar pickled baby corn on the cob, drained
1 (6-ounce) can pitted small ripe olives, drained

Sauté garlic and onion in hot oil in a large Dutch oven 3 minutes. Add carrot and peppercorns; sauté 5 minutes. Add vinegar; cover, reduce heat, and simmer 3 minutes. Stir in water and jalapeño peppers; cover and bring mixture to a boil. Add cauliflower and salt, stirring well; cover, reduce heat to medium, and cook 5 minutes. Add zucchini, bay leaves, marjoram, oregano, and thyme, stirring well; cook 2 minutes. Remove from heat; stir in corn and olives.

Transfer mixture to a large container; cover tightly, and chill at least 8 hours. Remove and discard bay leaves before serving. Yield: 12 servings.

Celebrate San Antonio
The Junior Forum of San Antonio, Texas

Acknowledgments

Special thanks to Dot Gibson and Ellen Rolfes for their support of this project and to the fund-raising groups who participated in this celebration of American cooking. America's best recipes have been selected and adapted from the following community cookbooks. The copyright for each of these is held by the sponsoring organization unless otherwise noted.

250 Years of Cooking in Harwinton, Friends of the Harwinton Library, 50 Burlington Rd., Harwinton, CT 06791

Academic Apron, Middlesex School, 1200 Lowell Rd., Concord, MA 01742

Angel Fare, St. Michael and All Angels Episcopal Church, 1704 Northeast 43rd Ave., Portland, OR 97213

Another Taste of Palm Springs, Tiempo de Los Niños, P.O. Box 195, Palm Springs, CA 92263

Around the World, Around Our Town: Recipes from San Pedro, Friends of San Pedro Library, 931 South Gaffey St., San Pedro, CA 90731

Artist's Palate Cookbook, New Orleans Museum of Art-Women's Volunteer Committee, P.O. Box 19123, City Park, New Orleans, LA 70179-0123

As You Like It, St. Bernard's School, 4 East 98th St., New York, NY 10029

Beyond the Village Gate, Parmadale Children's Village, 6753 State Rd., Parma, OH 44134

Biscayne Bights and Breezes, The Villagers, Inc., P.O. Box 14-1843, Coral Gables, FL 33114

The Bishop's Bounty, St. Mary's Training School for Retarded Children, P.O. Drawer 7768, Alexandria, LA 71306

Boston Tea Parties, Museum of Fine Arts, 465 Huntington Ave., Boston, MA 02115

Bound to Please, Junior League of Boise, P.O. Box 6126, Boise, ID 83707

The Brevillier Village Cookbook, Brevillier Village Auxiliary, 5416 East Lake Rd., Erie, PA 16511

California Heritage Continues, Junior League of Pasadena, 149 South Madison Ave., Pasadena, CA 91101. Recipes used by permission of Doubleday, a division of Bantam, Doubleday, Dell Publishing Group, Inc.

California Treasure, Junior League of Fresno, P.O. Box 16278, Fresno, CA 93755

Calling All Cooks Two, Telephone Pioneers of America, 3196 Hwy. 280 South, Room 301-NA, Birmingham, AL 35243

Calvary Collections, Nurture Committee of Calvary Lutheran Church, 2200 Hwy. 2 East, Kalispell, MT 59901

Celebrate San Antonio, Junior Forum of San Antonio, P.O. Box 791186, San Antonio, TX 78279-1186

Celebrated Seasons, Junior League of Minneapolis, 428 Oak Grove St., Minneapolis, MN 55403

Celebration: A Taste of Arkansas, Sevier County Cookbook Committee, P.O. Box 66, Lockesburg, AR 71846

Charleston Receipts Repeats, Junior League of Charleston, Inc., P.O. Box 177, Charleston, SC 29402

Compliments to the Cook, YWCA of Salt Lake City, 322 East 300 South, Salt Lake City, UT 84111

Con Mucho Gusto, Desert Club of Mesa, Inc., 331 East Hackamore, Mesa, AZ 85201

Concertos for Cooks, North Group, Symphony Women's Committee, Indiana State Symphony Society, Inc., 45 Monument Circle, Indianapolis, IN 46204

Cooking in Clover II, Jewish Hospital of St. Louis, 216 S. Kingshighway, St. Louis, MO 63108

Cooking with the Santa Fe Opera, Santa Fe Opera Guild, P.O. Box 2371, Santa Fe, NM 87504

A Cook's Book of Recipes from the Pacific Northwest, Rosehill Community Center, P.O. Box 81, Mukilteo, WA 98275

The Cooks' Book, Nightingale-Bamford School, 20 East 92nd St., New York, NY 10028

Cornsilk, Junior League of Sioux City, P.O. Box 2166, Northside Station, Sioux City, IA 51104

The Cove Cookery, Ladies Aid Society, St. John's Lutheran Church, Rt. 2, Box 15, Accident, MD 21520

Crème de Colorado Cookbook, Junior League of Denver, Inc., 6300 East Yale Ave., Suite 110, Denver, CO 80222

Crème de LA Coast, Small World Guild-Childrens Hospital of Orange County, 10 Jamestown, Irvine, CA 92720

A Dash of Down East, Junior Guild of Rocky Mount, P.O. 7912, Rocky Mount, NC 27804

Deep in the Heart, Junior Forum of Dallas, 2116 East Arapaho, Suite 721, Richardson, TX 75081

Delicious Decisions, Junior League of San Diego, 210 Maple St., San Diego, CA 92103

Diamonds in the Desert, Woman's League of Ozona, P.O. Box 1552, Ozona, TX 76943

Dining In, Young Woman's League of Westport, 10 Bay St., Suite 87, Westport, CT 06880

Down Home in High Style, Houston Academy Library Committee, P.O. Box 6046, Dothan, AL 36302

Elizabeth H. Brown Humane Society Cookbook, Elizabeth H. Brown Humane Society, Inc., P.O. Box 102, Orleans, VT 05820

Elvis Fans Cookbook, Volume 3, Elvis Presley Memorial Trauma Center of Memphis, P.O. Box 238, Welcome, NC 27374

Even More Special, Junior League of Durham and Orange Counties, 900 South Duke St., Durham, NC 27707

Favorite Recipes, Sponsor's Club, Robert Louis Stevenson School, P.O. Box 657, Pebble Beach, CA 93953

Favorite Recipes from Friends, Town Hill School, Interlaken Rd., Lakeville, CT 06039

Finely Tuned Foods, Symphony League, 9009 High Dr., Leawood, KS 66206

The Finishing Touch, Temple Israel Sisterhood, 1821 Emerson Ave., Dayton, OH 45406

Firehouse Favorites, Women's Auxiliary-Haddam Volunteer Fire Department, P.O. Box 471, Higganum, CT 06441

First There Must Be Food, Northwestern Memorial Hospital, 303 East Superior, Chicago, IL 60611

From Start to Finish, Rhode Island Special Olympics, 100 Jefferson Blvd., Warwick, RI 02886

From the Hills, Lutheran Church of Vestavia Hills, 201 South Montgomery Hwy., Vestavia Hills, AL 35216

The Gathering, Blue Bird Circle, 615 West Alabama, Houston, TX 77006

Gatherings, Junior League of Milwaukee, 626 North Broadway, Milwaukee, WI 53202

The Glory of Cooking, National Grange, 1616 H St. N.W., Washington, DC 20006

Good Cooking Cookbook, United Lutheran Church, Hwy. 5 West, Langdon, ND 58249

The Great Entertainer Cookbook, Buffalo Bill Historical Center, P.O. Box 3058, Cody, WY 82414

Home at the Range, Chapter EX-P.E.O., 429 Smokyhill, Oakley, KS 67748

Hunt to Harbor, Junior League of Baltimore, P.O. Box 11080, Baltimore, MD 21212

I Must Have That Recipe, Albert Einstein College of Medicine, Yeshiva University, 1300 Morris Park Ave., Suite B-802, Bronx, NY 10461

Keeping the Feast, Episcopal Church Women of St. Thomas Church, P.O. Box 627, Abingdon, VA 24210

The Kentucky Derby Museum Cookbook, Kentucky Derby Museum, 704 Central Ave., Louisville, KY 40208

Kitchen Sampler, Junior Service League of Bessemer, 605 Castlewood Dr., Bessemer, AL 35020

La Salette's Favorite Recipes, La Salette Shrine, 947 Park St., Attleboro, MA 02703

Let's Table It, Vermont Center for Independent Living, 174 River St., Montpelier, VT 05602

Libretto, Opera Society of Fort Lauderdale, 333 Southwest 2nd St., Fort Lauderdale, FL 33312

Lone Star Legacy II, Junior Forum of Austin, P.O. Box 26628, Austin, TX 78755

Lorimor Centennial Cookbook, Volume II, Centennial Committee, Box 125, Rt. 2, Lorimor, IA 50149

M.A.E.H. Cook Book, Michigan Association of Extension Homemakers, 301 South Michigan Ave., Hastings, MI 49058

Make It Miami, Guild of the Museum of Science, Inc., 3280 South Miami Ave., Miami, FL 33129

The Market Place, Junior Woman's Club of Augusta, Inc., P.O. Box 3133, Augusta, GA 30904

McComb's International Cuisine Affair, McComb Interdenominational Care Association, P.O. Box 7206, McComb, MS 39648

The Minnesota Ethnic Food Book, Minnesota Historical Society Press, 690 Cedar St., St. Paul MN 55101

Montgomery County Fair History Cookbook, Montgomery County Fair Association, Inc., P.O. Box 869, Conroe, TX 77305

. . . More Than Cookies!, Northwest Georgia Girl Scout Council, Inc., 100 Edgewood Ave. N.E., Suite 1100, Atlanta, GA 30335-4501

The Mystic Seaport All Seasons Cookbook, Mystic Seaport Museum Stores, 39 Greenmanville Ave., Mystic, CT 06355

Na Zdrowie II, Women's Auxiliary-Polish American Club of Agawam, P.O. Box 173, Feeding Hills, MA 01030

Necessities and Temptations, Junior League of Austin, Inc., 5416 Parkcrest, Suite 100, Austin, TX 78731

Noteworthy, a collection of recipes from the Ravinia Festival, Noteworthy Publications, 1575 Oakwood Ave., Highland Park, IL 60035

Off the Hook, Junior League of Stamford-Norwalk, 748 Post Rd., Darien, CT 06820

Old Irving Park Association Cookbook, Old Irving Park Association, P.O. Box 416736, Chicago, IL 60641

One Hundred Years of Sharing, Calvary Covenant Church Women, 404 Meeker St., Evansville, MN 56326

Our Favorite Recipes, E. J. Noble Hospital Staff and Friends, 77 West Barney St., Gouverneur, NY 13642

Out of Our League, Too, Junior League of Greensboro Publications, 220 State St., Greensboro, NC 27408

Out of This World Cookbook II, Woman's Club of Cocoa Beach, P.O. Box 32932-1104, Cocoa Beach, FL 32932

Palette to Palate, Junior League of St. Joseph and Albrecht Art Museum, 301 North 8th St., St. Joseph, MO 64501

Palm Country Cuisine, Junior League of Greater Lakeland, Inc., 2020 Crystal Grove Dr., Lakeland, FL 33801

Parishables, St. Paul's Episcopal Church, 2747 Fairmount Blvd., Cleveland Heights, OH 44106

Parker's Blue Ribbon Recipes, Parker Ward Relief Society, Rt. 2, Box 27-A, St. Anthony, ID 83445

Peachtree Bouquet, Junior League of DeKalb County, Inc., P.O. Box 183, Decatur, GA 30031

Pesach Potpourri, Sinai Akiba Academy, 10400 Wilshire Blvd., Los Angeles, CA 90024

A Pinch of Salt Lake, Junior League of Salt Lake City, P.O. Box 6163, Salt Lake City, UT 84106

Pot Luck, Village Green, P.O. Box 210, Temple, NH 03084

Purple Sage and Other Pleasures, Junior League of Tucson, Inc., 2099 East River Rd., Tucson, AZ 85718

A Rainbow of Recipes, Education Department/Regional Treatment Center, Box 157, Fergus Falls, MN 56537

Rave Revues, Lakewood Center Associates, Lakewood Center for the Arts, P.O. Box 274, Lake Oswego, OR 97034

Remembering Our Heritage, Herndon Covenant Church Women, Rt. 1, Herndon, KS 67739

Rockport Collection, Rockport Art Association, P.O. Box 987, Rockport, TX 78382

Royle Round-Up of Recipes, R.A.P.T., Royle Association of Parents and Teachers, Royle Rd., Darien, CT 06820

Santa Barbara: 200 Years of Good Taste, Santa Barbara Historical Society-Docent Council, 136 East De La Guerra St., Santa Barbara, CA 93102

The Share-Cropper, Central Delta Academy Parent-Teacher Organization, Rt. 1, Box 4, Inverness, MS 38753

Simply Sensational, TWIGS, Auxiliary of the Children's Medical Center, One Children's Plaza, Dayton, OH 45404-1815

Sinfully Good, Catholic Library Association, 461 West Lancaster Ave., Haverford, PA 19041

A Slice of Nantucket, St. Mary's Guild, St. Mary-Our Lady of the Isle Church, Federal St., Nantucket, MA 02554

Some Enchanted Eating, Friends of the West Shore Symphony Orchestra, P.O. Box 1603, Muskegon, MI 49443

Sooner Sampler, Junior League of Norman, Inc., 300 West Main, Norman, OK 73069

Sounds Delicious!, Volunteer Council of the Tulsa Philharmonic Society, Inc., 8177 South Harvard, Suite 431, Tulsa, OK 74137

South of the Fork, Junior League of Dallas, 8003 Inwood Rd., Dallas, TX 75209

Southern Elegance, Junior League of Gaston County, P.O. Box 3684, Gastonia, NC 28053

Southern Secrets, SouthTrust Corporation, P.O. Box 2554, Birmingham, AL 35290

The Spence Collection, Spence School, 22 East 91st St., New York, NY 10128

State Hospital Cooks, Patient/Staff Advocacy Committee, Vermont State Hospital, 103 South Main St., Waterbury, VT 05676

Steeped in Tradition, Junior Service League of DeLand, P.O. Box 1372, DeLand, FL 32721-1372

The Stenciled Strawberry Cookbook, Junior League of Albany, 419 Madison Ave., Albany, NY 12210

Stir Crazy!, The Junior Welfare League of Florence, P.O. Box 3715, Florence, SC 29502-0715

A Taste of Almost Heaven, Monongalia Arts Center, P.O. Box 239, Morgantown, WV 26505

A Taste of Salt Air and Island Kitchens, Ladies Auxiliary of the Block Island Volunteer Fire Department, Beach Ave., Block Island, RI 02807

Taste of Today, Brandeis University National Women's Committee, North Shore Illinois Chapter, P.O. Box 8117, Northfield, IL 60093

Temptations, Presbyterian Day School, 1100 West Sunflower Rd., Cleveland, MS 38732

Thou Preparest a Table Before Me, East Avenue United Methodist Church Women, 800 East Ave., York, NE 68467

Tidewater on the Half Shell, Junior League of Norfolk-Virginia Beach, Inc., P.O. Box 956, Norfolk, VA 23501

Treasured Recipes from Camargo to Indian Hill, Indian Hill Historical Society, 8100 Given Rd., Cincinnati, OH 45243

The True Essentials of a Feast, Library of Congress/LC Cooking Club, 101 Independence Ave., S.E., Washington, DC 20540

Truly Golden Recipes, Golden Congregational Church, Rt. 1, Ryan, Iowa 50126

Unbearably Good!, Junior Service League of Americus, 125 East Forsyth St., Americus, GA 31709

Upper Crust: A Slice of the South, Junior League of Johnson City, P.O. Box 1082, Johnson City, TN 37605

Uptown Down South, Junior League of Greenville, 17 West North St., Greenville, SC 29601

Very Innovative Parties, Loma Linda University School of Dentistry Auxiliary, P.O. Box 382, Loma Linda, CA 92354

Vintage Vicksburg, Junior Auxiliary of Vicksburg, P.O. Box 86, Vicksburg, MS 39180

VIP Cookbook, Volume VI, American Cancer Society, Virginia Division, 124 Park St. S.E., Vienna, VA 22180

A Visual Feast, Founders Society, Detroit Institute of Arts, 5200 Woodward Ave., Detroit, MI 48202

We, The Women of Hawaii Cookbook, We, The Women of Hawaii, 67-230 Kupahu St., Waialua, Oahu 96791

West Central Vegetarian Cookbook, West Central Seventh Day Adventist Church, 1154 Wisconsin, Oak Park, IL 60302

What's Cooking in the District?, Wildwood Fire Company Auxiliary, Inc., Wildes District, Kennebunkport, ME 04046

Wild Rice, Star of the North, The 1006 Summit Avenue Society, 1006 Summit Ave., St. Paul, MN 55105

Winning at the Table, Junior League of Las Vegas, 1100 East Sahara, Suite 311, Las Vegas, NV 89104

Index